Excel

Get the Results You Want!

Year 5 NAPLAN*-style Tests

Associate Professor James Athanasou
with Angella Deftereos

* This is not an officially endorsed publication of the NAPLAN program and is produced by Pascal Press independently of Australian governments.

© 2010 James Athanasou, Angella Deftereos and Pascal Press
Reprinted 2010 (twice)
Revised for NAPLAN Test changes 2011
New NAPLAN Test question formats added 2012
New NAPLAN Test question formats added 2013
Reprinted 2014
Conventions of Language questions updated 2017
Reprinted 2018

Revised in 2020 for the NAPLAN Online tests

Reprinted 2020, 2021, 2022, 2023, 2024

ISBN 978 1 74125 173 9

Pascal Press
PO Box 250
Glebe NSW 2037
(02) 9198 1748
www.pascalpress.com.au

Publisher: Vivienne Joannou
Project Editor: Mark Dixon
Edited by Joanne Innes, Mark Dixon and Rosemary Peers
Proofread and answers checked by Peter Little and Dale Little
Cover and page design by DiZign Pty Ltd
Typeset by Kim Webber and Grizzly Graphics (Leanne Richters)
Printed by Vivar Printing/Green Giant Press

CONTENTS

INTRODUCTION

Welcome to the ***Excel*** *Year 5 NAPLAN*-style Tests*. This book has been specially written to help parents and teachers of Year 5 students in their preparation for the Year 5 NAPLAN Tests. It is also helpful as a general revision for Year 5.

This book was first published in 2010 and has been revised for NAPLAN changes several times. It has been widely used and many thousands of copies have been published throughout the years. In this edition the content has been reorganised for the new online version of the NAPLAN Tests.

The aim of this brief introduction is to provide parents, guardians and teachers with some background to NAPLAN.

The book is a collaboration by a specialist in educational testing and an experienced NAPLAN marker. Both are trained teachers.

It is designed for use by parents who want to help their son or daughter, and by teachers who wish to prepare their class for the NAPLAN Tests. Some parents also use these books for general revision or when tutoring their son or daughter.

We hope that you will find this guide easy to use. In the following sections we will try to answer some frequently asked questions about the tests.

Associate Professor James Athanasou, LittB, MA, PhD, DipEd, MAPS

Angella Deftereos, BA, MTeach

What is different about this edition?

This is the latest and most thorough revision of the Year 5 book. It has been designed to accommodate the new online tests in an easy-to-use book format. The tests in this book contain excellent practice questions from very easy to very hard.

What is NAPLAN?

NAPLAN stands for *National Assessment Program—Literacy and Numeracy*. It is the largest educational testing program in Australia. It is conducted every year in March and the tests are taken by students in Year 3, Year 5, Year 7 and Year 9. All students in these year levels are expected to participate in the tests.

The tests cover Literacy—Reading, Writing, Conventions of Language (spelling, grammar and punctuation)—and Numeracy. In other words, they cover what are known to many people as the basic skills of reading, writing and arithmetic.

What is the purpose of NAPLAN?

Although NAPLAN has been designed mainly to provide administrators and politicians with information about Australian schools and educational systems, it is also relevant for each pupil. It provides a public record of their educational achievement.

Increasingly it is among the most valuable series of tests students will undertake in their primary schooling and probably their first formal and public examination.

What is being assessed?

The content of NAPLAN is based on what is generally taught across Australia. So do not be surprised if NAPLAN does not match exactly what each child is learning in their class. Most schools should be teaching more than the basic levels.

NAPLAN ONLINE AND THIS BOOK

NAPLAN covers only a specific range of skills. This is because literacy and numeracy are considered to be the basis of future learning in school. Of course we know that there are many other personal or social skills that are important in life.

We also realise that each child has their own special talents and aptitudes but at the same time governments also want to be able to assess their educational achievement in the fundamental skills. It is important to emphasise that there are many different kinds of literacy and numeracy, and that these tests cover only some aspects.

What is NAPLAN Online?

Until 2017 NAPLAN Tests were all paper-and-pencil tests. From 2022 all students have taken the NAPLAN tests on a computer or on a tablet. With NAPLAN paper-and-pencil tests, all students in each year level took exactly the same tests. In the NAPLAN Online tests this isn't the case; instead, every student takes a tailor-made test based on their ability.

In the NAPLAN Online tests a student is given specially selected questions that try to match their ability. This means that in theory a very bright student should not have to waste time answering very easy questions. Similarly, in theory, a student who is not so capable should not be given difficult questions that are far too hard for them.

Please visit the official ACARA site for a detailed explanation of the tailored test process used in NAPLAN Online and also for general information about the tests: https://nap.edu.au/online-assessment.

These tailor-made tests will mean broadly, therefore, that a student who is at a standard level of achievement will take a test mostly comprised of questions of a standard level; a student who is at an intermediate level of achievement will take a test mostly comprised of questions of an intermediate level; and a student who is at an advanced level of achievement will take a test mostly comprised of questions of an advanced level.

Do the tests in this book match those in NAPLAN Online?

The practice tests in this book are the same length as in NAPLAN Online.This book provides items across a wide range of difficulty.

Of course there is no way of predicting what actual questions will be asked but practice using these questions will help to familiarise a student with the content of the tests.

Naturally there will be some questions that can be presented on a computer that are harder to present in a book, but the content and skills will be similar.

Like in the NAPLAN Online tests, there are multiple-choice questions in this book but there are some differences. The spelling test is a good example. In the computer version the words are dictated by the computer. We cannot do this in a book but we have prepared a list of words for parents, guardians or teachers to dictate.

Are the questions in this book similar to those in NAPLAN Online?

Parents can have confidence that the questions in this book reflect the online NAPLAN. We believe that we have covered all the types of questions in a convenient book format.

On the whole it is our impression that some of the questions in this book will be much harder than those in NAPLAN. We have deliberately included some more challenging questions.

We have also made a special effort to cover as many different question formats as possible. For instance, spelling questions have been altered to be given orally to the student.

Naturally it is not possible to use the same processes as the online test, such as click and drag, but it is possible to use the same thinking processes.

The Check your skills pages after each test suggest the approximate level of difficulty of questions so you can see what levels of difficulty of questions a student is able to answer.

On the Check your skills pages, questions are divided into standard, intermediate or advanced. This will help you prepare for the standard, intermediate or advanced test that your child will sit. Please refer to page 34 to see an example of a checklist page from the book.

Please refer to the next page to see some examples of question types that are found in NAPLAN Online and how they compare to questions in this book. As you will see, the content tested is exactly the same but the questions are presented differently.

NAPLAN ONLINE QUESTION TYPES

NAPLAN Online question types	Equivalent questions in Numeracy Tests in this book
Online ruler How long is the piece of wood in this picture? Use the online ruler to measure the length of the wood. How wide is it? ☐ 30 cm ☐ 40 cm ☐ 50 cm ☐ 60 cm 0 10 20 30 40 50 60 cm	Here is a piece of wood. There is a tape under the wood. 0 10 20 30 40 50 60 This tape measure is marked in centimetres. How long is this piece of wood? 30 cm ○ 40 cm ○ 50 cm ○ 60 cm ○

NAPLAN Online question types	Equivalent questions in Reading Tests in this book
Dropdown Choose the words that best complete this sentence. *Dear Nicholas,* *Seasons greetings!* *Love,* *Mary-Ellen* The type of card on which you would find this greeting is a Christmas card. ↓ a birthday card. a get well card.	To answer this question colour in the circle with the correct answer. *Dear Nicholas,* *Seasons greetings!* *Love,* *Mary-Ellen* On which type of card would you find this greeting? ○ You might find it on a Christmas card. ○ You might find it on a birthday card. ○ You might find it on a get-well card.
Identifying/sorting Here are four steps for washing hands. • Rinse your hands. • Turn off the water. • Rub your hands together with soap until they are soapy. • Dry them with a clean towel. Sort them in order from first to last in each box. First ____ Second ____ Third ____ Fourth ____	Here are four steps for washing hands properly. Number them in order from 1 to 4. [ ] Rinse your hands. [ ] Turn off the water. [ ] Rub your hands together with soap until they are soapy. [ ] Dry them with a clean towel.

NAPLAN Online question types	Equivalent questions in Conventions of Language Tests in this book
Drag and drop Drag the correct word to fill in the space. **and** **but** **so** **or** I forgot to bring the batteries for my torch ______ I had to borrow some.	Read the sentences. They have some gaps. Choose the correct word or words to fill each gap. Colour in only one circle for each answer. I forgot to bring the batteries for my torch ______ I had to borrow some. and ○ but ○ so ○ or ○
Click Which underlined words can be replaced by *we're*? Click on the words. I asked the driver, "Where is the town?" I thought we were almost there but he said, "We are nearly there."	Colour in the circles with the correct answer. Which underlined words can be replaced with *we're*? I asked the driver, "Where is the town?" I thought we were almost there but he said, "We are nearly there."
Text entry The ______ of the fence is 120 centimetres. Click on the play button to listen to the missing word. 0.08 / 0.09 Type the correct spelling of the word in the box.	Ask your teacher or parent to read the spelling words for you. The words are listed on page 188. Write the spelling words on the lines below. **Test 3 spelling words** **26.** ______ **Spelling words for Conventions of Language Test 3** Word: **26.** height — Example: The height of the fence is 120 centimetres.

As you can see there are differences between the processes involved in answering the questions in NAPLAN Online and this book but we think they are minimal.

Nevertheless we **strongly advise** that students should practise clicking and dragging until they are **familiar** with using a computer or tablet to answer questions.

What are the advantages of revising for the NAPLAN Online tests in book form?

There are many benefits to a child revising for the online test using books.

- One of the most important benefits is that writing on paper will help your child retain information. It can be a very effective way to memorise. High quality educational research shows that using a keyboard is not as good as note-taking for learning.
- Students will be able to prepare thoroughly for topic revision using books and then practise computer skills easily. They will only succeed with sound knowledge of topics; this requires study and focus. Students will not succeed in tests simply because they know how to answer questions digitally.
- Also, some students find it easier to concentrate when reading a page in a book than when reading on a screen.
- Furthermore it can be more convenient to use a book, especially when a child doesn't have ready access to a digital device.
- You can be confident that ***Excel*** books will help students acquire the topic knowledge they need, as we have over 30 years experience in helping students prepare for tests. All our writers are experienced educators.

How *Excel Test Zone* can help you practise online

We recommend you go to www.exceltestzone.com.au and register for practice in NAPLAN Online–style tests once you have completed this book. The reasons include:

- for optimal performance in the NAPLAN Online tests we strongly recommend students gain practice at completing online tests as well as completing revision in book form
- students should practise answering questions on a digital device to become confident in this process
- students will be able to practise tailored tests like those in NAPLAN Online as well as other types of tests
- students will also be able to gain valuable practice in onscreen skills such as dragging and dropping answers, using an online ruler to measure figures and using an online protractor to measure angles.

Remember that ***Excel Test Zone*** has been helping students prepare for NAPLAN since 2009; in fact we had NAPLAN online questions even before NAPLAN tests went online!

We also have updated our website along with our book range to ensure your preparation for NAPLAN Online is 100% up to date.

What do the tests indicate?

They are designed to be tests of educational achievement; they show what a person has learnt or can do.

They are not IQ tests. Probably boys and girls who do extremely well on these tests will be quite bright. It is possible, however, for some intelligent children to perform poorly because of disadvantage, language, illness or other factors.

Are there time limits?

Yes, there are time limits for each test. These are usually set so that 95% of pupils can complete the tests in the time allowed.

If more than one test is scheduled on a day then there should be a reasonable rest break of at least 20 minutes between tests. In some special cases pupils may be given some extra time and allowed to complete a response.

Who does the NAPLAN Tests?

The NAPLAN Testing Program is held for pupils in Year 5 each year. The tests are designed for all pupils.

Some schools may exempt pupils from the tests. These can include children in special English classes and those who have recently arrived from non–English speaking backgrounds or children with special needs.

Our advice to parents and guardians is that children should only undertake the tests if it is likely to be of benefit to them. It would be a pity if a pupil was not personally or emotionally ready to perform at their best and the results underestimated their ability. The results on this occasion might label them inaccurately and it would be recorded on their pupil record card. Some parents have insisted successfully that their child be exempt from testing.

Who developed these tests?

The tests were developed especially by ACARA. These are large-scale educational tests in which the questions are trialled extensively. Any unsuitable questions will be eliminated in these trials. They should produce results with high validity and reliability.

How can the results be used?

The results of the NAPLAN Tests offer an opportunity to help pupils at an early stage. The findings can be used as early indicators of any problem areas.

It would be a pity to miss this chance to help boys or girls at this stage in their schooling when it is relatively easy to address any issues. The findings can also be used as encouragement for pupils who are performing above the minimum standard.

It is important for parents and teachers to look closely at the student report. This indicates the areas of strength and weakness. The report can be a little complex to read at first but it contains quite a helpful summary of the skills assessed in Reading, Writing, Conventions of Language and Numeracy. Use this as a guide for any revision.

If NAPLAN indicates that there are problems, then repeated testing with other measures of educational achievement is strongly recommended. It is also relevant to compare the results of NAPLAN with general classroom performance.

Remember that all educational test results have limitations. Do not place too much faith in the results of a single assessment.

Does practice help?

There is no benefit in trying to teach to the test because the questions will vary from year to year. Nevertheless a general preparation for the content of NAPLAN Tests should be quite helpful. Some people say that practising such tests is not helpful but we do not agree.

Firstly practice will help to overcome unfamiliarity with test procedures. Secondly it will help pupils deal with specific types of questions. Test practice should help students perform to the best of their ability.

Use the tests in this book to practise test skills and also to diagnose some aspects of learning in Year 5. In saying this parents should make sure their child is interested in undertaking these practice tests. There is no benefit in compelling children to practise.

Sometimes it is easy to forget that they are still young children. We recommend that you sit with them or at least stay nearby while they are completing each test. Give them plenty of praise and encouragement for their efforts.

How are students graded?

One of the big advantages of NAPLAN is that there is a clear scale of achievement. It is consistent from Year 3 right through to Year 9, which shows how much progress is being made.

There are now four levels of achievement:

- Exceeding
- Strong
- Developing
- Needs additional support.

This new grading system is simpler than the previous structure that had ten levels and was not always easy to interpret.

Exceeding describes students who are very proficient/advanced and have achieved at a level well beyond the limits expected at this stage of their schooling.

Strong indicates students who are of average to high-average competency. Their performance is solid and at the expected level of their school year.

Developing encompasses those students who are not yet proficient. These students are moving towards competency. They are progressing and their performance is towards the low-average level.

Needs additional support gives a firm indication that help is needed.

It is important to track each student's development from Year 3 through Year 5, Year 7 and Year 9 to see whether they are exceeding, strong, developing or need additional support in each area of NAPLAN.

NAPLAN shows how a student compares with the national average and provides other useful information for students, parents/guardians and teachers.

What results are provided?

Parents receive comprehensive test results, as do teachers and schools. The results are first reported against the four levels of achievement (Exceeding, Strong, Developing, Needs additional support). For students to be proficient they need to be at the Exceeding or Strong levels.

It is easy to look only at the level reached on these tests but it is more important to see what the student knows or can do. The levels are not a percentage score or the number of questions answered correctly.

Instead they describe the level of achievement. Descriptors are included that make clear each pupil's literacy and numeracy skills. The national average is also provided; this is a useful comparison.

A band covering the middle 60% of students is shown. Despite the considerable difference in ability between the pupils at the top and bottom of this band, it still indicates whether a student is performing above, below or within the typical range of performance.

So check to see what students know or can do to identify the areas in which they need extra help. Also look at their strengths in the areas of literacy and numeracy. It is important to use the results for the benefit of the students.

Are the tests in Year 3 and Year 5 the same?

The tests increase in difficulty but the general content is much the same. Some questions might be repeated. This is to allow the test developers to standardise the results across Years 3 and 5. The similar questions act like anchors for all the other questions.

When are the tests held?

The tests are planned for May on an agreed date. The actual timetable is listed on the official website at www.nap.edu.au. They may be spread over several days. Ideally the tests should be given in the mornings.

How is NAPLAN related to *My School*?

The My School website reports the NAPLAN results for around 10 000 Australian schools. *My School* is available at www.myschool.edu.au.

Will children be shown what to do?

The testing program is normally very well organised with clear instructions for schools and teachers. Teachers receive special instructions for administering the tests.

Teachers will probably give children practice tests in the weeks before the NAPLAN Tests.

How our book's grading system works

Step 1

In this book you will notice that we have provided Check your skills pages. These pages provide you with information about the content of each question.

Step 2

Once you have completed the checklists you will be able to see the content that was easy for the student or the questions that were difficult.

• • • • • • • • •

Please note that it is not possible to accurately predict the content of the NAPLAN Tests. NAPLAN focuses on the 'essential elements that should be taught at the appropriate year levels'.

Thank you for your patience in working through this introduction. We hope you find this guide helpful. It is designed to be easy to use and to help pupils prepare. We wish every pupil well in the NAPLAN Tests and in their future studies.

Associate Professor James A Athanasou, LittB, MA, PhD, DipEd, MAPS
Angella Deftereos, BA, MTeach

INSTRUCTIONS FOR PARENTS AND TEACHERS USING THIS BOOK

How is this book organised?

It is divided into sample questions and practice tests. We start with samples of the numeracy and literacy (reading and conventions of language) questions. Work through these examples so that every student knows what needs to be done. At the very least please ensure that your child is familiar with the sample questions.

This is followed by four practice tests for numeracy, four practice tests for reading and four practice tests for conventions of language. There is also a sample writing task and four practice tests for writing. At the very least try to revise the samples if you do not have enough time to do the practice tests.

Numeracy Tests

The Numeracy Tests in this book have 42 questions and should take up to 50 minutes. Some children will finish quickly while others will need all the time available.

Try not to explain terms during the testing. This can be done after the test session. If a question is still too hard, it is better to leave it at this stage. Some students may not be ready for the task.

Literacy Tests

Literacy is divided into three tests: Reading, Conventions of Language and Writing.

The Writing Test offers help with aspects of writing using prompts and stimulus materials.

Allow up to 50 minutes for Reading Tests, 45 minutes for Conventions of Language Tests and 42 minutes for Writing Tests, with a break in between.

- In the Reading Test students will read stories, letters and non-fiction writing. There will be supporting pictures and charts. Students will be asked to find information, make conclusions, find the meaning and look at different ideas.
- The Conventions of Language Test is divided into two parts: grammar and punctuation, and spelling. Students must be able to use verbs and punctuation, such as speech marks and commas, correctly. Also they will be asked to spell words.
- In the Writing Test students will write a specific type of text. They will be judged on the structure of their writing, as well as their grammar, punctuation and spelling.

Test materials

All test materials are contained in this book. There are answers for scoring the responses.

Equipment

Students will not need white-out, pens or calculators. It is best to use a pencil. Children should be provided with a pencil, an eraser and a blank sheet of paper for working out.

Time limits

Try to keep roughly to the time limits for the tests. You may give some students extra time if they are tired. Even a short break every 20 minutes is appropriate.

Instructions to students

Explain patiently what needs to be done. Students should only attempt these tests if they wish to and do no more than one test in a session.

Recording answers

Show students the way to mark the answers. They have to colour in circles, shapes or numbers, or write the answers in the boxes or on the lines provided.

SAMPLE QUESTIONS—NUMERACY

Here are some sample Numeracy questions. Make sure you read each question carefully so that you know exactly:

- **what information is given to you in the question**
- **what the question is asking you to find.**

Then make sure you read each answer option carefully in order to choose the correct answer. There is no time limit for the sample questions.

If you aren't sure what to do, ask your teacher or your parents to help you. Don't be afraid to ask if it isn't clear to you.

To answer these questions, write the answer in the box or colour in the circle with the correct answer. Colour in only one circle for each answer.

1. Here is a table of numbers. Some squares are white and some are shaded. There is a pattern in these numbers.

1	2	3	4	5	6	7
8	9	10	11	12	13	14
15	16	17	18	19	20	21
22	23	24	25	26	27	28
29	30	31	32	33	34	35
36	37	38	39	40	41	42

What is the next number that should be shaded?

34 ○ 36 ○ 38 ○ 40 ○

2. Here is a clock which shows 24-hour time.

Which clock shows this time?

○ ○ ○ ○

3. Here are five shapes. They are used to make a design.

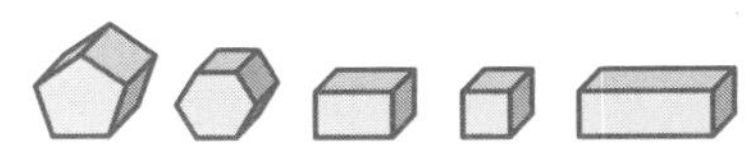

Which design uses all of the five shapes?

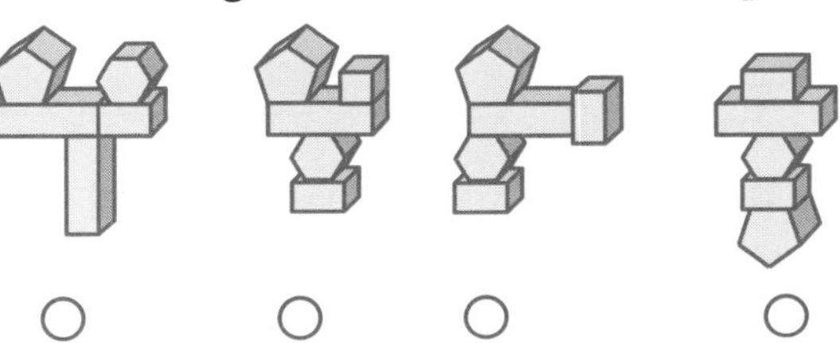

○ ○ ○ ○

4. What is the value of 9 in 1948?

- ○ 9 thousands
- ○ 9 hundreds
- ○ 9 tens
- ○ 9 ones

5. Which is the largest angle?

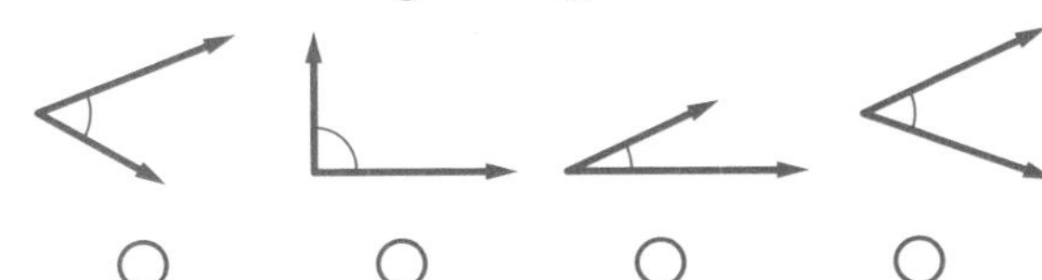

○ ○ ○ ○

6. There is a pattern in these numbers. Write in the number that is missing.

60 → +100 → [ ] → +100 → 260

7. This table shows some weight measurements for cooking. All weights are approximate.

Imperial weights	Metric weights
$\frac{1}{4}$ ounce	7 g
$\frac{1}{2}$ ounce	14 g
$\frac{3}{4}$ ounce	21 g
1 ounce	28 g
$1\frac{1}{4}$ ounce	35 g
$1\frac{1}{2}$ ounce	42 g

Approximately how many grams (g) will the $\frac{1}{2}$ ounce and the $1\frac{1}{4}$ ounce make altogether?

8. Part of this grid is shaded. The grid is made up of squares. Count the number of squares or parts of squares that are shaded.

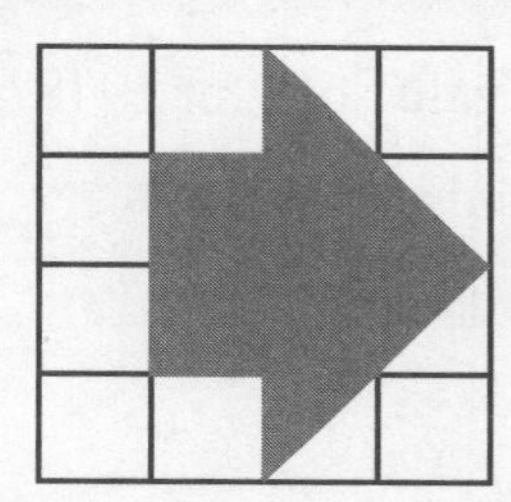

How many squares are shaded?

4	6	8	10
○	○	○	○

9. How many blocks make up this shape? (Note: The pattern in front is continued throughout.)

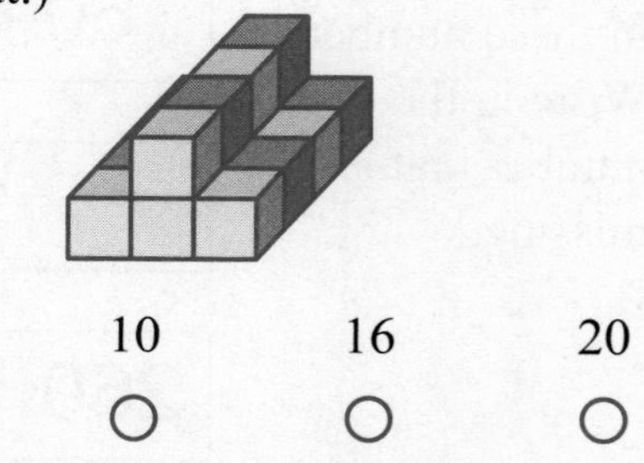

8	10	16	20
○	○	○	○

10. Here is a shape made out of some blocks.

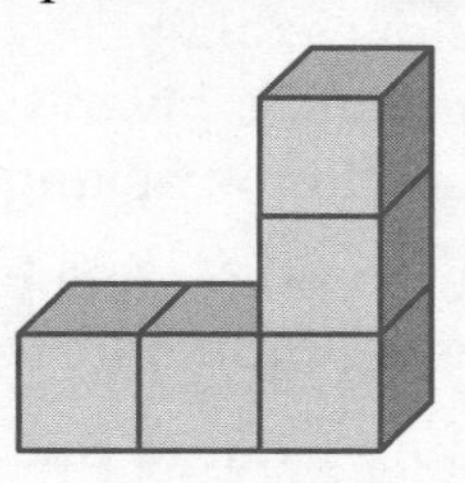

Which one of the four shapes below is the same as the one above? Is it A, B, C or D?

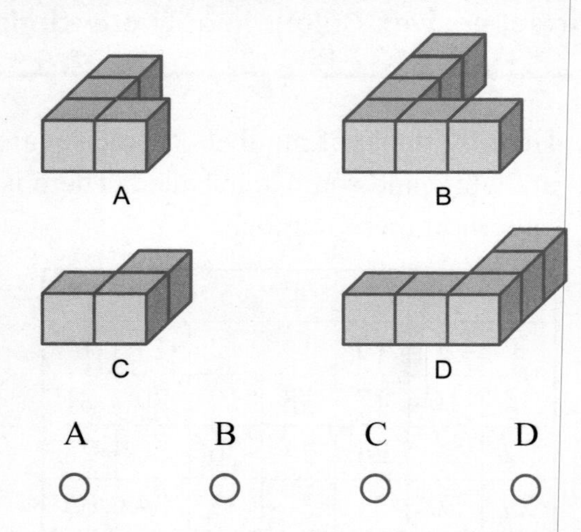

A	B	C	D
○	○	○	○

11. A chicken snack pack costs \$2. A boy buys 4 packs for his family.

Fill in the number sentence below to show how much he spent.

4 × \$ ☐ = \$ ☐

Write your answers in the boxes.

12. Here are some presents. There is a telescope, a helmet and a ball. Their prices in the shop are also shown.

Here are four sums. They show a quick way to guess or estimate the price of the three presents. Which sum is the best way to estimate the total cost of the three presents altogether?

- ○ $80 + $120 + $30
- ○ $80 + $130 + $30
- ○ $90 + $130 + $30
- ○ $90 + $130 + $40

13. There are different types of galaxies. Some are spiral such as our Milky Way. Others are irregular spiral, elliptical or irregular. This chart shows the number of local groups of galaxies.

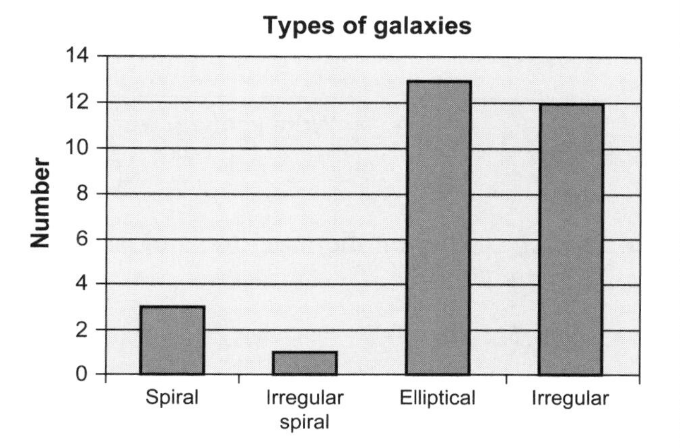

Which answer is correct?

- ○ There are more spiral than irregular spiral.
- ○ There are more spiral than elliptical.
- ○ There are fewer elliptical than irregular.
- ○ There are fewer spiral than irregular spiral.

14. Here are some objects in a box.

One object is chosen without looking. What is the chance of choosing a pencil?

- ○ certain
- ○ more than half
- ○ less than half
- ○ impossible

15. Two triangular prisms have been joined together.

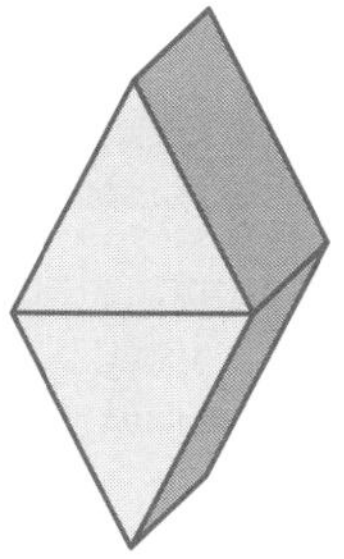

How many separate faces does the new shape have? (Hint: Count the faces that have been joined and that are flat or vertical as one face.)

3	4	6	9
○	○	○	○

You are about halfway through the sample questions—well done!

16. Complete this calculation.

$763 - 289 =$ ☐

Write your answers in the boxes.

17. Complete this calculation.

$2.6 + 3.9 =$ ☐

18. Complete this calculation.

$1401 \div 3 =$ ☐

☞ Answers and explanations on pages 7–8

19. Write one number in each space to complete this calculation.

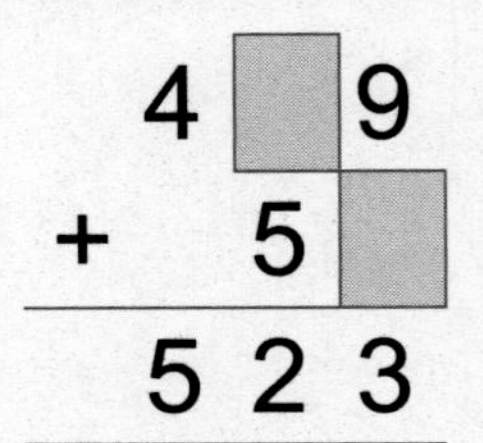

20. Here is a piece of wood. There is a tape measure under the wood.

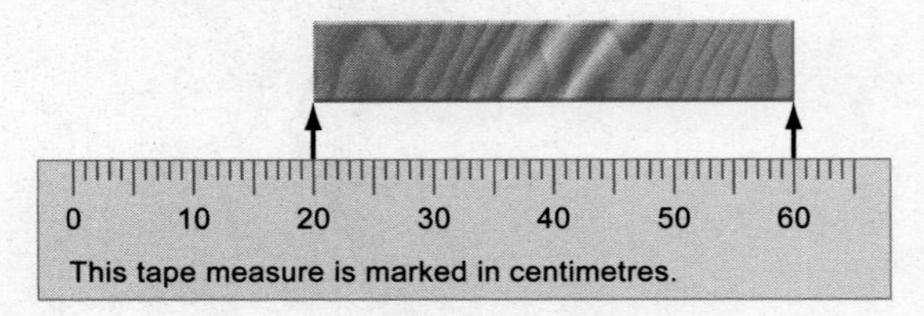

How long is this piece of wood?

30 cm ○ 40 cm ○ 50 cm ○ 60 cm ○

21. I fold this pattern in half.

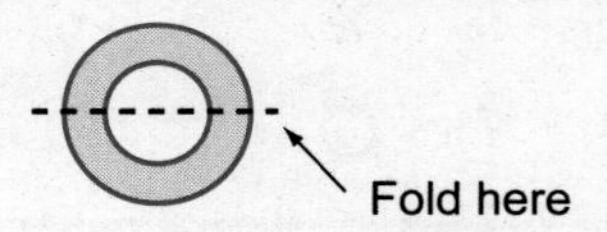

Which shape will I see?

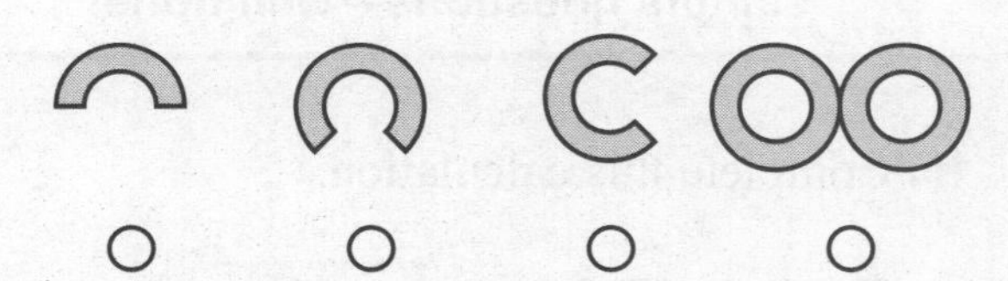

22.

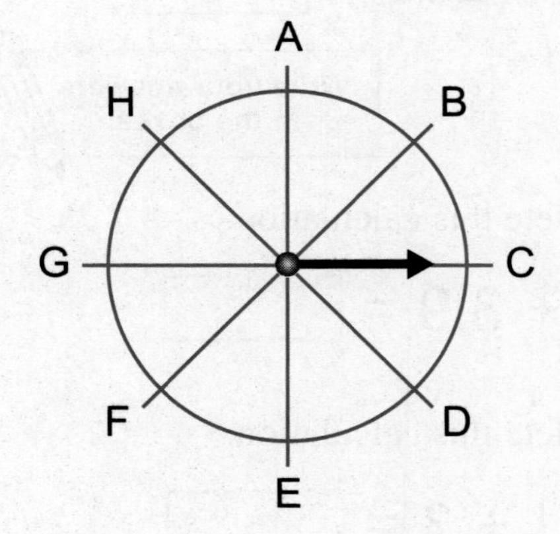

To which letter would the arrow be pointing if it is moved two spaces clockwise?

A ○ B ○ D ○ E ○

23. Pressure is the force on an area. To find the pressure, divide the force by the area.

$$\text{Pressure} = \frac{\text{Force}}{\text{Area}}$$

For example, if the pressure was noticed as 8 and the force was measured at 16, then the area must be 2.

Here is a problem: if the force is 250 and the pressure is 25, then what is the area?

24. Which of the numbers below is closest to 0.7?

0.5 ○ 0.8 ○ 0.2 ○ 0.4 ○

25. In many countries wood is burned for fuel. Often the main use of this wood is for cooking.

The chart below shows which countries are the major producers of wood for fuel.

Altogether, about 600 million cubic metres of wood is burnt per year.

Major producers of wood for fuel

Ethiopia 5%
Nigeria 15%
India 35%
Brazil 22%
Indonesia 23%

About how many million cubic metres does Ethiopia produce? (Remember: Altogether these countries produce about 600 million cubic metres.)

5	15	30	45	60
○	○	○	○	○

26. What is the perimeter (the distance around the outside edges) of this figure?

The perimeter is shown by the dark line. (Note: Some of the lengths are not shown in the figure.)

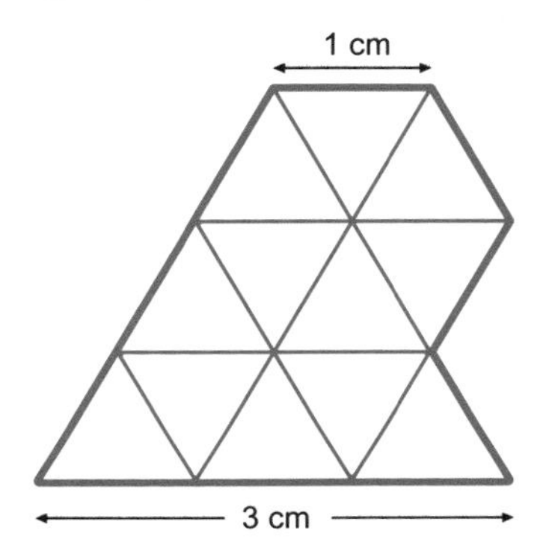

4 cm	6 cm	9 cm	10 cm	12 cm
○	○	○	○	○

27. Here is a map. It shows three cities. The map is divided into sections.

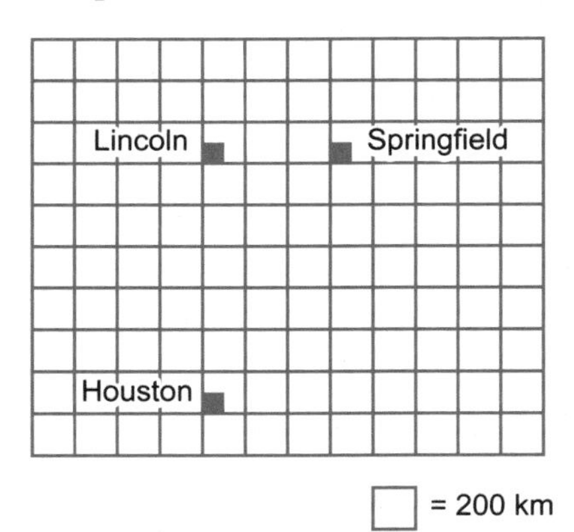

The distance from Lincoln to Houston is 1200 km.

How far is it from Lincoln to Springfield on this map?

○ 300 km
○ 400 km
○ 500 km
○ 600 km
○ 700 km

28. Here is a shape. Some parts are coloured and some are blank.

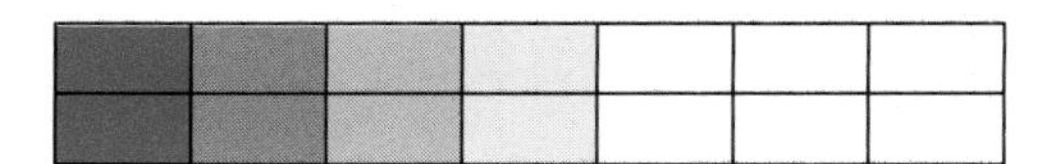

How many parts are coloured?

○ 6 out of 8 parts
○ 8 out of 8 parts
○ 6 out of 14 parts
○ 8 out of 14 parts
○ 14 out of 14 parts

29. The sides of this shape are folded upwards to make a square pyramid. Each triangle has the same pattern on both sides.

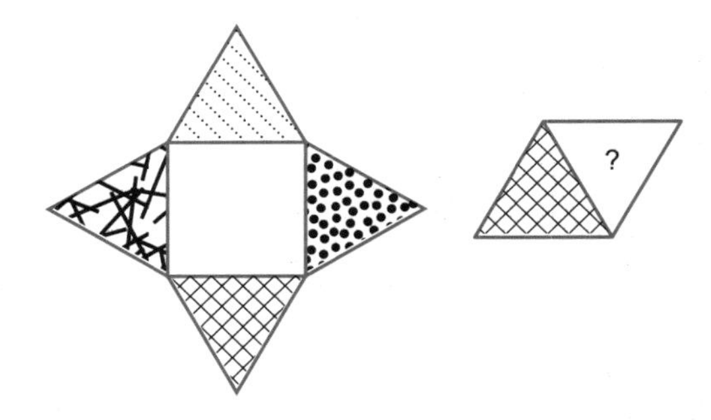

Which pattern fills the space shown with the question mark?

 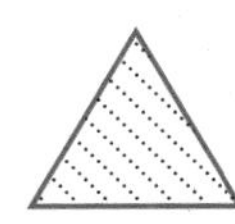  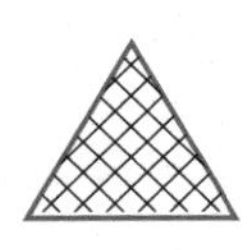

30. The length of this car from the front to the back is 3 metres (3.0 m).

The size of the wheel is half a metre (0.5 m).

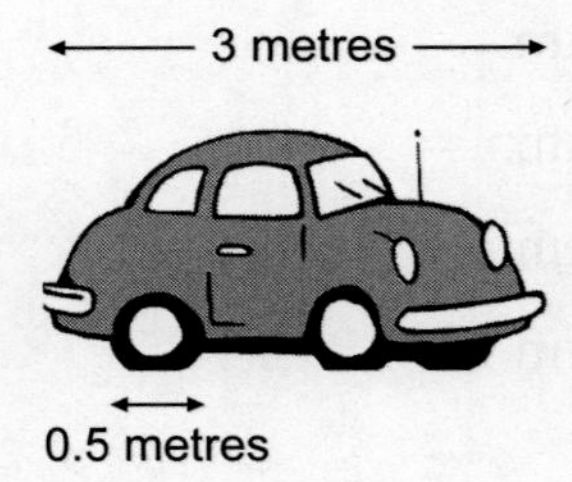

How long is the car compared to its wheel?

- ○ 3 times as long
- ○ 4 times as long
- ○ 5 times as long
- ○ 6 times as long

31. There are 12 people in this picture. Some are the same.

What fraction of the 12 people have beards?

$\frac{12}{4}$	$\frac{1}{3}$	$\frac{1}{4}$	$\frac{4}{8}$
○	○	○	○

END OF TEST

Well done! You have completed the sample questions for Numeracy. Even if you don't practise any others, at least you will have some familiarity with the method used in the NAPLAN Tests.

How did you go with these sample questions? Check to see where you did well and where you had problems. Try to revise the questions that were hard for you.

There are now four more Numeracy Tests to practise, each containing 42 questions. They include many of the same types of questions, plus a few other types.

 ☞ Answers and explanations on pages 7–8

ANSWERS TO SAMPLE QUESTIONS—NUMERACY

1. **38.** The numbers increase by six. They start with 2 then 8, 14, 20, 26, 32 then 38. With these questions have a guess if you are not sure, as there is no penalty for guessing incorrectly.
2. The **second clock**, (clock). The time is 8.00 pm. Do you know how to convert 24-hour time to analogue time? If not, ask your teacher or your parents to help you. It isn't difficult. You just subtract 12 if the number on the display is larger than 12:00. So 20 – 12 becomes 8 pm.
3. Only the **second design** uses all of the five blocks. All the other designs use five blocks but they don't use every one in the top picture. They use one block twice. The design has been broken into pieces to make it easier for you to see.

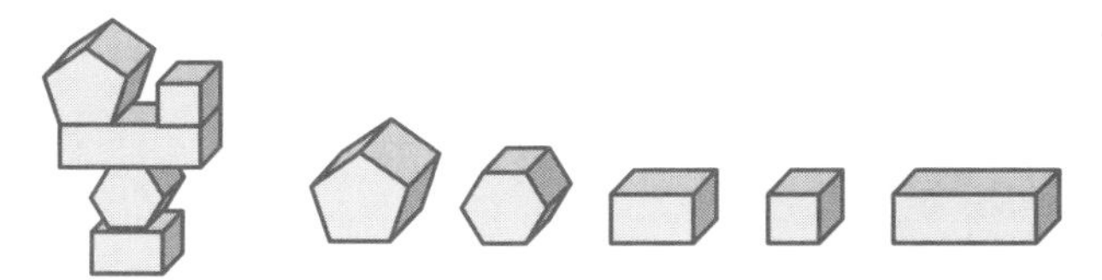

4. **9 hundreds.** The number is made up of 1 thousand, 9 hundreds, 4 tens and 8 ones. This should have been easy for you.
5. The **second answer** is correct. It's the largest angle.

   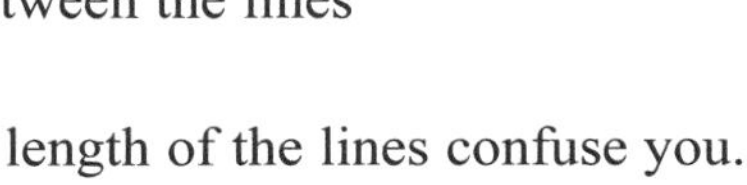

   The space between the lines is widest.

   Don't let the length of the lines confuse you.

   It's the size of the opening that is important.
6. **160.** The numbers increase by 100. You start with 60 then add 100 to make 160. Then you add 100 to 160 to make 260. Did you write your answer in the box?
7. **49 g.** The $\frac{1}{2}$ ounce is 14 g and the $1\frac{1}{4}$ ounce is 35 g. Add these together to make 49 g. Imperial weights were used in Australia before the change to the metric system in the mid-1970s.
8. **6.** There are four whole squares and four half squares. When you add the four whole squares plus the four half squares, you get six squares altogether.
9. **16.** There are four blocks in each section and there are four sections. It may not be easy for you to see because of how it's drawn and you need to visualise or imagine some parts of the diagram.
10. **D.** This is L-shaped with five blocks. The others are quite different. Sometimes you will find these easy to see and sometimes it's a little hard. It may help if you try to draw the shape and then rotate it.
11. **4 × $2 = $8.** The snack packs cost $2. The boy buys four snack packs, so the sum is 4 × $2 = $8. Did you write your answers in the boxes?
12. **$90 + $130 + $30.** You need to round the numbers up or down before adding them to estimate the answer quickly. So $87 becomes $90 (it is closest to $90); $128 becomes $130 (it is closest to $130); and $32 becomes $30 (it is closest to $30). If the number ends in five or more then round it up, otherwise round it down.
13. **There are more spiral than irregular spiral.**
14. **less than half**. There are 10 objects and there are 4 pencils. So the chance of choosing a pencil is 4 out of 10. This is less than half.
15. **6.** Each prism has five faces but when they are joined, there are only six faces.
16. **474.** 763 – 289 = 474. This question came from my son, Nicholas, who is in Year 8. Make sure that you know how to do these types of calculations.
17. **6.5** (2.6 + 3.9 = 6.5)
18. **467.** 1401 ÷ 3 = 467.
19. The missing numbers are **6** and **4** and the sum is 469 + 54 = 523.
20. **40 cm.** The wood starts at 20 cm and finishes at 60 cm which makes a difference of 40 cm.
21. The **first answer** is correct. We have tried to show this for you (it isn't drawn to scale). When you put both halves together, you get a circle.

    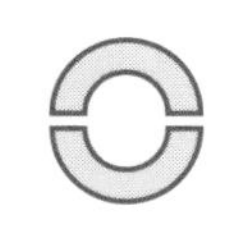
22. **E.** After one space the arrow points to D then after another space it points to E.
23. **10.** Pressure is force divided by area. So if the force is 250 and the pressure is 25, then the area must be 10 because 25 = 250 ÷ 10. Pressure is measured in newtons per square metre. This is actually an easy question but the wording of the problem may have been unclear to you.
24. **0.8** (This number is closest to 0.7)

ANSWERS TO SAMPLE QUESTIONS—NUMERACY

25. **30.** There are 600 million cubic metres altogether so 5% for Ethiopia is 30. A quick way of working this out is to take 10% which is 60, then dividing that by 2 to get 5%, which is 30.

26. **10 cm.** The perimeter is 3 cm along the bottom, 3 cm along the left-hand side, 1 cm across the top and 3 cm on the right-hand side.

27. **600 km.** You need to count the squares. The six squares from Lincoln to Houston equal 1200 km, so the length of each square is 200 km. There are three squares from Lincoln to Springfield, which means that this distance is 3×200 km = 600 km.

28. **8 out of 14 parts.** There are 14 rectangles and 8 are coloured.

29. 

The **first answer** is correct. The pattern shown above completes the picture. You have to imagine how it will look when each part is folded to make the pyramid.

30. **6 times as long**

31. $\frac{1}{3}$. This is because 4 out of the 12 have beards and four twelfths is one-third.

SAMPLE QUESTIONS—READING

Here are some sample Reading questions. You will need to look at or read a text. Make sure you read each question carefully so that you know exactly what the question is asking. Then find the relevant section in the text. Finally make sure you read each answer option carefully in order to choose the correct answer. There is no time limit for the sample questions.

To answer these questions, write the answer in the box or colour in the circle with the right answer. Colour in only one circle for each answer.

If you aren't sure what to do, ask your teacher or your parents to help you. Don't be afraid to ask if it isn't clear to you.

Read *The Life Cycle of a Butterfly* and answer questions 1 to 4.

The Life Cycle of a Butterfly

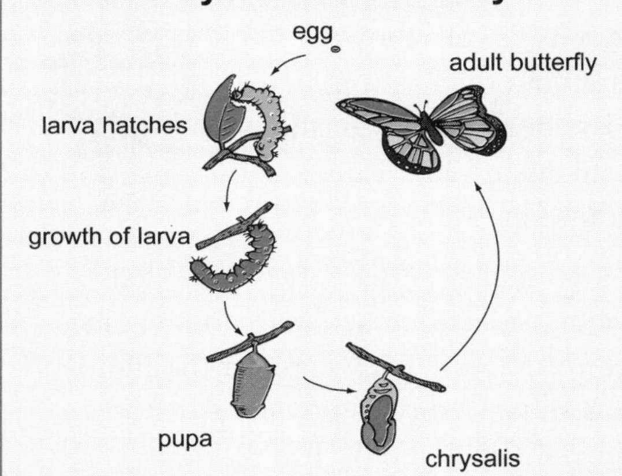

Butterflies have a life cycle in which they change their form. They start as eggs, then become caterpillars and finally become butterflies.

A butterfly lays many eggs on a plant. From these eggs come small larvae, which are familiar to you as caterpillars. The caterpillars eat the plants and shed their skin several times until they turn into a pupa. They then spin silk that clings to a plant and their skin peels off until an object called a chrysalis or cocoon appears.

After some weeks or a few months, the pupa slowly emerges from its cocoon becoming a full-grown butterfly. The parts of the caterpillar change into the wings, legs, head and body of the butterfly.

Finally, the butterfly becomes free of its cocoon. Some butterflies live for only a few days, but others can live for many months.

1. What does this diagram show?

- ◯ It shows the stages in the growth of a butterfly.
- ◯ It explains how a caterpillar is born.
- ◯ It shows the life of all insects.
- ◯ It is all about caterpillars and cocoons.

2. What is a chrysalis?

- ◯ A chrysalis is like a cocoon.
- ◯ A chrysalis is a caterpillar.
- ◯ A chrysalis is a pupa.

3. How many stages in the life cycle of a butterfly are shown in the diagram above?

4	5	6	7
◯	◯	◯	◯

4. How long does it take for the pupa to emerge from its cocoon?

- ◯ It takes a few days to some weeks for the pupa to emerge.
- ◯ It takes some weeks for the pupa to emerge.
- ◯ It takes some weeks to a few months for the pupa to emerge.
- ◯ It takes a few months for the pupa to emerge.

☞ **Answers and explanations on page 16**

Read the text about Boy Scouts and answer questions 5 to 8.

The best food for the Boy Scout is shredded wheat because it has all the muscle-building, bone-making material in the whole wheat grain. It is prepared in a digestible form. It supplies all the strength needed for work and play.

It is ready-cooked and ready-to-eat. It has the greatest amount of body-building nutriment in the smallest bulk. Its crispness compels thorough mastication, and the more you chew it the better you like it.

Shredded wheat is the favourite food of athletes. The records show that the winners of many brilliant rowing and track events have been trained on shredded wheat.

From The Project Gutenberg e-book of *Boy Scouts Handbook* by Boy Scouts of America, 1911

5. A good title for this text could be

- ◯ Shredded Wheat.
- ◯ Boy Scouts.
- ◯ My Favourite Food.

6. What is the aim of the text?

- ◯ to inform
- ◯ to entertain
- ◯ to warn
- ◯ to suggest

7. What is the meaning of *mastication*?

- ◯ chewing
- ◯ flying
- ◯ seeing

8. What role model is used to convince people to try the food?

- ◯ The example that is used is the Boy Scout.
- ◯ The example that is used is that it is ready to eat and nutritious.
- ◯ The example that is used is sports performance.

Read *Legacy* and answer questions 9 to 13.

Legacy

Legacy is a well-known Australian organisation that has been caring for the dependants of deceased veterans since 1923.

It is a voluntary service. It is provided by veterans, servicemen and women, and other volunteers. They care for the families of Australian Army, Navy and Air Force members if they die during service.

Legacy currently cares for 115 000 widows and 1900 children and dependants throughout Australia.

Legacy is dedicated to improving the lives and opportunities of families. It does this through:

- looking after individual and family needs;
- supporting the rights and benefits of families; and
- helping families with their sadness.

There are over 6100 volunteers around Australia who look after the widows and their families. They ensure Legacy's promise to care for the families of deceased veterans is kept.

Adapted from www.legacy.com.au

☞ Answers and explanations on page 16

9. Which sentence gives you the best idea of the content of this passage?

- ◯ Legacy cares for the dependants of deceased veterans.
- ◯ Legacy improves the lives and opportunities of families.
- ◯ Legacy has over 6100 volunteers around Australia.

10. For how many children does Legacy care?

- ◯ 115 000
- ◯ 1923
- ◯ 6100
- ◯ 1900

11. Who volunteers for Legacy?

- ◯ children
- ◯ returned soldiers
- ◯ widows
- ◯ dependants

12. Which sentence is true?

- ◯ Legacy assists Australian Army, Navy and Air Force members.
- ◯ Legacy assists volunteers.
- ◯ Legacy assists dependants.

13. How could you describe Legacy?

- ◯ Legacy is part of the government.
- ◯ Legacy is a charity.
- ◯ Legacy is part of the Army, Navy and Air Force.

Read *Currumbin Sanctuary* and answer questions 14 to 23.

Currumbin Sanctuary

If you want to see some examples of Australian wildlife then you may wish to visit the Currumbin Wildlife Sanctuary in Queensland. It is on the Gold Coast Highway at Currumbin just a few kilometres south of Surfers Paradise and is open daily from 8 am to 5 pm. The sanctuary features wildlife shows, lorikeet feeding, koala photos and a play park.

There are many scenes of Australia at Currumbin Sanctuary. The Aboriginal dancers take visitors back to the Dreamtime, through ancient myths, dances and songs.

The sanctuary is set in some 27 hectares of tropical grounds. It claims to have the largest collection of native Australian animals in the world and is well known for its colourful lorikeets that visit twice daily. There are also chances to see kangaroos, koalas, emus, cassowaries, platypuses, wombats, wallabies, dingoes and crocodiles in this wildlife park.

There is a small train for visitor transport. It takes them on a trip through the landscaped grounds to Koala Junction or Kangaroo Crossing. The sanctuary's attractions include snake shows, an animal nursery and photos with koalas.

☞ Answers and explanations on page 16

SAMPLE QUESTIONS—READING

14. How big is the sanctuary?

- ○ 25 hectares
- ○ 27 hectares
- ○ 9 hectares

15. What is the main reason that is given to visit Currumbin Sanctuary?

- ○ for a holiday at Surfers Paradise
- ○ to ride the train
- ○ to see Australian wildlife

16. Which features of the sanctuary are mentioned in the first paragraph?

- ○ kangaroos, koalas, emus, cassowaries, platypuses, wombats, wallabies, dingoes and crocodiles
- ○ snake shows, an animal nursery, and chances for photographs with koalas
- ○ wildlife shows, lorikeet feeding, koala photos, and a play park
- ○ wildlife shows, lorikeet feeding, koala photos

You are about halfway through the sample questions—well done!

17. What is the main claim made by the sanctuary?

- ○ It claims to have the largest collection of Australian wildlife in the world.
- ○ It claims to take visitors back to the Dreamtime through ancient myths, dances and songs.
- ○ It claims that the attractions include snake shows, an animal nursery and chances for photos with koalas.

18. What is another word for sanctuary?

- ○ show
- ○ shelter
- ○ farm
- ○ zoo

19. There are two large flightless birds mentioned. Colour in the two circles next to these birds.

- ○ lorikeets
- ○ kangaroos
- ○ koalas
- ○ emus
- ○ cassowaries
- ○ platypus
- ○ wombats
- ○ wallabies
- ○ dingoes
- ○ crocodiles

20. Colour in the circles next to the animals that are marsupials.

- ○ lorikeets
- ○ kangaroos
- ○ koalas
- ○ emus
- ○ cassowaries
- ○ platypus
- ○ wombats
- ○ wallabies
- ○ dingoes
- ○ crocodiles

21. Colour in the circles next to the animals that are amphibious.

- ○ lorikeets
- ○ kangaroos
- ○ koalas
- ○ emus
- ○ cassowaries
- ○ platypus
- ○ wombats
- ○ wallabies
- ○ dingoes
- ○ crocodiles

22. Which is the closest capital city to Currumbin Sanctuary?

- ○ Adelaide
- ○ Sydney
- ○ Brisbane
- ○ Melbourne
- ○ Hobart
- ○ Canberra
- ○ Darwin

☞ Answers and explanations on page 16

23. In what type of publication would you expect to see an article like this on Currumbin Sanctuary?

- ○ I would expect to see it in a book on reptiles.
- ○ I would expect to see it in a children's book.
- ○ I would expect to see it in a tourist guide.
- ○ I would expect to see it in a daily newspaper.

Read *Role of a Newsreader* and answer questions 24 to 33. In this passage the writer talks to a newsreader.

Role of a Newsreader

Elizabeth Halley: When the cameras are on you, are you reading from your script or have you learnt it by heart?

Geraldine Doogue: No, there's a real danger in doing that. I used to try to learn it by heart years ago, and that's fatal because you find there's just far too much to memorise. When you're sitting in a small studio with all the lights on you, it's a bit like a pressure cooker, and you find that if you forget one word it throws you, you end up looking terrified, with your eyes popping out. I've seen people do this.

EH: Do you have someone prompting you?

GD: No, you have what's called an autocue. The script is put onto a screen electronically, using a set of mirrors. The autocue operator sits about six metres away from you at a machine where he or she tapes all the pages together. It's like a giant message, like a long piece of paper which is fed into a sort of turntable. When we look at the cameras, the script rolls around in front of us. What is awful is if suddenly the autocue breaks down.

EH: Has that ever happened?

GD: Yes, you can see the newsreader following the autocue and they suddenly look at the camera and their eyes go wide and they go, 'Er, er' and look down at their script—you always have your script in front of you. I always make sure, having been through this that I have the right page open, because your script is very thick, you've got pages and pages of it. I have seen people who haven't bothered to keep up—they look down and their script is pages behind where they are on the autocue.

EH: And so they have to quickly flip through?

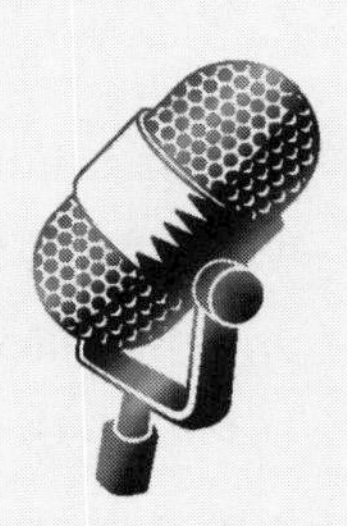

GD: Oh, yes—they are frantically thinking, 'I'll find this in a moment'—it's terrible, just terrible!

EH: If something goes wrong like that, do they switch to something else, put a bit of music on or switch to another story? Or is it up to the newsreader to cover up what's going wrong?

GD: Well, that's an interesting thing. That differs from channel to channel. Usually commercial channels will go to a commercial break, which can get you out of any number of holes.

 ☞ **Answers and explanations on page 16**

Generally I think it would be fair to say that you're very rarely asked to ad lib, just talk off the cuff, for any longer than thirty seconds to a minute. It would be considered a minor disaster if a newsreader had to do that, because it's a very tightly constructed little operation, very contrived. You know, everything has its place, everything …

From *TV News: An Interview with Geraldine Doogue* by Elizabeth Halley, HBJ, 1992

24. Who is the interviewer in this passage?

- ○ the newsreader
- ○ Geraldine Doogue
- ○ Elizabeth Halley

25. Who is *GD* in the interview?

- ○ *GD* is a short way of writing Geraldine Doogue.
- ○ *GD* is the name of the interviewer.
- ○ *GD* is the name of the writer.
- ○ *GD* is a short way of writing Geraldine.

26. What is a newsreader doing when the cameras are on them?

- ○ A newsreader has learnt the news by heart.
- ○ A newsreader is reading from the script.
- ○ A newsreader has someone prompt them.
- ○ A newsreader is looking at the autocue.

27. What is the problem for a newsreader in learning the news by heart?
Write your answer on the lines.

____

____

____

____

____

28. What is an *autocue*?

- ○ An autocue displays the script off camera.
- ○ An autocue displays the script on camera.
- ○ An autocue is a set of mirrors.

29. What is a newsreader supposed to do when the autocue breaks down?

- ○ A newsreader should look at the camera.
- ○ A newsreader should go 'Er, er'.
- ○ A newsreader should look at their script.

30. What does the newsreader advise about the script?

- ○ to keep ahead of the autocue
- ○ to keep up with the autocue
- ○ to keep behind the autocue

31. What happens when the autocue is not working?

- ○ Some channels will go to a commercial break.
- ○ Some channels cover up what has gone wrong.
- ○ Some channels put on music.

 ☞ Answers and explanations on page 16

32. What is the meaning of *ad lib*?

- ○ make up something to say
- ○ read from the script
- ○ apologise

33. What would be a good subtitle for this text?

- ○ Presenting Opinions
- ○ The Timing of the News
- ○ Live Reports from Newsreaders
- ○ Presenting the News

END OF TEST

Well done! You have completed the sample questions for Reading. Even if you don't practise any other Reading Tests, at least you will have some familiarity with the method used in the NAPLAN Tests.

How did you go with these sample questions? Check to see where you did well and where you had problems. Try to revise the questions that were hard for you.

There are four more Reading Tests, each containing 39 questions. They include many of the same types of questions, plus a few other types.

The spelling, grammar and punctuation questions are in the Conventions of Language sample test. You can do this test now or you can leave it until later. Now take a break before you start any more tests.

Answers and explanations on page 16

ANSWERS TO SAMPLE QUESTIONS—READING

1. **It shows the stages in the growth of a butterfly.**
2. **A chrysalis is like a cocoon.**
3. **6.**
4. **It takes some weeks to a few months for the pupa to emerge.** (Read the passages carefully—the answer is there somewhere.)
5. **Shredded Wheat** could be a good title of this text in the book.
6. The aim of the text is **to suggest**.
7. *Mastication* means **chewing**. You may not have known this word.
8. **The example that is used is sports performance.**
9. **Legacy cares for the dependants of deceased veterans.**
10. **1900**
11. **Returned soldiers** volunteer for Legacy.
12. **Legacy assists dependants.**
13. **Legacy is a charity.**
14. **27 hectares**
15. **to see Australian wildlife**
16. **wildlife shows, lorikeet feeding, koala photos and a play park**
17. **It claims to have the largest collection of Australian wildlife in the world.**
18. **shelter**
19. **emus, cassowaries**
20. **koalas, wombats, kangaroos, wallabies** (Note: a marsupial is an animal that carries its young in a pouch.)
21. **platypus, crocodile** (Note: Amphibious means the animal is able to live or operate on both land and water.)
22. **Brisbane**
23. **I would expect to see it in a tourist guide.**
24. **Elizabeth Halley**
25. ***GD* is a short way of writing Geraldine Doogue.**
26. **A newsreader is looking at the autocue.**
27. **There is too much for a newsreader to learn.**
28. **An autocue displays the script off camera.**
29. **A newsreader should look at their script.**
30. **to keep up with the autocue**
31. **Some channels will go to a commercial break.**
32. **make up something to say**
33. **Presenting the News**

SAMPLE QUESTIONS—CONVENTIONS OF LANGUAGE

Instructions for parents and teachers

This section tests whether students can spell words and find spelling, grammar and punctuation errors in a text.

The first series of questions are multiple-choice grammar and punctuation questions just as in NAPLAN Online. Then we have provided spelling words that are to be read out to the student. The words are read by the teacher or a parent. The student writes their answer on the lines we have provided below. This is similar to NAPLAN Online.

Read the sentences. They have some gaps. Colour in the circle with the correct answer. Colour in only one circle for each answer.

1. ______ recess and lunch we went to the library to hear the author.

○ From ○ Along ○ Through ○ Between

2. My button fell off ______ it was not sewn on properly.

○ unless ○ because ○ although ○ until

3. I looked around but my friends ______ gone.

○ was ○ were ○ has ○ are

4. Tomas is ______ than Luke.

○ stronger ○ more stronger ○ strong ○ strongest

5. I woke up with an ______ headache.

○ gigantic ○ huge ○ colossal ○ incredible

Colour in the circle with the correct answer.

6. Which sentence is correct?

○ I reached the top of the stairs and just stand still.
○ I reached the top of the stairs and just stooded still.
○ I reached the top of the stairs and just stood still.
○ I reached the top of the stairs and just standing still.

7. Which sentence is correct?

○ Mum, Dad and I went to the park.
○ Mum, Dad and myself went to the park.
○ Mum, Dad and me went to the park.

Did you colour in one of the circles?

☞ Answers and explanations on pages 23–24

8. Shade one circle to show where the missing question mark (**?**) should go.

I asked him where the car was ○
Why do you want to know ○
he said ○

9. Shade the circles to show which words should start with a capital letter. Shade more than one circle if necessary.

ms r french visited the school at stanwell harbour.

○ ○ ○ ○ ○ ○ ○

10. Shade **four** circles to show where the speech marks (“ and ”) should go.

○ ○ ○ ○ ○○

I like green vegetables, said Georgia, but I also like potatoes .

11. Which sentence has the correct punctuation?

○ That Wednesday which happens to be my birthday, is the only day I am available to meet.
○ That Wednesday which, happens to be my birthday is the only, day I am available to meet.
○ That Wednesday, which happens to be my birthday, is the only day I am available to meet.
○ That Wednesday which happens, to be my birthday, is the only day I am available to meet.

Read the sentences and colour in the circle with the correct word or words to complete the sentence. Colour in only one circle for each answer.

12. All of the ▬▬ were ready for the exam.

○ student’s ○ students’ ○ students ○ students’s

13. My cold is definitely ▬▬ this morning.

○ worser ○ worst ○ worse ○ more worser

14. Mikhail dressed ▬▬ this morning.

○ him ○ himself ○ his ○ hisself

15. ▬▬ fight continuously.

○ She and her brother
○ Her and her brother
○ She and him
○ She and himself

☞ Answers and explanations on pages 23–24

SAMPLE QUESTIONS—CONVENTIONS OF LANGUAGE

Colour in the circle with the correct answer.

16. Which sentence has the correct punctuation?

- ○ John said "I don't want to play today", so Nicholas cried.
- ○ John said, "I don't want to play today," so Nicholas cried.
- ○ "John said I don't want to play today", so Nicholas cried.
- ○ John said I "don't want to play today, so Nicholas cried."

Did you colour in one of the circles?

Read the sentences. They have words missing. Colour in the circle next to the word that completes the sentence. Colour in only one circle for each answer.

17. Tuesday ______ another of our special days. ○ has ○ is

18. Dieu was class monitor last ______. ○ weak ○ week

19. Mrs Bramble teaches Grade ______. ○ For ○ Four ○ Fore

20. Pat ______ how they laughed at her joke. ○ forgot ○ remembered

21. You can see the ______ in the back garden. ○ goanna ○ Go Anna

22. ______ dog is black, brown and white. ○ Marios ○ Mario's ○ Marios'

23. The quick brown fox jumped ______ the lazy dog. ○ in ○ under ○ over

24. ______ played tennis in the street. ○ david ○ David ○ Davids

You are about halfway through the sample questions—well done!

☞ Answers and explanations on pages 23–24

Sample spelling questions 25 to 36

To the teacher or parent

First read and say the word slowly and clearly. Then read the sentence with the word in it. Then repeat the word again.

If the student is not sure, ask them to guess. It is okay to skip a word if it is not known.

Sample Conventions of Language spelling words

Word	Example
25. although	I am going shopping although I would rather play with my friends.
26. recognise	My aunt did not recognise me after all these years.
27. getting	It was getting very hot in the kitchen.
28. eight	There were eight people in the waiting room.
29. ankle	I hurt my ankle playing tennis yesterday.
30. goes	Dad goes to work at 6 am every day.
31. illegal	It is illegal to park across the footpath.
32. decided	We decided to go to the library.
33. yelling	The fans were excited and yelling loudly.
34. voting	The voting for school prefects is now complete.
35. stopping	There is no way of stopping.
36. driveway	They parked in the driveway.

Write your answer on the line.

25. ____________________

26. ____________________

27. ____________________

28. ____________________

29. ____________________

30. ____________________

31. ____________________

32. ____________________

33. ____________________

34. ____________________

35. ____________________

36. ____________________

 Answers and explanations on pages 23–24

Look at the labelled drawing of the human body. The spelling mistakes on the labels have been underlined. Write the correct spelling for each word in the boxes.

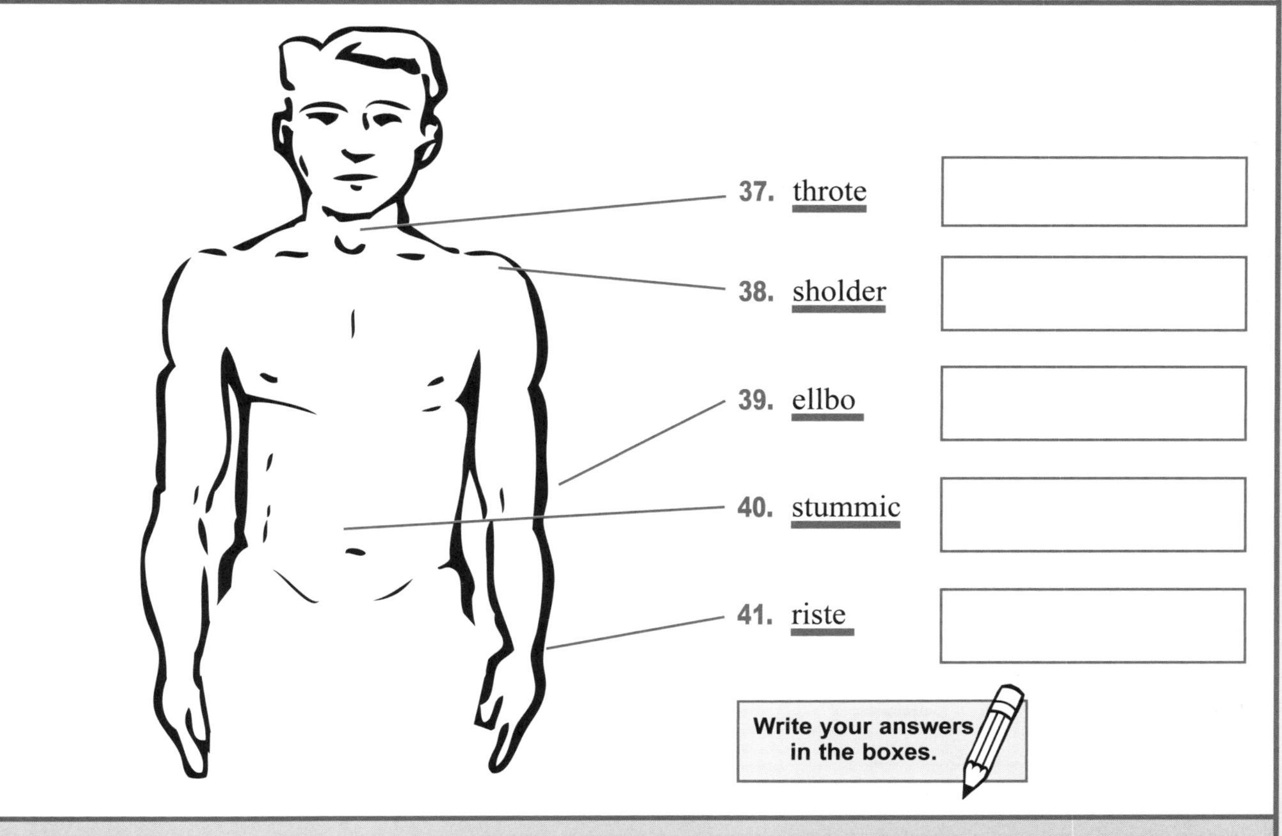

Read the text *Fish*. The spelling mistakes have been underlined. Colour in the circle next to the correct answer. Colour in only one circle for each answer.

Fish

42. Fish live in water. Fish can breethe under water.
- ○ breathe ○ breath ○ brethe

43. Gills let oxigen from the water into the fish's blood.
- ○ oxegen ○ oxygen ○ oxigun

44. All fish are coverd with scales.
- ○ covered ○ cuvered ○ kovered

45. Most babie fish hatch out of eggs.
- ○ baby ○ babe ○ babie

46. Many fish eat tiny plants called plankton that grou in the sea.
- ○ groe ○ grow ○ gro

47. Some fish eat otha fish.
- ○ other ○ othe ○ utha

Answers and explanations on pages 23–24

Read the text *A Scare at the Beach*. The spelling mistakes have been underlined.
Write the correct spelling for each underlined word in the boxes.

A Scare at the Beach

Write your answers in the boxes.

An ien man champion was knocked off his surfboard by a shark. **48.**

Bystanders thort the shark was around three metres long. **49.**

They saw to other large sharks. **50.**

A helicopter chased a ways the other sharks. **51.**

Read the text *Kidneys*. Each sentence has one word that is incorrect.
Write the correct spelling for each word in the boxes.

Kidneys

The kidneys are nessesary organs of the human body. **52.**

Kidneys come in pears and each is about 13 cm long. **53.**

One of the jobs of the kidney is to filter waiste out of the blood. **54.**

END OF TEST

Well done! You have completed the sample questions for Conventions of Language. Even if you don't practise any other Conventions of Language Tests, at least you will have some familiarity with the method used in the NAPLAN Tests.

How did you go with these sample questions? Check to see where you did well and where you had problems. Try to revise the questions that were hard for you.

There are four more Conventions of Language Tests to practise. These contain around 55 questions. They include many of the same types of questions, plus a few other types.

Answers and explanations on pages 23–24

ANSWERS TO SAMPLE QUESTIONS—CONVENTIONS OF LANGUAGE

1. **Between**
2. **because**
3. **were**
4. **stronger**
5. **incredible.** Remember: After the word *an*, the next word must start with a vowel.
6. **I reached the top of the stairs and just stood still.**
7. **Mum, Dad and I went to the park.** Does that sentence sound OK to you? Perhaps it does, but the others have a pronoun error. If you are having trouble, say the sentence as separate clauses: *Mum went to the park; Dad went to the park; Me/I went to the park. Me went to the park* is clearly not right, so *I went to the park* is correct.
8. We have underlined where the question mark should appear, to make it easier to see: **I asked him where the car was. 'Why do you want to know?' he said.**
9. The sentence should look like this: **Ms R French visited the school at Stanwell Harbour.**
10. **"I like green vegetables," said Georgia, "but I also like potatoes."** Full stops, question marks and commas always go inside the quotation marks. Only put the question mark outside the speech marks if the quotation is not a question, e.g. *Did George say, 'I don't know'?*
11. **That Wednesday, which happens to be my birthday, is the only day I am available to meet.** A pair of commas is used in the middle of a sentence to identify clauses, phrases and words that are not essential to the meaning of the sentence. One comma is used before to indicate the beginning of the pause and one at the end to indicate the end of the pause. A good hint is that if you leave out the clause, phrase or word, does the sentence still make sense? That Wednesday (which happens to be my birthday) is the only day I am available to meet.
12. **students**
13. **worse**
14. **himself**
15. **She and her brother** fight continuously.
16. **John said, "I don't want to play today," so Nicholas cried.**
17. **is**
18. **week**
19. **Four**
20. **remembered**
21. **goanna**
22. **Mario's**
23. **over**. Ask your teacher or parents why this is an unusual sentence. Hint: See if it uses every letter in the alphabet.
24. **David**
25. **although**
26. **recognise**
27. **getting**
28. **eight**
29. **ankle**
30. **goes**
31. **illegal**
32. **decided**
33. **yelling**
34. **voting**
35. **stopping**
36. **driveway**
37. **throat**. Notice that in these questions you had to write the answer in the boxes. If you make an error, cross out the wrong answer neatly and write in the new answer.
38. **shoulder**
39. **elbow**
40. **stomach**
41. **wrist**
42. **breathe**
43. **oxygen**
44. **covered**
45. **baby**
46. **grow**
47. **other**. These last few should have been quite easy for you.
48. **ironman.** Don't spend too much time on any one question. Allow around one minute for each question.
49. **thought**
50. **two**

51. **away.** Remember that if you make an error, cross out the wrong answer neatly and write in the new answer.
52. **necessary.** Please note that there are no tricks intended in any of these questions. In the NAPLAN Tests, the questions are specially selected and designed to test your ability to spell.
53. **pairs.** Although the word *pears* is spelt correctly, it isn't the right word for this context. The English language includes many words that sound the same but are spelt differently depending upon the context in which they are used. Be careful of these words and get to know the context in which they should be used, e.g. *too/to/two*.
54. **waste**

An important note about the NAPLAN Online tests

The NAPLAN Online Numeracy test will be divided into different sections. Students will only have one opportunity to check their answers at the end of each section before proceeding to the next one. This means that after students have completed a section and moved onto the next they will not be able to check their work again. We have included reminders for students to check their work at specific points in the practice tests from now on so they become familiar with this process.

NUMERACY TEST 1

This is the first Numeracy Test. There are 42 questions.

If you aren't sure what to do, ask your teacher or your parents to help you. Don't be afraid to ask if it isn't clear to you.

Allow around 50 minutes for this test.

Write the answer in the box or colour in the circle with the correct answer. Colour in only one circle for each answer.

1. Here is a table of numbers. Some squares are white and some are shaded. There is a pattern in these numbers.

1	2	3	4	5	6	7
8	9	10	11	12	13	14
15	16	17	18	19	20	21
22	23	24	25	26	27	28
29	30	31	32	33	34	35
36	37	38	39	40	41	42

What is the next number that should be shaded?

○ 38 ○ 39 ○ 40 ○ 41 ○ 42

2. Here is a digital clock.

Which analogue clock shows this time?

○ ○ ○ ○

3. Here is a shape made from different pieces. How many of the pieces are triangular prisms?

○ 2 ○ 4 ○ 9 ○ 6

4. What is the value of 4 in 9481?

- ○ 4 thousands
- ○ 4 hundreds
- ○ 4 tens
- ○ 4 ones

5. Which is the largest angle?

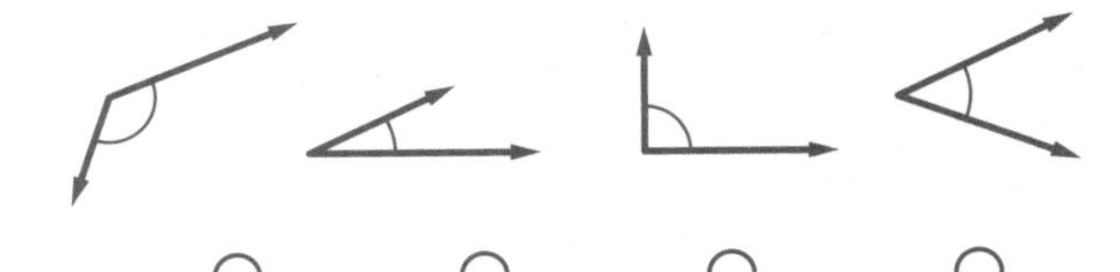

○ ○ ○ ○

☞ Answers and explanations on page 169

6. Add the travelling times for this bus journey in peak hour.

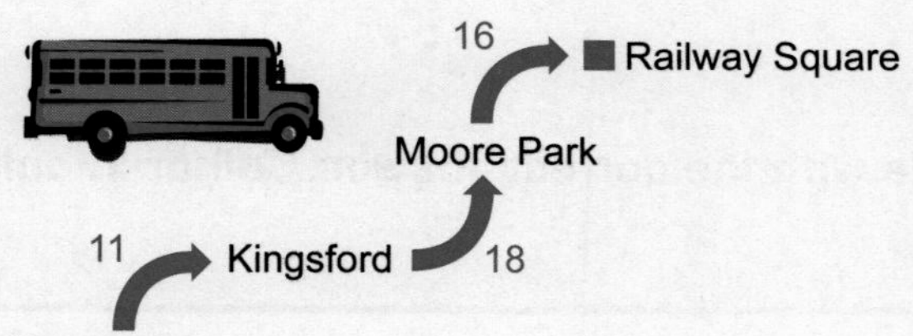

Maroubra to Kingsford 11 minutes
Kingsford to Moore Park 18 minutes
Moore Park to Railway Square 16 minutes

How long is the bus trip from Maroubra to Railway Square?

☐ minutes

Write your answer in the box.

7. There is a pattern in these numbers. Write in the number that is missing.

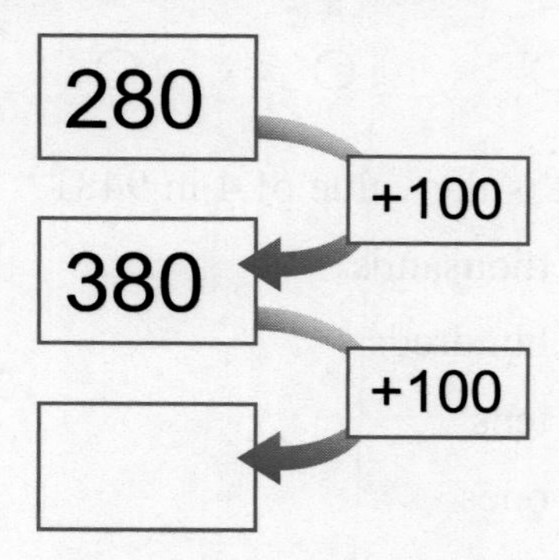

8. Use the table below to answer this question.

Birds in my backyard today

Type of bird	Number of birds
Rosellas	13
Magpies	19
Pigeons	16
Galahs	12

How many magpies and pigeons are there?

☐

Write your answer in the box.

9. You have these coins.

You buy a ticket for $2.50. How much do you have left?

$1 ○ $1.15 ○ $1.25 ○ $1.35 ○

10. Here are four shapes. They are called A, B, C and D. Each shape has part of it coloured.

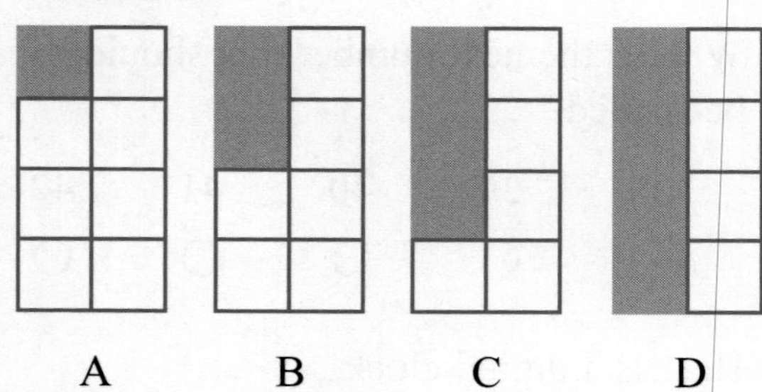

Which shape has one-quarter of its surface coloured?

A ○ B ○ C ○ D ○

11. Here is a shape made up of some blocks.

Which one of the four shapes on the next page is the same as the one above? Is it A, B, C or D?

 ☞ Answers and explanations on page 169

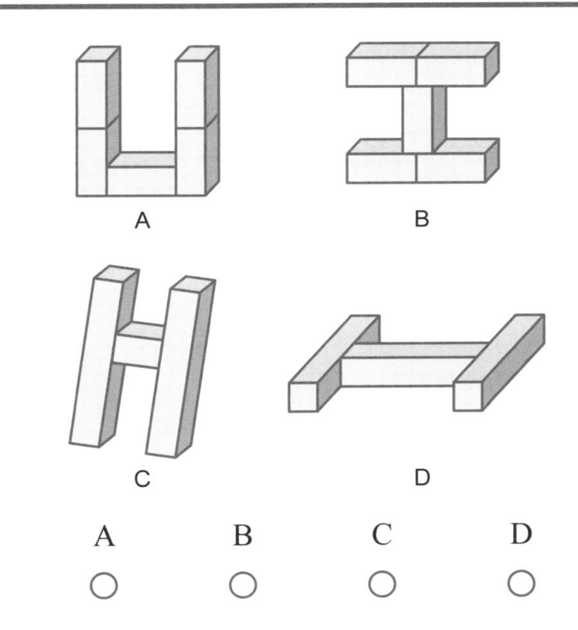

A B C D

○ ○ ○ ○

12. CS Lewis wrote the Narnia series, including *The Lion, the Witch and the Wardrobe*. He was born in 1898 and died in 1963.

Which sum would you use to show how old he was when he died?

○ 1898 + 1963

○ 1898 – 1963

○ 1963 – 1898

13. This football costs $3.50.

How much will 3 footballs cost? Fill in the number sentence below.

3 × $ ☐ = $ ☐

14. Here are some foods from a cafe. There is a slice of cake, some toast and a piece of fish. Their price in the cafe is also shown.

$3.70 $3.20 $15.10

Here are four sums. They round off the prices and show a quick way to guess or estimate the price of the three foods. Which is the best way?

○ $3 + $3 + $15 ○ $4 + $3 + $15

○ $3 + $3 + $16 ○ $4 + $4 + $16

It would be a good idea to check your answers to questions 1 to 14 before moving on to the other questions.

15. This chart shows the length of some objects.

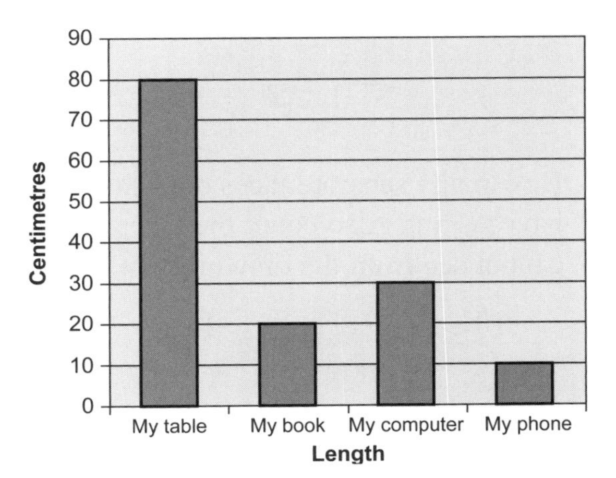

Which sentence is correct?

○ My computer and phone together are the same length as my table.

○ My table is the same length as my book and my computer and my phone together.

○ My book and computer together are the same length as my table.

○ My book and phone together are the same length as my computer.

 ☞ Answers and explanations on page 169

16. There are six spaces that have a number. Spin the arrow and it will land on one of the spaces with a number.

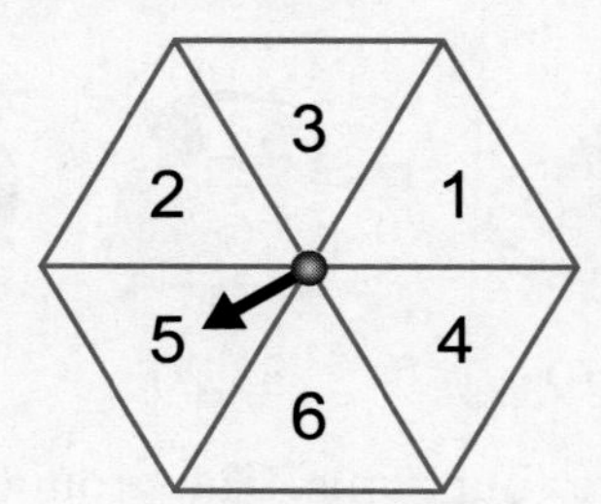

If I spin this arrow, what is the chance it will land on the space with the number 5?

- ◯ 1 out of 6 chances
- ◯ 4 out of 6 chances
- ◯ 6 out of 1 chances
- ◯ 5 out of 6 chances

17. Here is a prism.

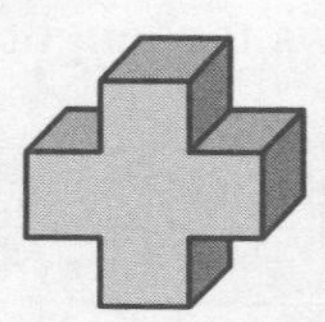

How many separate faces does the shape have? (Hint: Also count the faces that you cannot see from the drawing.)

10	12	14	16
◯	◯	◯	◯

18. Complete this calculation.

$784 - 269 = \square$

19. Complete this calculation.

$4.6 + 5.8 = \square$

20. Complete this calculation.

$1904 \div 8 = \square$

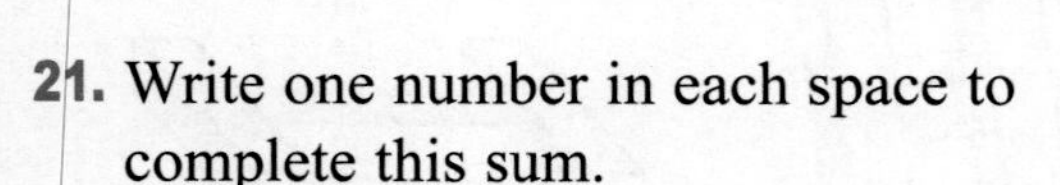

21. Write one number in each space to complete this sum.

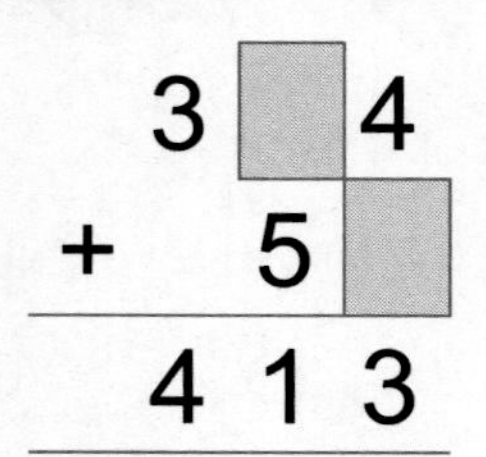

22. Here is a piece of wood. There is a tape under the wood.

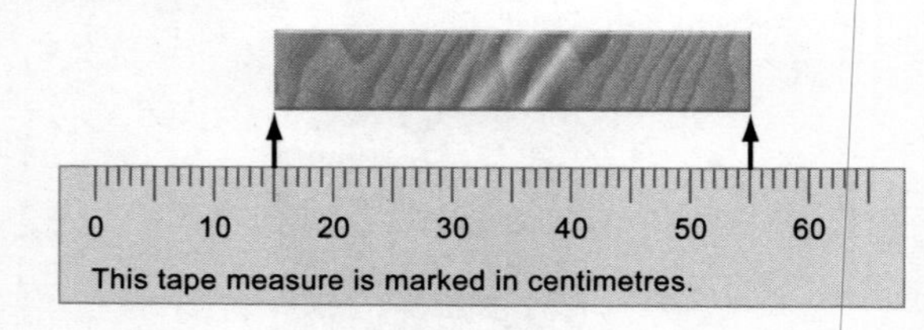

How long is this piece of wood?

30 cm	40 cm	50 cm	60 cm
◯	◯	◯	◯

23. I folded this pattern in half.

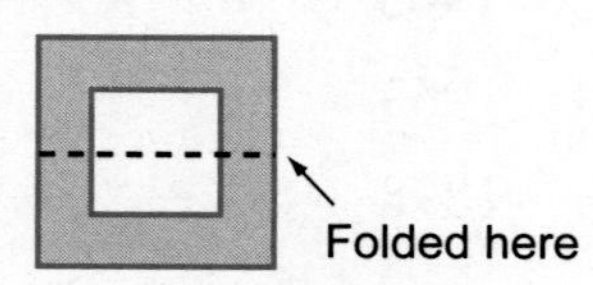

Which shape will I see?

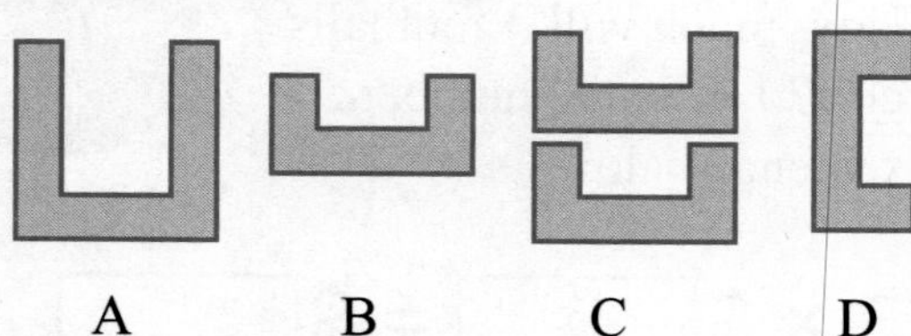

A	B	C	D
◯	◯	◯	◯

☞ Answers and explanations on page 169

24.

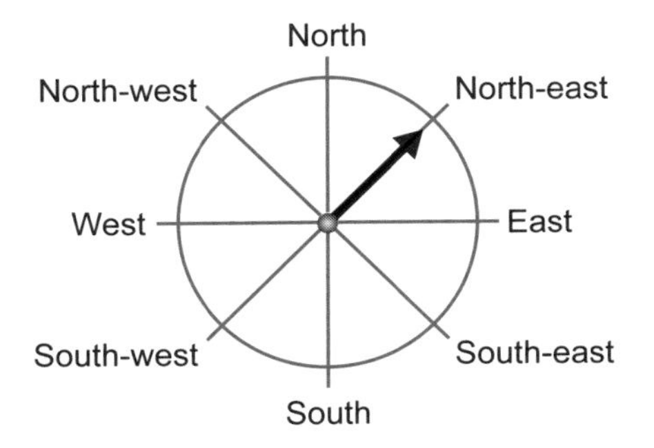

To which direction would the arrow be pointing if it was moved two spaces clockwise?

East	South-east	South	South-west
○	○	○	○

25. An improper fraction has a *numerator* that is larger than a *denominator*.

Which one of these fractions is an improper fraction?

$\frac{1}{4}$	$\frac{5}{4}$	$1\frac{1}{4}$	$\frac{4}{9}$
○	○	○	○

26. Speed is equal to the distance travelled divided by the time taken. To find the speed, divide the distance by the time.

$$\text{Speed} = \frac{\text{Distance}}{\text{Time}}$$

For example, if the distance I covered was 100 km and it took me two hours then my speed would be 50 km per hour (100 ÷ 2 = 50).

Here is a problem: If I travelled 160 km and the time taken was four hours, then what is my speed?

☐ km per hour

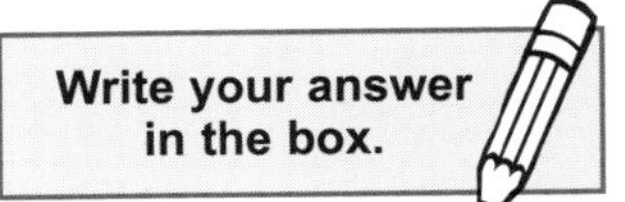

27. Which of the numbers indicated below is closest to 0.1?

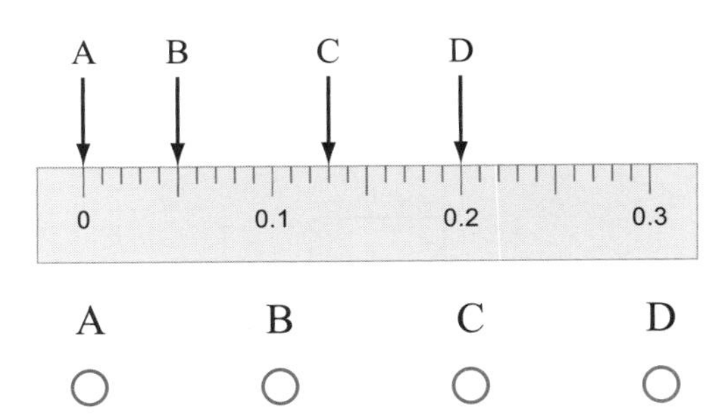

A	B	C	D
○	○	○	○

28. There are 11 nations in Oceania. The land size varies from 7.6 million square km for Australia to a tiny 21 square km for Nauru. (Note: All percentages have been rounded.)

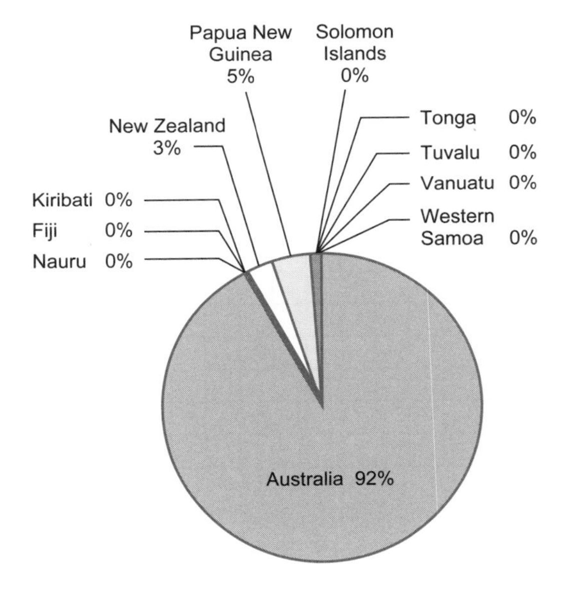

Which country has the second-largest area?

○ Solomon Islands
○ Papua New Guinea
○ New Zealand
○ Fiji
○ Australia

It would be a good idea to check your answers to questions 15 to 28 before moving on to the other questions.

 ☞ Answers and explanations on pages 169–170

29. What is the perimeter (the distance around the outside edges) of this figure?

(Note: Some of the lengths are not shown in the figure.)

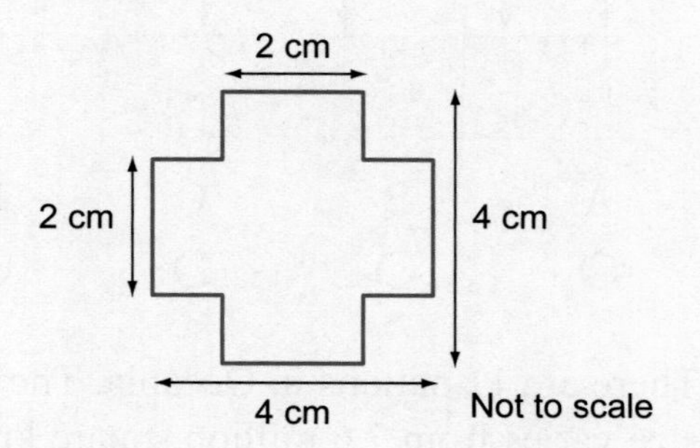

12 cm ○ 14 cm ○ 16 cm ○ 18 cm ○ 20 cm ○

30. Here is a map. It shows three suburbs. The map is divided into sections.

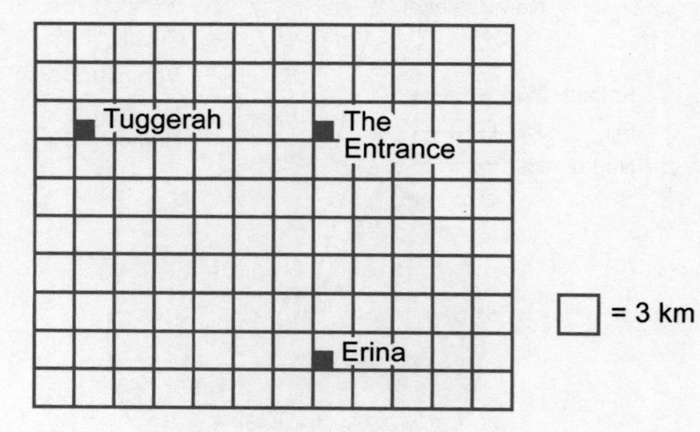

The distance from Tuggerah to The Entrance is 18 km.

How far is it from The Entrance to Erina on this map?

6 km ○ 12 km ○ 15 km ○ 18 km ○ 24 km ○

31. Here is a shape. Some parts are coloured and some are blank.

How many parts are coloured?

- ○ 10 out of 15 parts
- ○ 10 out of 25 parts
- ○ 15 out of 25 parts
- ○ 25 out of 25 parts

32. The sides of this shape are folded upwards to make a triangular pyramid. Each triangle has the same pattern on both sides.

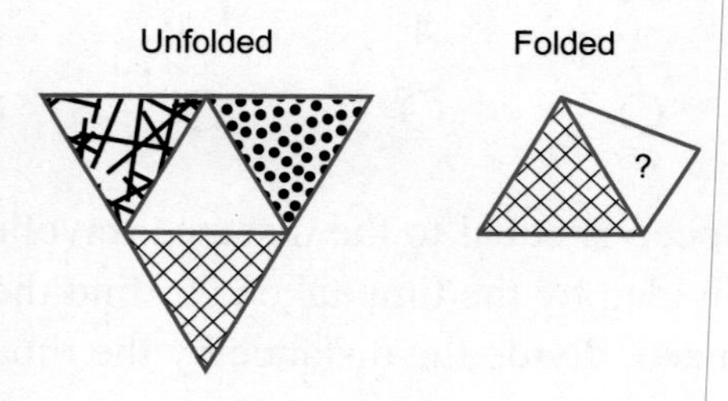

If the shape is not moved after it has been folded, which pattern fills the space shown with the question mark?

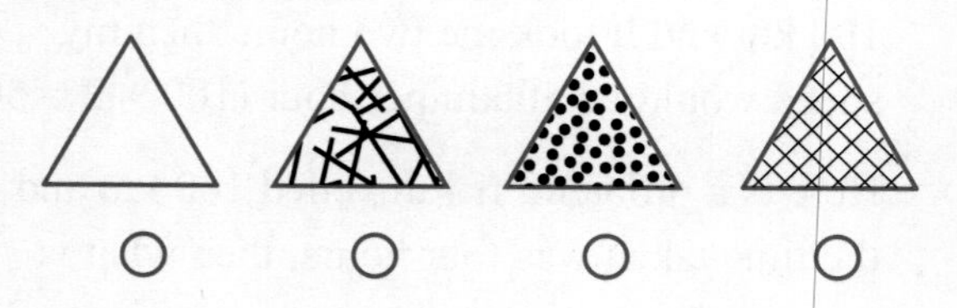

○ ○ ○ ○

☞ Answers and explanations on page 170

Here is a small water bottle.
It holds 10 litres.
It is part full.

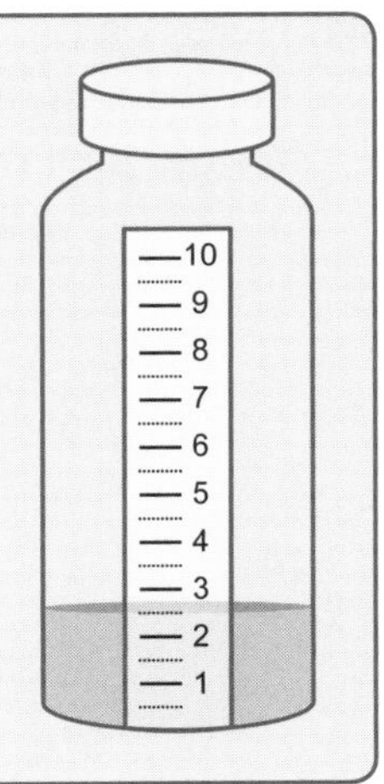

33. How many litres are in this bottle now?

- ◯ 1 litre
- ◯ 1.5 litres
- ◯ 2 litres
- ◯ 2.5 litres
- ◯ 3 litres

34. How full is this bottle?

- ◯ one-sixth
- ◯ one-fifth
- ◯ one-quarter
- ◯ one-third
- ◯ one-half

35. There are 12 animals in these pictures. Some are the same.

What fraction of the 12 animals are dogs?

$\frac{9}{3}$	$\frac{1}{3}$	$\frac{1}{4}$	$\frac{12}{3}$
◯	◯	◯	◯

36. Some numbers are triangular. This means that they have the pattern of a triangle. Here are some examples.

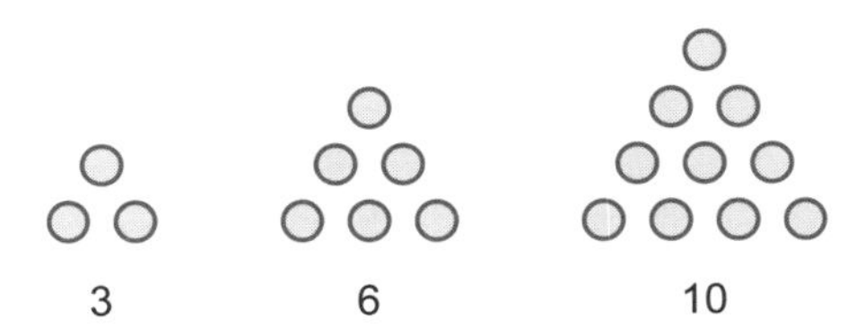

What would be the next triangular number?

12	15	16	21	24
◯	◯	◯	◯	◯

37. Without looking, you choose a shoe from a box at random (this means any shoe). There are four black shoes, four grey shoes and two blue shoes.

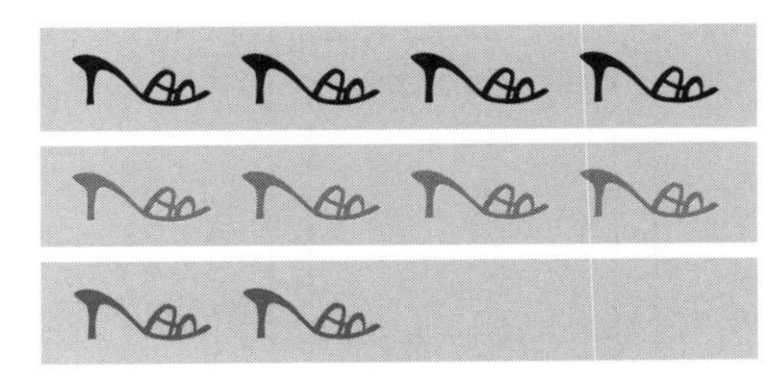

The first shoe that you pick is black. What are the chances that the next shoe you pick will be black?

- ◯ 1 in 10
- ◯ 3 in 10
- ◯ 4 in 10
- ◯ 1 in 9
- ◯ 3 in 9
- ◯ 4 in 9

38. Three cats all weigh the same and together the three of them weigh 15 kg.
Four dogs also weigh the same and together the four of them weigh 32 kg.

You take out just one cat and one dog. What would be the average weight of just one cat and one dog together?

5.5 kg	6 kg	6.5 kg	7 kg	7.5 kg
◯	◯	◯	◯	◯

☞ Answers and explanations on page 170

39. Look at this rectangle. It is not drawn to scale.

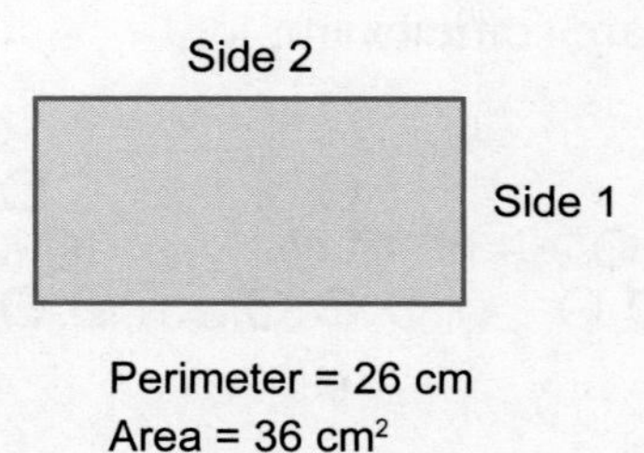

The perimeter of the rectangle is 26 cm and its area is 36 cm^2. What are the lengths of its two sides?

40. This box is one-quarter full of cricket balls.

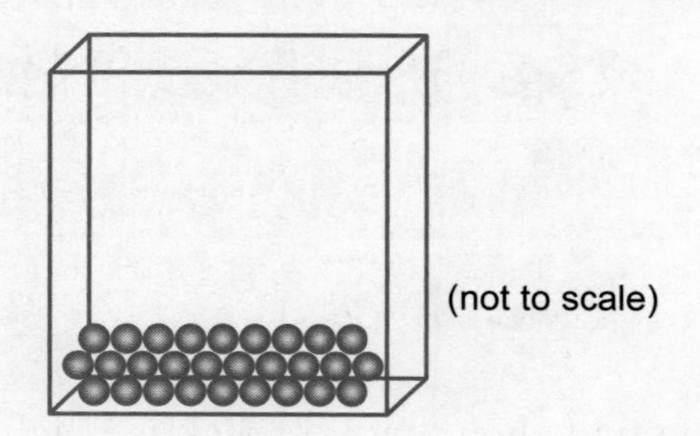

You put in another 60 cricket balls and now it is three-quarters full.

How many cricket balls does the box hold when it is full?

41. Here is a puzzle. Find the two missing numbers in this diamond puzzle. You follow the arrows to find the answers.

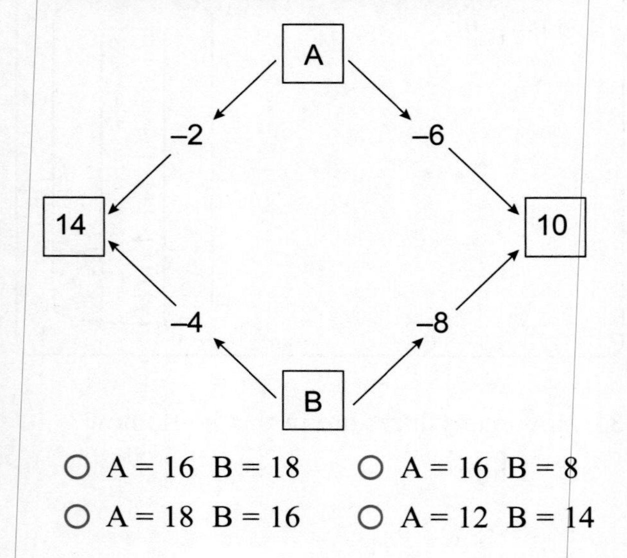

○ A = 16 B = 18 ○ A = 16 B = 8

○ A = 18 B = 16 ○ A = 12 B = 14

42. Here is a grid with some squares that are fully shaded and some that are partly shaded.

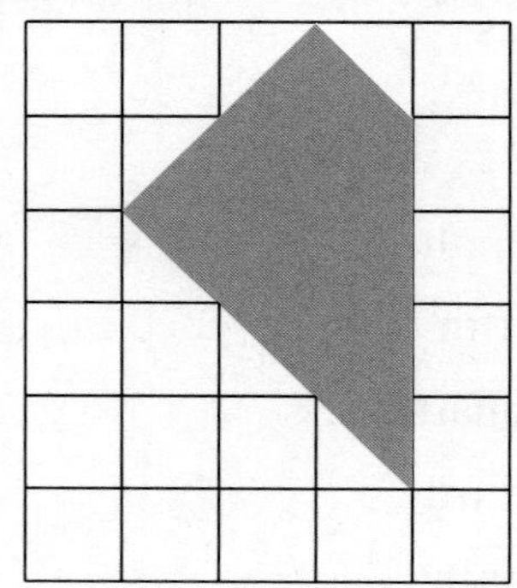

Estimate the number of shaded squares on this grid.

○ 10 ○ 8 ○ 6 ○ 7

END OF TEST

Well done! You have completed the first Numeracy Test. Even if you don't practise any others, at least you will have done a fair sample of the questions.

How did you go with these test questions? Some were harder than the sample questions. Check to see where you did well and where you had problems. Try to revise the questions that were hard for you.

Use the diagnostic chart on pages 34–35 to see which level of ability you reached. This is only an estimate. Don't be surprised if you answered some difficult questions correctly or even missed some easier questions.

There are now three more practice tests, each containing 42 questions. We will start to include new types of questions in each of these tests.

 ☞ Answers and explanations on page 170

Check the answers

As you check the answer for each question, mark it as correct (✓) or incorrect (✗). Mark any questions that you omitted or left out as incorrect (✗) for the moment.

Then look at how many you answered correctly in each band. Your achievement band is probably somewhere up to the point where you answered most questions correctly. You can ask your parents or your teacher to help you do this if it isn't clear.

We expect you to miss some easy questions and also to answer some hard questions correctly, but your level of ability should be where you are starting to find the questions too hard. Some students will reach the top band—this means that their ability cannot be measured by these questions or even the NAPLAN Tests. They found it far too easy.

Understanding the different levels

We have divided the questions into three levels of difficulty:

- Standard
- Intermediate
- Advanced.

For each question we have described the skill involved in answering the question. Then, depending on what sort of skill is involved, we have placed it into one of the three levels. It should make sense, especially when you go back and look at the type of question. The Standard level includes the easiest tasks and then they increase in difficulty.

Don't worry about the level of ability in which you are located. We expect students to be spread across all of the three bands. Also numeracy may or may not be your strongest subject.

The purpose of these practice tests is to help you be as confident as possible and perform to the best of your ability. The purpose of the NAPLAN Tests is to show what you know or can do. For the first time it allows the user to estimate their level of ability before taking the actual test and also to see if there is any improvement across the practice tests.

Remember that the levels of ability are only a rough guide. No claim is made that they are perfect. They are only an indicator. Your level might change as you do each practice test. We hope that these brief notes are of some help.

CHECK YOUR SKILLS: NUMERACY TEST 1

Instructions

As you check the answer for each question, mark it as correct (✓) or incorrect (✗). Mark any questions that you omitted or left out as incorrect (✗) for the moment.

Then look at how many you answered correctly in each level. You will be able to see what level you are at by finding the point where you started having consistent difficulty with questions at a certain level. For example, if you answer most questions correctly up to the Intermediate level and then get most questions wrong from then onwards, it is likely your ability is at the Intermediate level. You can ask your parents or your teacher to help you do this if it isn't clear to you.

Am I able to ...

	SKILL	ESTIMATED LEVEL	✓ or ✗
1	Interpret a chart to continue a number pattern involving single-digit numbers?	Standard	
2	Convert digital time to analogue time?	Standard	
3	Identify a 3D composite model from objects (cylinders, rectangular or triangular prisms)?	Standard	
4	Identify place value in a 4-digit number?	Standard	
5	Identify the size of an angle?	Standard	
6	Solve an addition of three two-digit numbers?	Standard	
7	Continue a number pattern involving counting by hundreds?	Standard	
8	Interpret data in two-way tables?	Standard	
9	Calculate the change from coins?	Standard	
10	Use informal units to measure the area of a shape?	Standard	
11	Recognise a 3D model made from rectangular prisms from a different perspective?	Standard	
12	Recognise how to solve a difference in dates?	Standard	
13	Solve everyday money problems involving addition or multiplication?	Intermediate	
14	Select the best addition strategy for estimating a total?	Intermediate	
15	Interpret data from column graphs to confirm a statement?	Intermediate	
16	Use chance to describe the outcome in a simple experiment with random selection?	Intermediate	
17	Identify the faces of a 3D model?	Intermediate	
18	Solve a three-digit subtraction?	Intermediate	
19	Solve a problem with place values for decimals?	Intermediate	
20	Solve division involving four-digit numbers?	Intermediate	
21	Use problem-solving strategies to complete a number problem?	Intermediate	
22	Use a scale in metric units to solve a length problem?	Intermediate	
23	Identify symmetry in a design?	Intermediate	
24	Specify direction using clockwise quarter turns?	Intermediate	
25	Recognise an improper fraction?	Intermediate	

CHECK YOUR SKILLS: NUMERACY TEST 1

	SKILL	ESTIMATED LEVEL	✓ or ✗
26	Solve problems by applying knowledge of arithmetic operations?	Advanced	
27	Find the position of decimals on a number line?	Advanced	
28	Interpret a sector graph?	Advanced	
29	Calculate the perimeter of a composite rectangular shape?	Advanced	
30	Use a scale to determine distance on a grid?	Advanced	
31	Describe probability using numerical values?	Advanced	
32	Visualise a shape to match a given net?	Advanced	
33	Read the volume of a container?	Advanced	
34	Determine the fraction of a quantity?	Advanced	
35	Identify the simplest equivalent fraction to represent part of a twelfth?	Advanced	
36	Find the next number in a series?	Advanced	
37	Describe the probability of a random selection?	Advanced	
38	Find the average of a composite?	Advanced	
39	Find the dimensions of a figure given the perimeter and area?	Advanced	
40	Solve a problem involving unknown fractions?	Advanced	
41	Solve a dual calculation problem?	Advanced	
42	Estimate the shaded area in a grid?	Advanced	
	TOTAL		

NUMERACY TEST 2

This is the second Numeracy Test. There are 42 questions.

If you aren't sure what to do, ask your teacher or your parents to help you. Don't be afraid to ask if it isn't clear to you.

Allow around 50 minutes for this test.

Write your answer in the box or colour in the circle with the correct answer. Colour in only one circle for each answer.

1. Here are two rows of numbers. There is a pattern in the numbers in both rows. The numbers in the first and second rows are also related. Write the last three numbers in the boxes below.

First row	0	1	2	3	4	5
Second row	4	5	6			

2. It is morning (am). Which clock shows the latest possible time in the morning?

○ ○ ○ ○

3. Here is a shape that is cut exactly into two equal pieces.

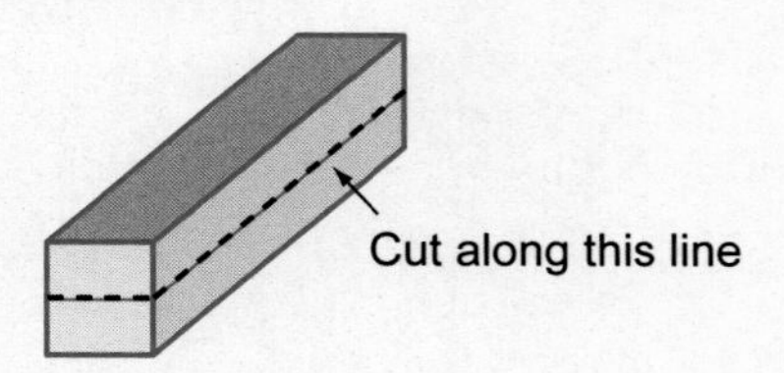

Which shape will the two faces have?

Square ○ Rectangle ○ Cube ○ Trapezium ○

4. What is the numeral for 25 000 + 500 + 40 + 9?

25 459 ○ 25 549 ○ 25 490 ○ 2549 ○

5. Which angle is a right angle?

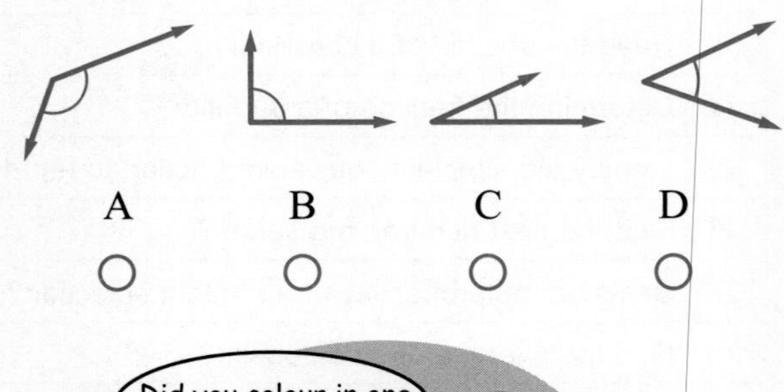

○ ○ ○ ○

6. I have an ancient book that mentions many animals.

Sheep	45
lamb	35
Lion	9
Ox	10
Horse	27

How many animals are mentioned in this book?

[ ] animals

Write your answer in the box.

7. There is a pattern in these numbers.
Write in the number that is missing.

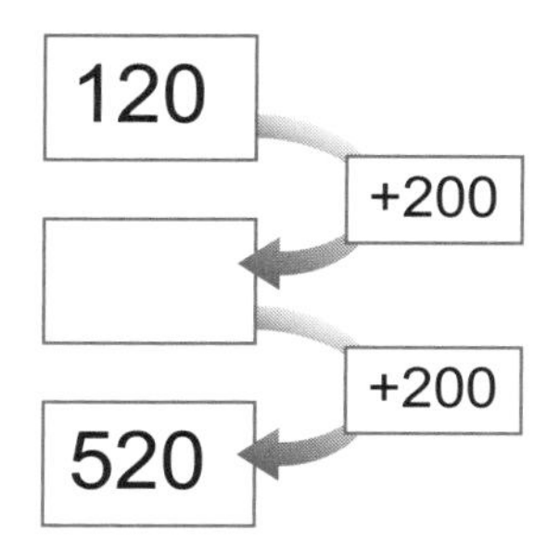

8. Use the table below to answer this question.

Household water usage

Activity	Litres (approximately)
Brushing teeth	3
Shower (per minute)	20
Washing machine	120
Bath	150
Watering garden (1 hour)	600

Draw in the column for the bath.

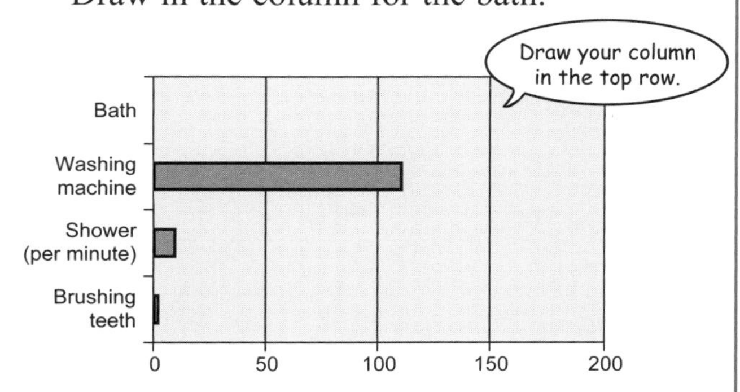

9. Here is a shape that covers some dots.

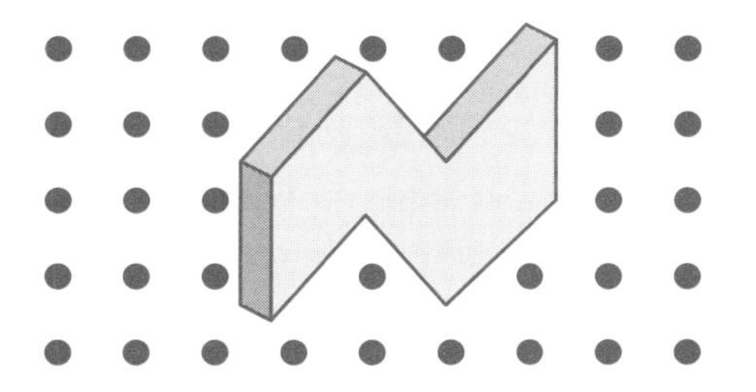

How many dots are covered by the shape?

☐ dots

Write your answer in the box.

10. This grid is made up of squares. There is a coloured shape on this grid.

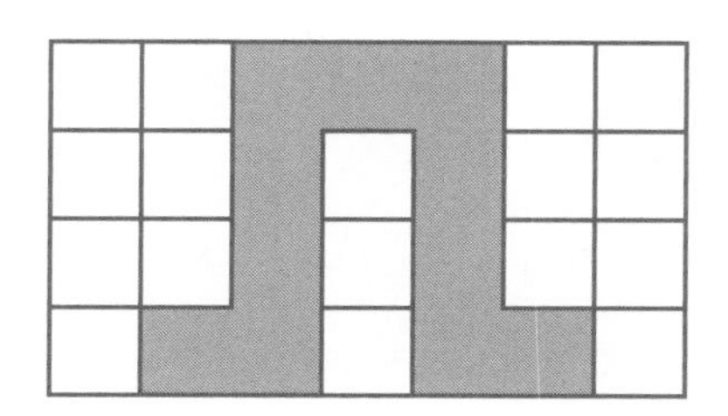

How many squares are covered by the coloured shape?

28 ○ 12 ○ 17 ○ 11 ○

11. Here is a shape made up of some blocks.

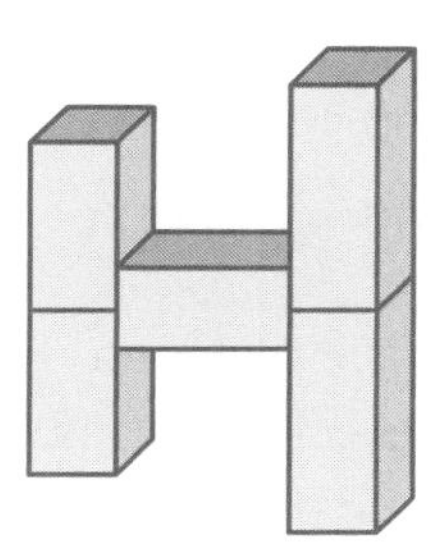

Which one of the four shapes below is the same as the one above? Is it A, B, C or D?

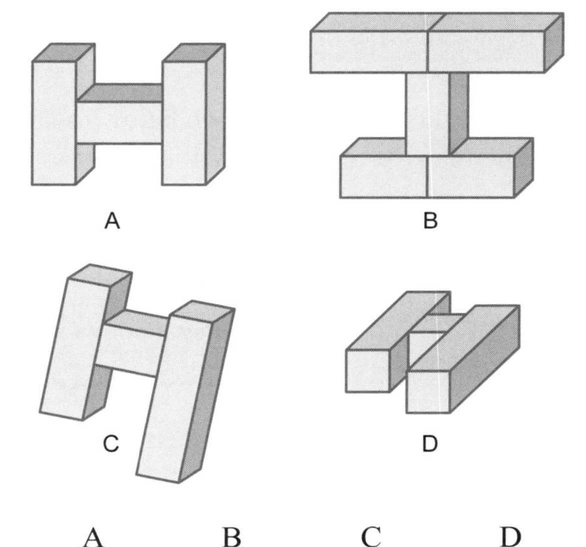

A ○ B ○ C ○ D ○

Answers and explanations on page 171

12. China has an army of 1 600 000 and the USA has an army of 502 000.

Which of these sums would you use to show the difference between these armies?

- ○ 1 600 000 + 502 000
- ○ 502 000 – 1 600 000
- ○ 1 600 000 – 502 000
- ○ 1 600 000 ÷ 502 000
- ○ 1 600 000 × 502 000

13. Here is a piece of wood. It is cut into pieces that are 10 centimetres long. How many pieces can be cut from it altogether?

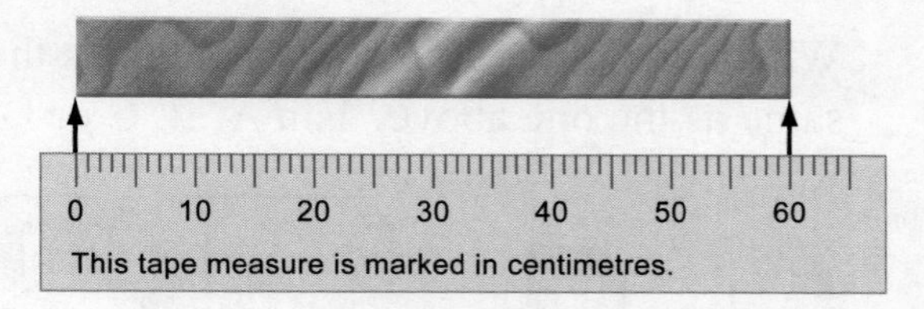

Fill in the number sentence below to show how many pieces there will be.

☐ ÷ 10 = ☐ pieces

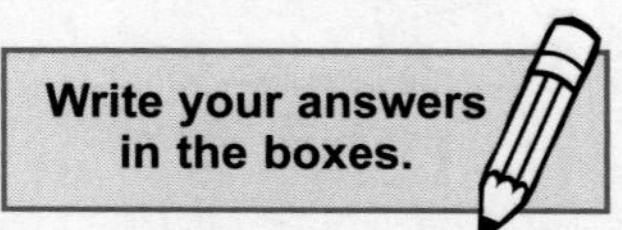

14. An estimate is your best guess. It can be the closest answer to a question. Here is an example:

For the sum 21 + 8 an estimate could be around 30. The correct answer is 29.

Why did we pick 30? We sort of guessed—you can round off the numbers to end in a 0.

This way they are easy to add and also to guess. The estimated sum would be: 20 + 10 = 30. We did this because 21 is close to 20 and 8 is close to 10. The answer of 30 is fairly close but not perfectly accurate. It is an estimate.

Now estimate the answer to this sum:

31 + 28 = ?

50	55	60	65
○	○	○	○

It would be a good idea to check your answers to questions 1 to 14 before moving on to the other questions.

15. This table shows the temperature at 2 pm on 25 November in a particular year throughout Australia.

It shows the temperature now. It also shows the highest temperature or likely highest temperature for the day.

City	Temperature now	Likely highest temperature
Adelaide	28 °C	26 °C
Brisbane	27 °C	28 °C
Canberra	19 °C	20 °C
Darwin	34 °C	35 °C
Hobart	13 °C	16 °C
Melbourne	23 °C	25 °C
Perth	21 °C	22 °C
Sydney	20 °C	20 °C

Which answer is correct?

- ○ The temperature in Adelaide is now more than the predicted high for the day.
- ○ The temperature in Darwin is now at its highest for the day.
- ○ The temperature in Sydney and Melbourne is now the same.
- ○ The temperature in Sydney and Canberra is now the same.

☞ Answers and explanations on page 171

16. Here are three rows. On each row there are some glasses.

Row	Objects
Top	
Middle	
Bottom	

On which row (top, middle or bottom) would I have the best chance of picking up the glasses if I choose only one article from each row?

○ Top
○ Middle
○ Bottom

17. You can flip, slide or turn shapes.

Here is an example. Look closely at what happens to the coloured shape.

Flip

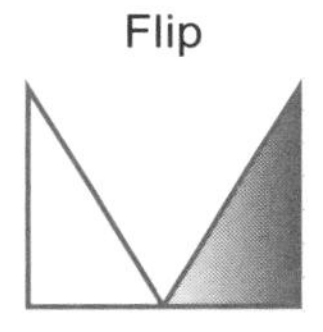

Slide

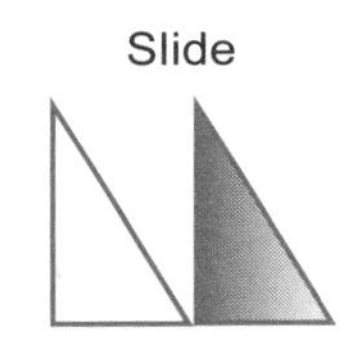

Turn

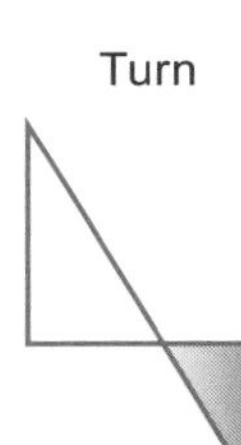

Has a flip, a slide or a turn been done with this coloured shape?

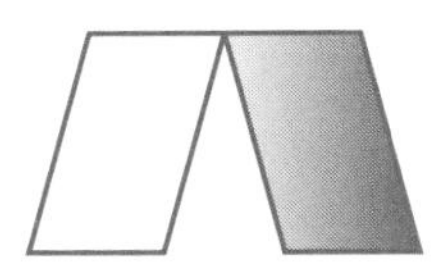

Flip	Slide	Turn
○	○	○

18. Complete this calculation.

$764 - 279 = \square$

19. Complete this calculation.

$\$3.70 + \$8.90 = \square$

20. Complete this calculation.

$2568 \div 8 = \square$

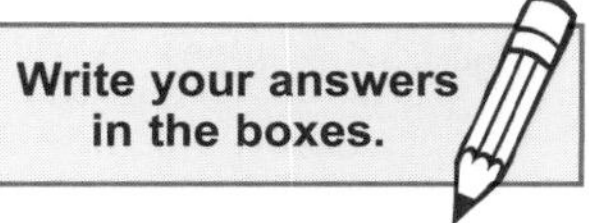

21. Some children catch this bus to school.

At the first stop, 8 get on.
At the second stop, 7 get on and 3 get off.
At the third stop, half get off.

How many children are left on the bus now?

5	6	7	8
○	○	○	○

22. Here is a house. There is a tape measure used to measure the width of the house.

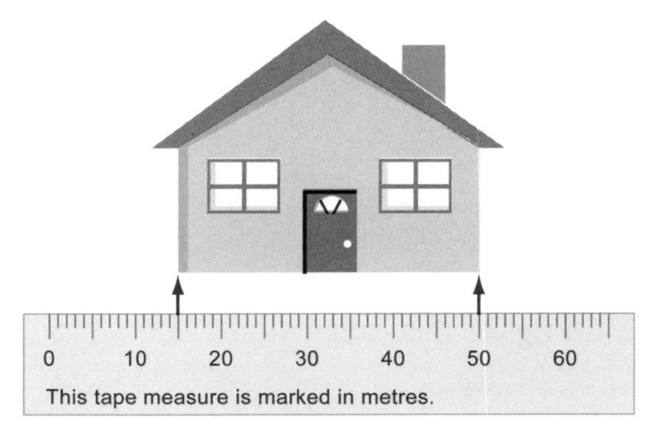

How wide is this house?

30 m	35 m	40 m	50 m
○			○

NUMERACY TEST 2

23. I folded this pattern in half.

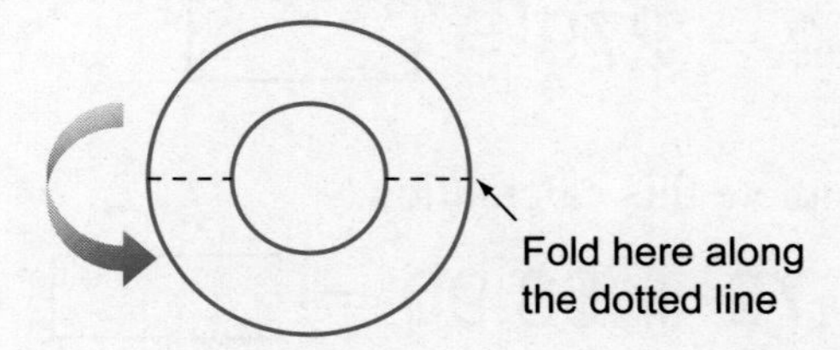

Which shape could I see?

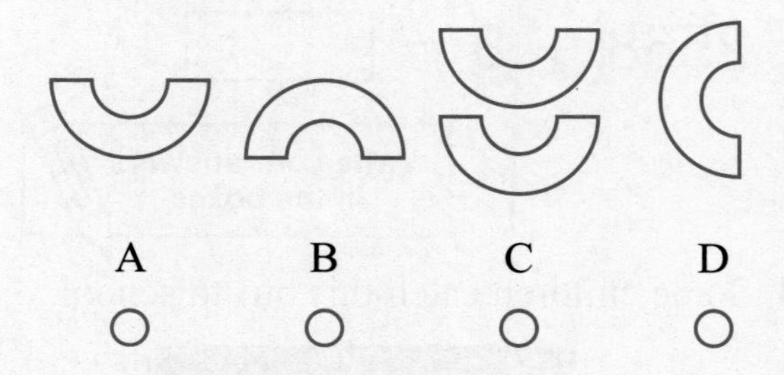

A	B	C	D
○	○	○	○

24. The arrow moves two spaces anticlockwise.

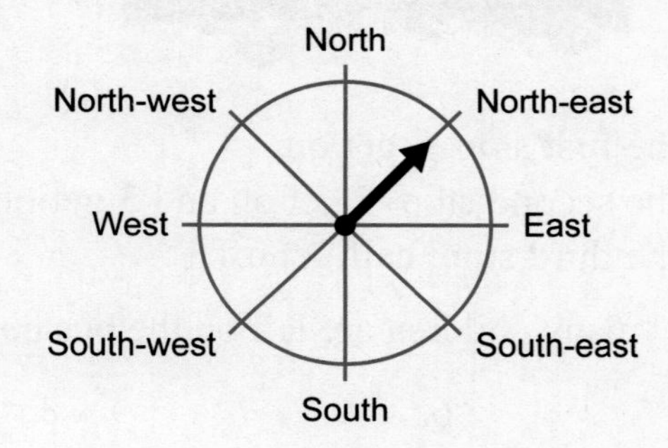

To which direction would the arrow be pointing if it moved two spaces anti-clockwise?

- ○ North-west
- ○ West
- ○ South-east
- ○ East
- ○ North

25. Complete this calculation.

$$2 - \frac{1}{4} = \square$$

Write your answer in the box.

26. This triangle is made up of numbers from 6 to 11. Some numbers have been filled in for you.

When you add the three numbers on each side, each of the three sides of this triangle adds to 26.

Write the numbers 6, 7 and 8 in the circles.

27. Today is Monday 30 July.

I go to the doctor every 3 weeks.

When is my next visit?

- ○ 19 August
- ○ 20 August
- ○ 21 August
- ○ 22 August

28. A skyscraper is a building taller than 152 metres. Only the five cities with the most skyscrapers are shown in this chart.

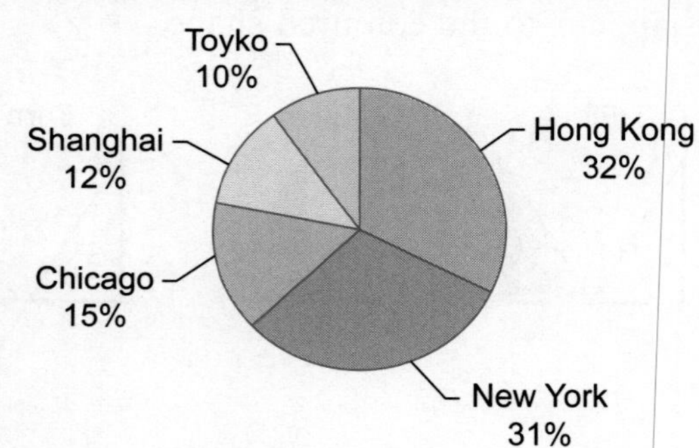

Which of these five cities has the second largest number of skyscrapers?

- ○ Hong Kong
- ○ Tokyo
- ○ Shanghai
- ○ Chicago
- ○ New York

It would be a good idea to check your answers to questions 15 to 28 before moving on to the other questions.

☞ Answers and explanations on pages 171–172

29. What is the perimeter (the distance around the outside edges) of this figure?

(Note: Some of the lengths are not shown in the figure.)

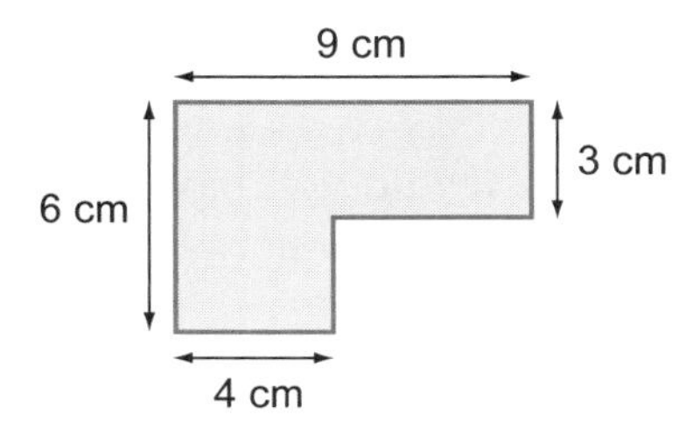

22 cm ◯ 30 cm ◯ 27 cm ◯ 36 cm ◯

30. Here is a map. It shows four towns in Syria, Jordan and Israel.

The map is divided into sections. Each section is 20 km. For instance, the distance from Bethlehem to Madaba is 40 km.

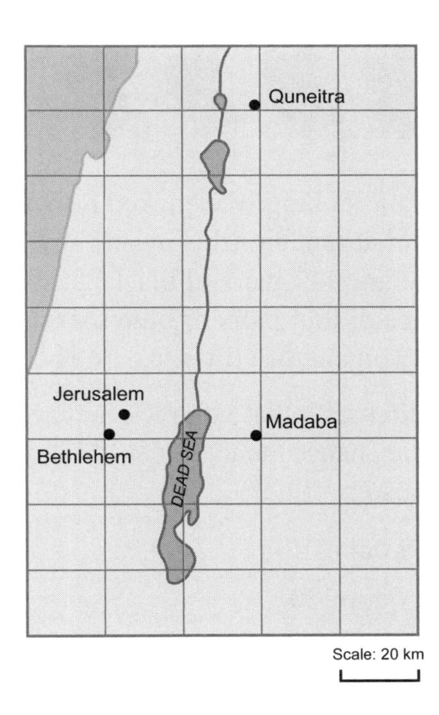

How far is it from Madaba to Quneitra on this map?

80 km ◯ 100 km ◯ 110 km ◯ 120 km ◯ 130 km ◯

31. The scores on a dice are shown on the faces. They can be any number from 1 to 6.

If you throw a dice, which sentence is correct?

◯ It is more likely you will score an even number than an odd number.

◯ It is more likely you will throw a 6 rather than a 1.

◯ It is more likely you will score a number from 1 to 4 rather than a 5 or 6.

◯ It is more likely you will score an odd number than an even number.

32. The sides of this shape are folded upwards to make a square pyramid. Each triangle has the same pattern on both sides.

Unfolded

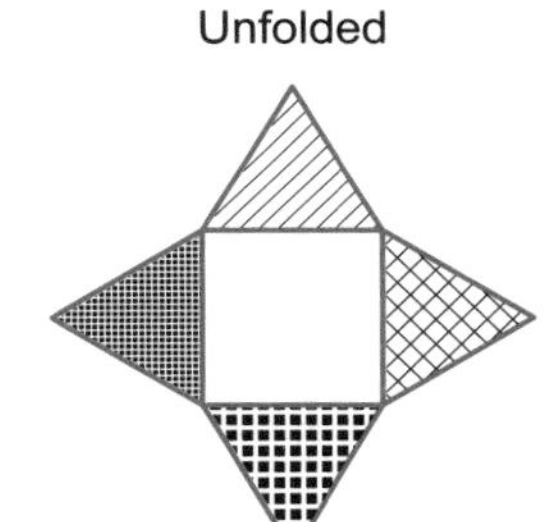

Folded

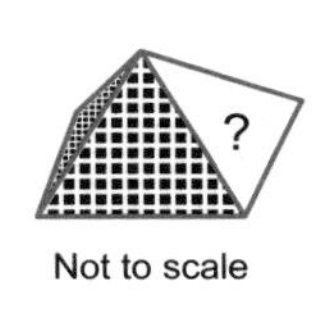

Not to scale

Which pattern fills the space shown with the question mark?

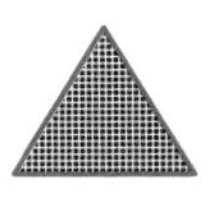 ◯  ◯ 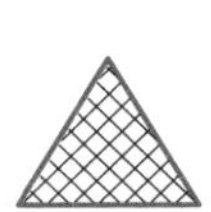 ◯  ◯

33. Here is a small water bottle. It holds 10 litres. It is part full.

About how full is the bottle?

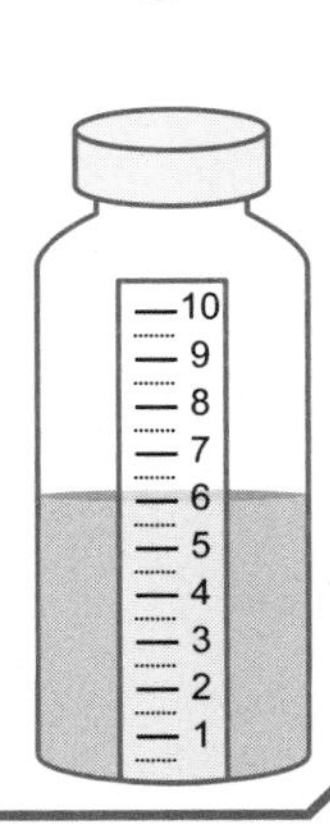

◯ one-sixth

◯ one-tenth

◯ ten sixths

◯ three fifths

☞ Answers and explanations on page 172

34. A square number is any number that can be formed into a square of dots. Here are some square numbers.

What is the square number that is missing (in the place of the question mark)?

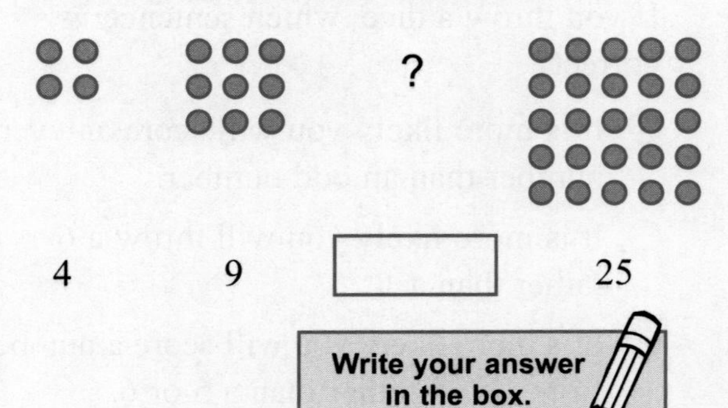

35. There are 15 forms of transport in this picture. There are buses, cars, aeroplanes, bicycles and ocean liners. Some are the same.

What fraction of the 15 methods of transport are bicycles?

○ $\frac{15}{5}$ ○ $\frac{10}{15}$ ○ $\frac{1}{4}$ ○ $\frac{1}{3}$

36. Here is a table of symbols. The direction North is also shown on the side. You are going to travel through the squares.

Go to the square one space to the north of the symbol ≈, and then one square to the east of that one, then one square to the north again, and finally one square to the east again. The steps are north, east, north and east.

In what direction would you have to move to return to the starting symbol?

- ○ North
- ○ North-west
- ○ North-east
- ○ South
- ○ South-west
- ○ South-east

37.

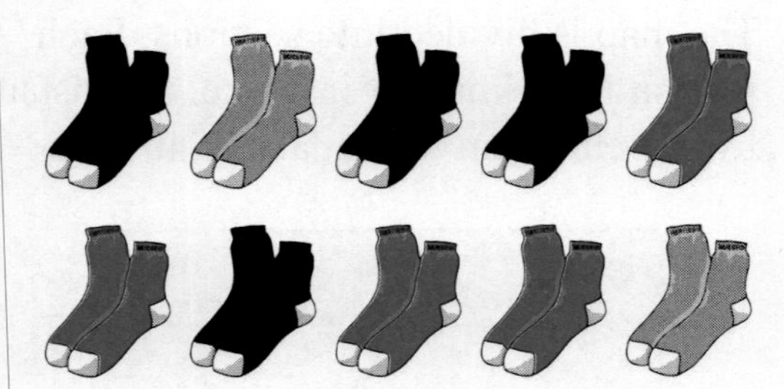

Without looking, you picked a sock from a drawer at random (this means any sock). There are four pairs of black socks (8 socks), four pairs of blue socks (8 socks) and two pairs of grey socks (4 socks).

The first sock that you pick is blue. What are the chances that the next sock you pick will also be blue?

- ○ 19 out of 19
- ○ 2 out of 20
- ○ 18 out of 20
- ○ 7 out of 19
- ○ 7 out of 20

☞ Answers and explanations on page 172

38. Three workers take 15 days to finish a big job. How long will it take five workers if they work at the same speed?

- ○ 10 days
- ○ 9 days
- ○ 8 days
- ○ 7 days
- ○ 6 days

39. Look at this rectangle. It is not drawn to scale.

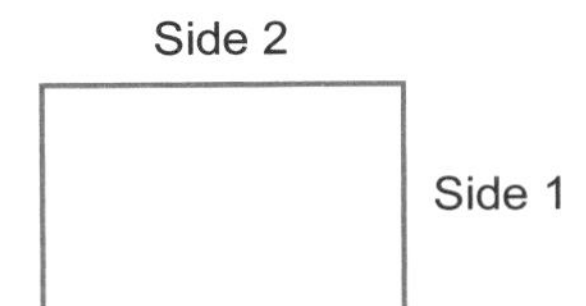

Perimeter = 18 cm
Area = 18 cm^2

What are the lengths of its two sides?

Side 1 ☐

Side 2 ☐

Write your answers in the boxes.

40. A grandson is 12 years old and is now one-fifth of his grandfather's age. In 12 years time, when the grandfather will be 72, the grandson will be one-third of his grandfather's age.

At what age will the grandson be if he is exactly half the age of the grandfather?

- ○ 48 years
- ○ 60 years
- ○ 36 years
- ○ 24 years
- ○ 50 years

41. $1976 \div 8 =$

248	247	246	244
○	○	○	○

42. Which of these numbers is the largest in value?

0.91	9.01	9.1	1.91
○	○	○	○

END OF TEST

Well done! You have completed the second Numeracy Test. We tried to change the questions and some were a little harder.

How did you go with these test questions? Check to see where you did well and where you had problems. Try to revise the questions that were hard for you.

Use the diagnostic chart on pages 44–45 to see which level of ability you reached. This is only an estimate. Don't be surprised if you answered some difficult questions correctly or even missed some easier questions.

There are now two more practice tests, each containing 42 questions. We have included some new types of questions in this test.

☞ Answers and explanations on page 172

CHECK YOUR SKILLS: NUMERACY TEST 2

Instructions

As you check the answer for each question, mark it as correct (✓) or incorrect (✗). Mark any questions that you omitted or left out as incorrect (✗) for the moment.

Then look at how many you answered correctly in each level. You will be able to see what level you are at by finding the point where you started having consistent difficulty with questions at a certain level. For example, if you answer most questions correctly up to the Intermediate level and then get most questions wrong from then onwards, it is likely your ability is at the Intermediate level. You can ask your parents or your teacher to help you do this if it isn't clear to you.

Am I able to ...

	SKILL	ESTIMATED LEVEL	✓ or ✗
1	Continue a number pattern involving single-digit numbers?	Standard	
2	Identify latest analogue time in terms of am?	Standard	
3	Identify a shape from a rectangular prism that is bisected?	Standard	
4	Complete a five-digit numeral?	Standard	
5	Identify a right angle?	Standard	
6	Solve an addition of five numbers?	Standard	
7	Continue a number pattern involving counting by 200?	Standard	
8	Convert data to a chart?	Standard	
9	Visualising hidden information?	Intermediate	
10	Use informal units to measure the area of a shape?	Standard	
11	Recognise a model viewed from a different perspective?	Standard	
12	Recognise how to solve a difference?	Standard	
13	Complete a number sentence involving division?	Intermediate	
14	Use an estimate to describe the outcome?	Intermediate	
15	Interpret data from a chart to confirm a statement?	Intermediate	
16	Estimate the chances of selecting an object?	Intermediate	
17	Recognise the property of a shape that has been flipped or turned?	Intermediate	
18	Solve a three-digit subtraction?	Intermediate	
19	Solve a money problem with dollars and cents?	Intermediate	
20	Solve division involving four-digit numbers?	Intermediate	
21	Solve a sequential problem?	Intermediate	
22	Use a scale in metric units to solve a length problem?	Intermediate	
23	Identify symmetry in a design?	Intermediate	
24	Specify direction using counter clockwise quarter turns?	Intermediate	
25	Subtract a fraction from a whole number?	Intermediate	
26	Solve an incomplete problem?	Advanced	
27	Find a future date?	Advanced	

CHECK YOUR SKILLS: NUMERACY TEST 2

	SKILL	ESTIMATED LEVEL	✓ or ✗
28	Interpret a sector graph?	Advanced	
29	Calculate the perimeter of an irregular shape?	Advanced	
30	Use a scale to determine distance on a grid?	Advanced	
31	Calculate the likelihood of an event?	Advanced	
32	Visualise a shape to match a given net?	Advanced	
33	Determine the fraction of a quantity?	Advanced	
34	Find the missing square of a number?	Advanced	
35	Identify the simplest equivalent fraction to represent part of a fifteenth?	Advanced	
36	Trace a series of directions?	Advanced	
37	Describe the probability of a random selection?	Advanced	
38	Find a composite amount and apply it to a new situation?	Advanced	
39	Find the dimensions of a figure given the perimeter and area?	Advanced	
40	Solve a problem involving relations?	Advanced	
41	Solve a division?	Intermediate	
42	Determine the largest decimal?	Advanced	
	TOTAL		

NUMERACY TEST 3

ADAPTED FOR ONLINE FORMAT

This is the third Numeracy Test. There are 42 questions.

If you aren't sure what to do, ask your teacher or your parents to help you. Don't be afraid to ask if it isn't clear to you.

Allow around 50 minutes for this test.

Write the answer in the box or colour in the circle with the correct answer. Colour in only one circle for each answer.

1. Here is a pattern made up of pentagons (shapes with five sides: ⬠).
How many more pentagons are needed to cover all the area in the white rectangle?

The rectangle is shown with a black border.
(Hint: Use the pentagons that are outside to help you.)

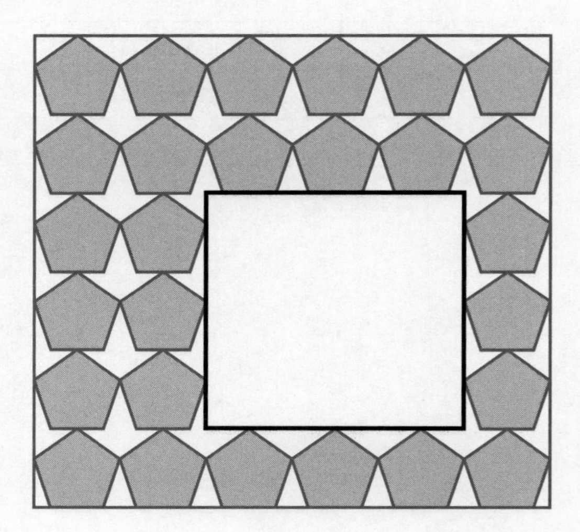

How many pentagons are needed?

☐ pentagons

Write your answer in the box.

2. Which clock shows the time at around 7:30?

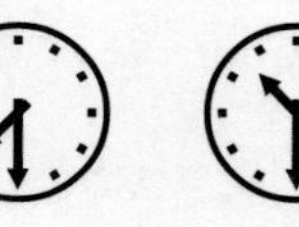

○ ○ ○ ○

3. Name the shapes in this figure.

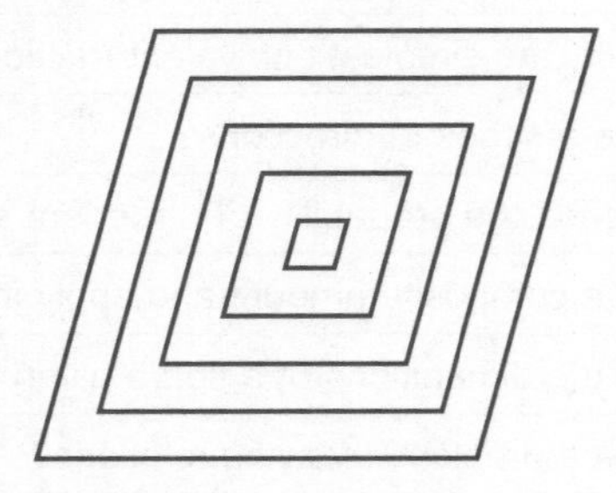

○ They are all squares.
○ They are all cubes.
○ They are all rectangles.
○ They are all parallelograms.

4. Write the number eight thousand and twenty-six in figures (numerals).

☐

Write your answer in the box.

5. Here is a picture with different types of triangles. How many right-angled triangles can you find? Include any triangles inside another triangle.

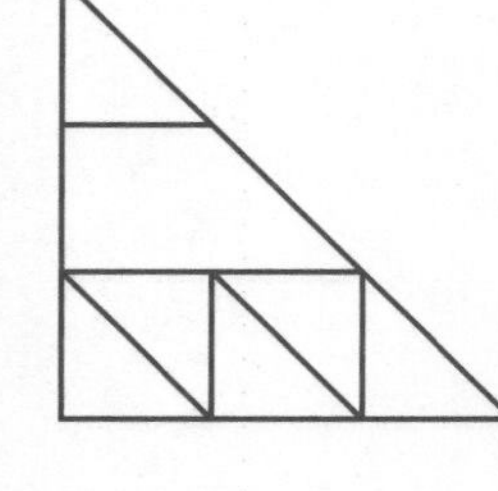

4	5	6	7	8
○	○	○	○	○

☞ Answers and explanations on page 173

6. Add the following amounts

$$
\begin{array}{r}
\$18.50 \\
+\ \$12.50 \\
\hline
\end{array}
$$

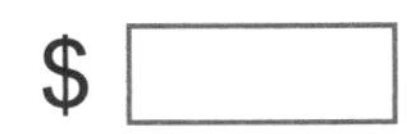

Write your answer in the box.

7. There is a pattern in these numbers. Write in the number that is missing.

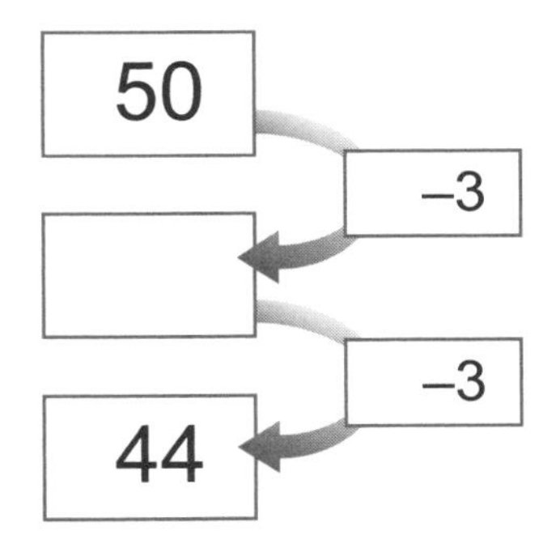

8. Use the table below to answer this question.

Languages spoken in most countries

Language	Number of countries
English	57
French	33
Arabic	23
Spanish	21
Portuguese	7

How many more countries speak English than French?

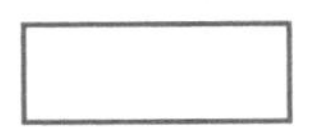 countries

Write your answer in the box.

9. Here are some shapes. Colour one-fifth of these shapes.

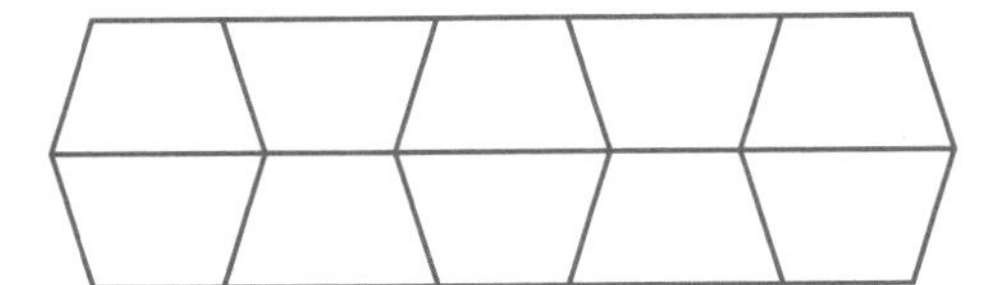

10. How many of these coins are worth twice as much as one of the other coins?

2	3	4	5
○	○	○	○

11. Here is a shape made up of some blocks.

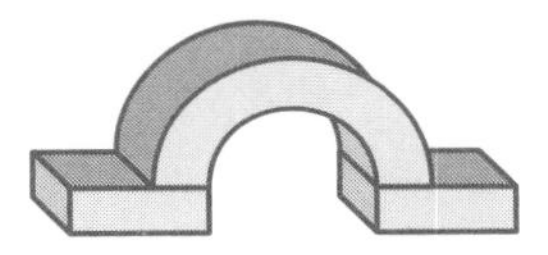

Which one of the four shapes below is the same as the one above? Is it A, B, C or D?

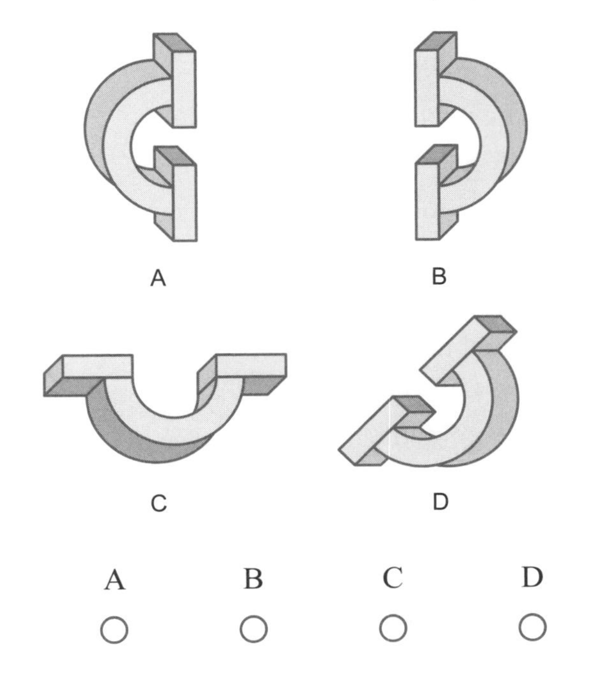

A	B	C	D
○	○	○	○

12. A farm is 900 hectares in area. It is divided into three blocks, one of 300 hectares, one of 200 hectares and one more block.

Which sum should be used to show how large the last block is?

- ○ Last block = 900 – 300 – 200
- ○ Last block = 300 + 200 + 400
- ○ Last block = 900 ÷ 3
- ○ Last block = 900 + 300 + 200

13. A prime number is a number that can only be divided by itself and one.

Numbers like 2, 3, 5, 7, 11 and 13 are prime numbers. There are many other prime numbers.

Numbers like 4, 6, 8 and 9 are not prime numbers.

Now choose the correct answer for numbers from 1 to 20:

- ○ There are more prime numbers than odd numbers.
- ○ There are more prime numbers than even numbers.
- ○ There is one even number which is a prime number.
- ○ All the odd numbers are prime numbers.
- ○ All the even numbers are prime numbers.

14. Here is part of a receipt from a shop. Five items are bought.

fresh food
AS FRESH AS IT GETS

MAROUBRA
SHOP 458 PACIFIC SQUARE
ABN 93 496 2486
TAX INVOICE

1 Carrots **Bag**	$4.29
1 Chinese Cabbage Half	$0.99
0.8kg Royal Gala Apple SML	$2.82
0.67kg Nectarine White	$4.29
0.54kg Banana	$1.63
5 Items(s) SUB-TOTAL	$14.02
Cash tendered	$20.00
ROUND CASH	$14.00
Change	$6.00

Tuesday 3–2–2019 #2285 L0004 Lina

THANK YOU
FOR SHOPPING AT FRESHFOOD

Here are four sums. They round off the prices and show a quick way to guess or estimate the price of the five foods. Which is the best way?

- ○ $4 + $1 + $3 + $5 + $2
- ○ $4 + $0 + $2 + $4 + $1
- ○ $5 + $1 + $3 + $5 + $1
- ○ $4 + $1 + $3 + $4 + $2

It would be a good idea to check your answers to questions 1 to 14 before moving on to the other questions.

☞ Answers and explanations on page 173

15. This chart shows the number of wins for different companies in the Formula One racing championships (up to 2006).

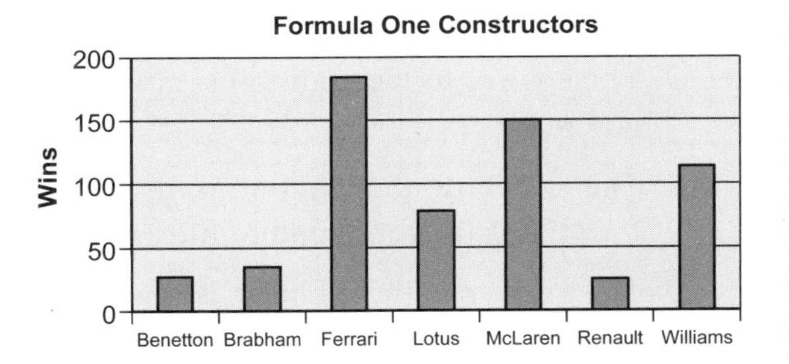

Which answer is correct?

- ○ McLaren has about twice as many wins as Brabham.
- ○ Lotus has about twice as many wins as Brabham.
- ○ Williams has about twice as many wins as Brabham.
- ○ Renault has about twice as many wins as Brabham.

16. A coin can land on heads or tails when it is tossed in the air.

Two coins are tossed. What is the chance they will both land on heads (heads for coin 1 and heads for coin 2)?

- ○ 1 out of 4 chances
- ○ 2 out of 4 chances
- ○ 2 out of 2 chances
- ○ 3 out of 4 chances
- ○ 3 out of 8 chances

17. A shape can be made to flip, slide or turn.

Has a flip, a slide or a turn (rotate) been done to this coloured shape?

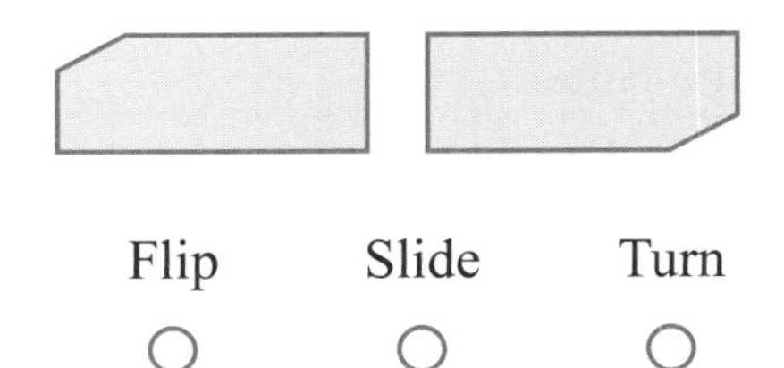

Flip ○ Slide ○ Turn ○

18. Complete this calculation.

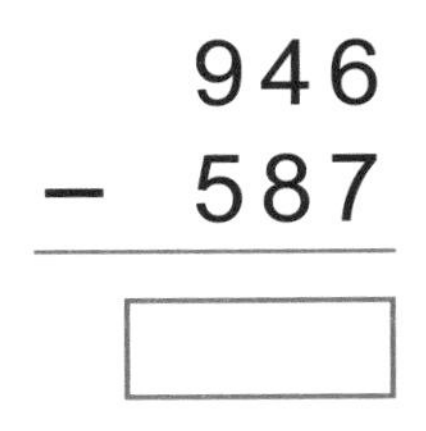

Write your answer in the box.

19. Complete this calculation.

$6.80 × 3 = ☐

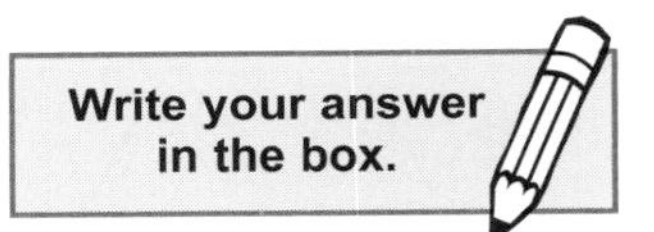

20. Which is the smallest angle?

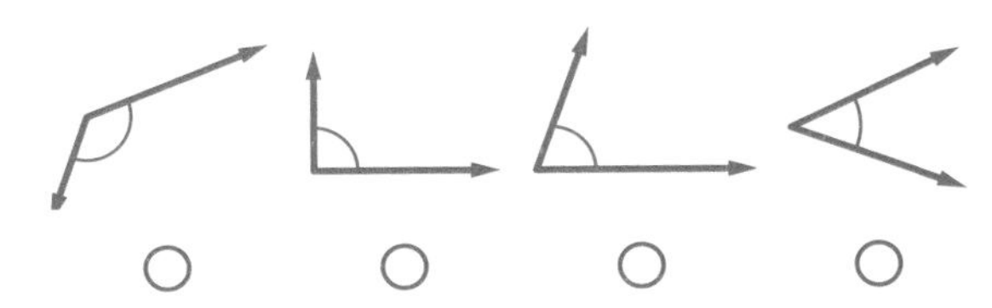

○ ○ ○ ○

21. There are signs missing in this calculation. Use + − × or ÷ to fill the spaces. The spaces are shown with dots.

7 … (10 … 4) = 42

Write your answers over the sets of 3 dots.

Answers and explanations on page 173

22. Look at this drawing. There is a pattern but one part is missing. This is shown with a question mark (?).

Pick which piece (A, B, C or D) will complete the pattern.

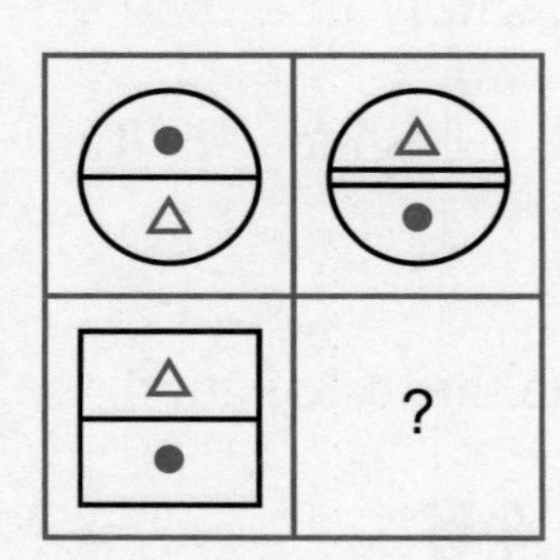

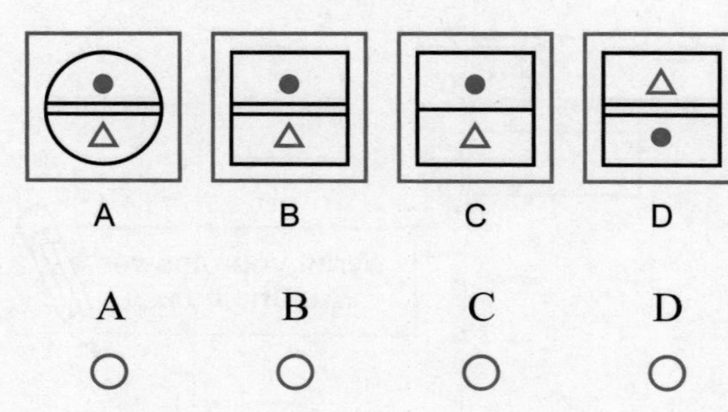

A B C D

○ ○ ○ ○

23. I folded this pattern in half.

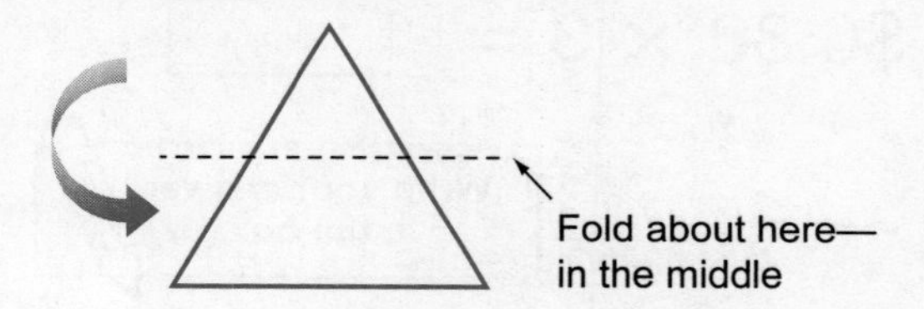

Which shape could I see?

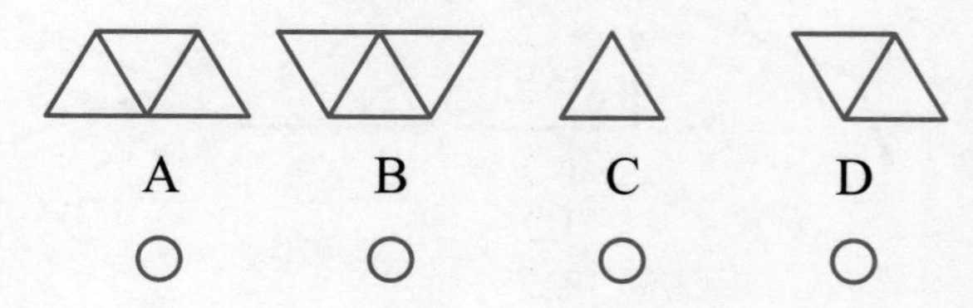

A B C D

○ ○ ○ ○

24. What is the area of the shaded part of this figure?

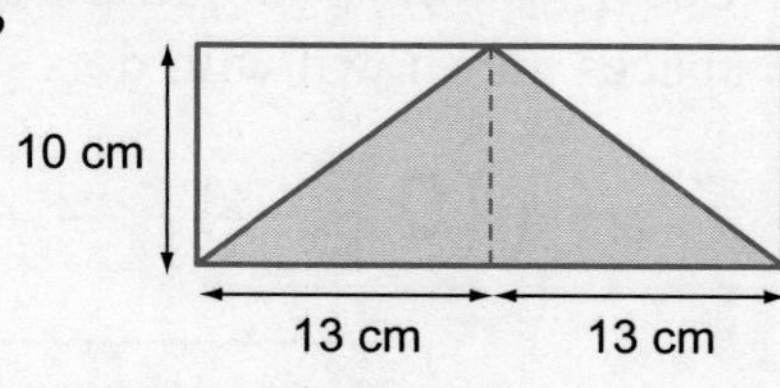

36 cm² ○ 130 cm² ○ 169 cm² ○ 260 cm² ○

25. Add any four numbers in a row. It could be 1 + 2 + 3 + 4 or 2 + 3 + 4 + 5 or even 20 + 21 + 22 + 23 or even 98 + 99 + 100 + 101.

Choose the correct answer.

- ○ The answer to the addition is always an odd number.
- ○ The answer to the addition is always four times the first number plus six.
- ○ The answer to the addition is always a multiple of four.
- ○ The answer to the addition is always four times the fourth number minus eight.

26. In this puzzle there are only numbers from 2 to 8. Each row, column and diagonal adds up to 15.

Part of it has been completed for you.

Fill in the even numbers 2, 4, 6 and 8 to complete the diagram.

Remember that every line has to add up to 15.

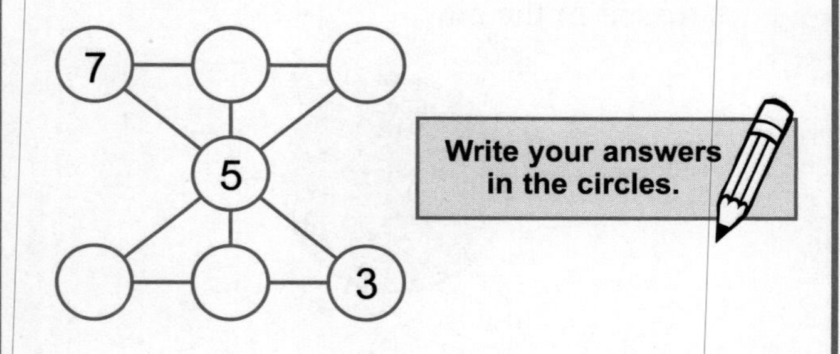

27. Which of the numbers below is closest to 0.02?

A B C D

○ ○ ○ ○

☞ Answers and explanations on page 174

28. This pie chart shows seven major religions. There are many other smaller religious groups.

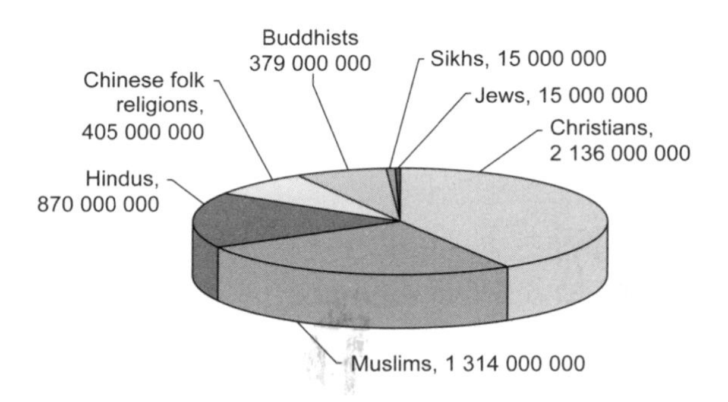

Which is the third-largest religious group?

- ○ Muslims
- ○ Hindus
- ○ Chinese folk religions
- ○ Buddhists
- ○ Sikhs

It would be a good idea to check your answers to questions 15 to 28 before moving on to the other questions.

29. This is a rectangular prism. The volume of this figure is 650 cm^3.

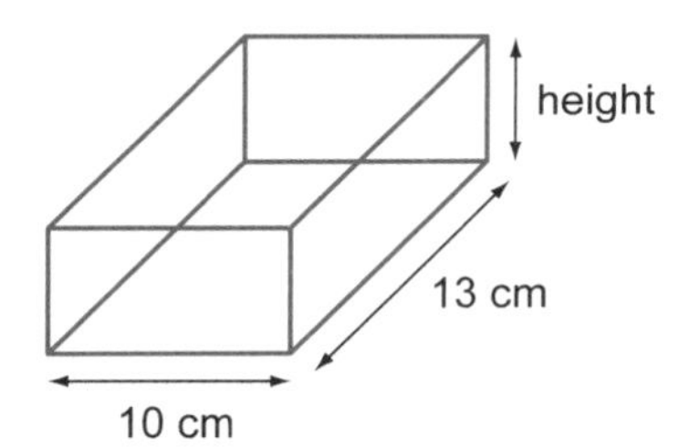

Not to scale

The height of the rectangular prism is not shown in the figure.

What is the height of the prism?

○ 1 cm	○ 5 cm
○ 2 cm	○ 10 cm
○ 3 cm	○ 13 cm

30. Here is a map. It shows three cities on an island. The map is divided into sections. Each section or square is 2 km.

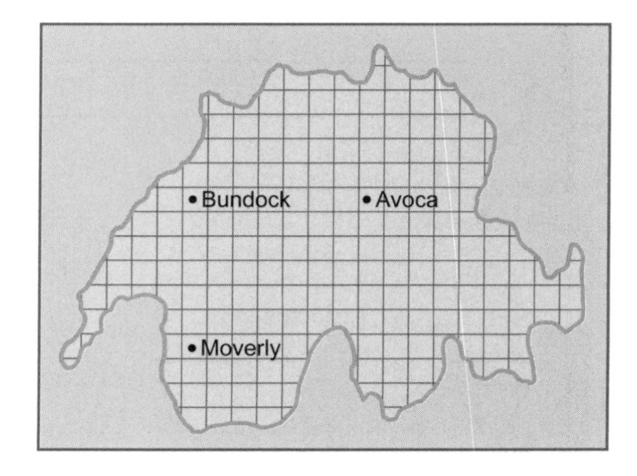

How far is it from Moverly to Bundock, then from Bundock to Avoca, on this map?

6 km	13 km	19 km	26 km	39 km
○	○	○	○	○

31. Here is a shape. It contains squares. Some of the squares are white while some are half coloured and half white.

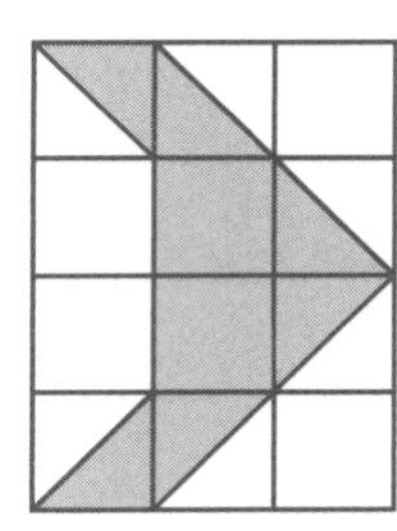

What fraction of the shape is made up of half-coloured squares?

$\frac{1}{2}$	$\frac{1}{3}$	$\frac{1}{4}$	$\frac{2}{3}$	$\frac{3}{4}$
○	○	○	○	○

☞ Answers and explanations on page 174

32. This net is folded to make a solid shape.

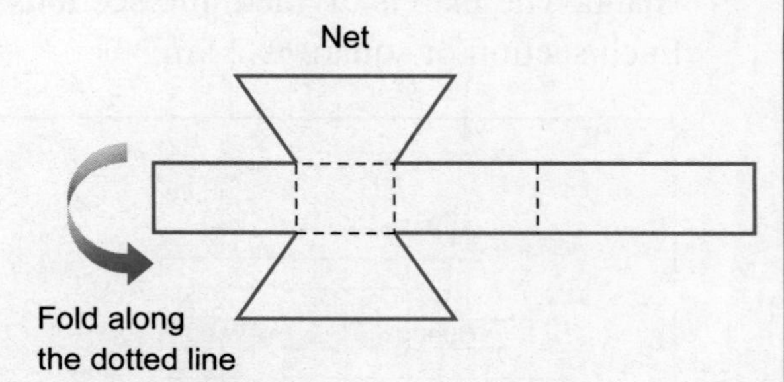

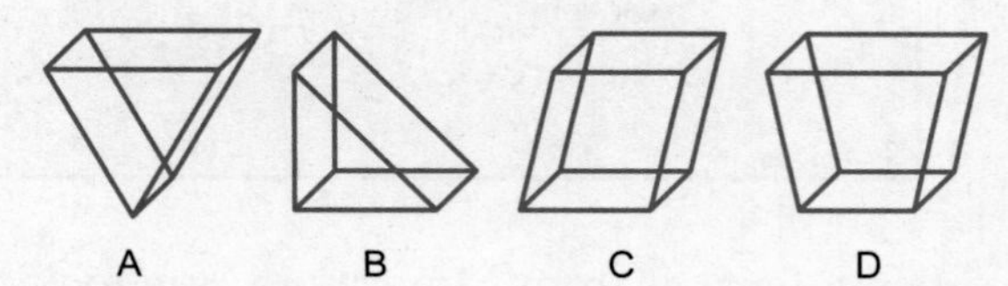

Which solid shape matches the net above?

A ○ B ○ C ○ D ○

33. A pole that is 10 metres high casts a shadow of 15 metres. Another pole casts a shadow of 7.5 metres.

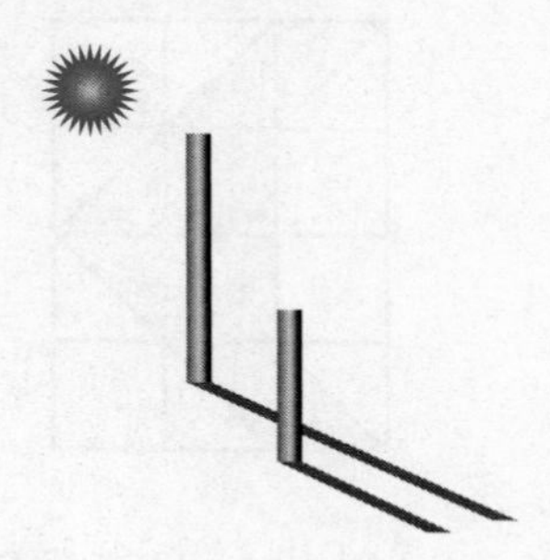

How tall is the pole with a shadow of 7.5 metres?

2.5 m ○ 5 m ○ 7.5 m ○ 10 m ○ 12.5 m ○

34. A floor has 1 white tile for every 3 black tiles. There are 72 tiles used on the floor. How many white tiles are needed?

6 ○ 12 ○ 18 ○ 24 ○

35. What is the next number in the series 2, 4, 6, 10, 16, ...?

○ 22 ○ 30
○ 24 ○ 32
○ 26 ○ 34
○ 28

36. There are 20 numbers from 1 to 20 in a box. You select a number at random.

The first number that you pick is an even number. What are the chances that the next number you pick is also an even number?

○ 1 in 20 ○ 1 in 9
○ 1 in 19 ○ 9 in 19
○ 1 in 10 ○ 9 in 20

37. Three young people have an average age of 13. There are 2 girls aged 13 years and 15 years.

How old is the boy?

○ 10 ○ 13
○ 11 ○ 14
○ 12 ○ 15

☞ Answers and explanations on page 174

38. It costs $50 to make the first 100 phone calls every month and then 17 cents for every extra phone call.

How much would it cost to make 300 calls in a month?

$34	$67	$77	$84	$94
○	○	○	○	○

39. If $\frac{3}{4}$ of a number is 375, what is the number?

- ○ 125
- ○ 250
- ○ 375
- ○ 500
- ○ 625
- ○ 750

40. Here are some descriptions. These chances are numbered from 1 to 5.

1 certain
2 quite likely
3 an even chance
4 unlikely
5 impossible

There are some sentences below. Put a (1) next to the sentence if something is certain; put a (2) if something is quite likely to happen; put a (3) if there is an even chance; put a (4) next to a sentence if it is unlikely to happen; and put a (5) if something is impossible to happen.

Chances	Sentences
	When I toss a coin once, it will land on heads.
	I will eat some take away food next week.
	I will be involved in an accident next week.
	I am zero centimetres tall.
	I was born.

Write your answers in these spaces.

41. This target has three areas called A, B and C.

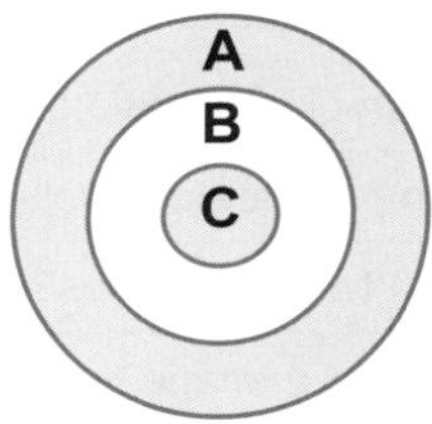

If you throw a ball at this target, which area are you most likely to hit?

○ A ○ B ○ C

42. 450 was divided by a number and the answer was 15.

What was the number?

END OF TEST

Well done! You have completed the third Numeracy Test. We tried to change the questions and some were a little harder. Don't worry if you didn't finish it in time as we added some new types of questions.

How did you go with these test questions? Check to see where you did well and where you had problems. Try to revise the questions that were hard for you.

Use the diagnostic chart on pages 54–55 to see which level of ability you reached. This is only an estimate. Don't be surprised if you answered some difficult questions correctly or even missed some easier questions.

There is now one last practice test that contains 42 questions.

☞ Answers and explanations on pages 174–175

CHECK YOUR SKILLS: NUMERACY TEST 3

Instructions

As you check the answer for each question, mark it as correct (✓) or incorrect (✗). Mark any questions that you omitted or left out as incorrect (✗) for the moment.

Then look at how many you answered correctly in each level. You will be able to see what level you are at by finding the point where you started having consistent difficulty with questions at a certain level. For example, if you answer most questions correctly up to the Intermediate level and then get most questions wrong from then onwards, it is likely your ability is at the Intermediate level. You can ask your parents or your teacher to help you do this if it isn't clear to you.

Am I able to ...

	SKILL	ESTIMATED LEVEL	✓ or ✗
1	Use informal units to measure the area of a grid?	Standard	
2	Identify analogue time on a clockface?	Standard	
3	Identify a shape composed of parallelograms?	Standard	
4	Write a 4-digit number?	Standard	
5	Identify right-angled triangles?	Standard	
6	Solve an addition of two two-digit decimals?	Standard	
7	Continue a number pattern involving subtracting by threes?	Standard	
8	Interpret data in two-way tables?	Standard	
9	Find the fraction of a shape?	Standard	
10	Recognise money that is double in value?	Standard	
11	Recognise a model viewed from a different perspective?	Standard	
12	Recognise how to set out a solution?	Standard	
13	Identify prime numbers?	Intermediate	
14	Select the best addition strategy for estimating a total?	Intermediate	
15	Interpret data from column graphs to confirm a statement?	Intermediate	
16	Use chance to describe the outcome in a simple experiment?	Intermediate	
17	Recognise the property of a shape that has been turned?	Intermediate	
18	Solve a three-digit subtraction?	Intermediate	
19	Multiply a decimal?	Intermediate	
20	Identify the smallest angle?	Intermediate	
21	Use problem-solving strategies to complete a number sentence?	Intermediate	
22	Find a sequence in a matrix?	Intermediate	
23	Recognise a folded design?	Intermediate	
24	Find the area of a triangle?	Intermediate	
25	Find a pattern in the sum of consecutive numbers?	Intermediate	
26	Complete vertical, horizontal and diagonal additions of even numbers?	Advanced	
27	Find the position of decimals on a number line?	Advanced	

CHECK YOUR SKILLS: NUMERACY TEST 3

	SKILL	ESTIMATED LEVEL	✓ or ✗
28	Interpret a sector graph?	Advanced	
29	Calculate the height of a rectangular prism given length, breadth and volume?	Advanced	
30	Use a scale to determine distance on a grid?	Advanced	
31	Describe a proportion using a fraction?	Advanced	
32	Visualise a shape to match a given net?	Advanced	
33	Solve a problem involving a relation between two quantities?	Advanced	
34	Determine the number of items from the ratio of a quantity?	Advanced	
35	Find the next number in a series?	Advanced	
36	Find the probability of randomly selecting an object?	Advanced	
37	Solve a problem given the average of three numbers and two of the numbers?	Advanced	
38	Calculate the cost of additional quantities?	Advanced	
39	Find a whole number given the fraction?	Advanced	
40	Determine the likelihood of an event?	Advanced	
41	Estimate the area of concentric circles?	Intermediate	
42	Solve a problem using division?	Advanced	
	TOTAL		

NUMERACY TEST 4

This is the fourth Numeracy Test. There are 42 questions. The questions show you what to do. Write your answers in this book.

If you aren't sure what to do, ask your teacher or your parents to help you. Don't be afraid to ask if it isn't clear to you.

These questions will be harder than the earlier Numeracy Tests so don't worry if you can't answer all the questions. Allow around 50 minutes for this test.

Write your answer in the box or colour in the circle with the correct answer. Colour in only one circle for each answer.

1. What is the numeral for 6000 + 80 + 7?

○ 6087 ○ 6870 ○ 60 807 ○ 6807

2. Colour or shade $\frac{3}{4}$ of the figure below.

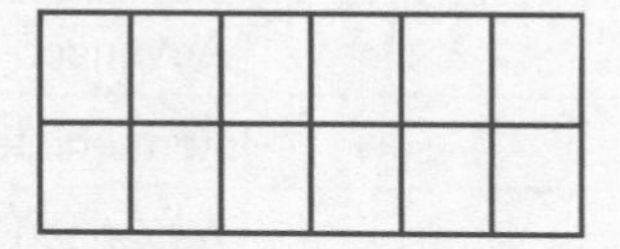

3. How many of these numbers can be rounded off to 48 000?

47 550	48 550	47 123
47 600	48 499	47 750
48 123	48 250	47 500

○ 6 ○ 7 ○ 8 ○ 9

4. Here are some scores on a test.

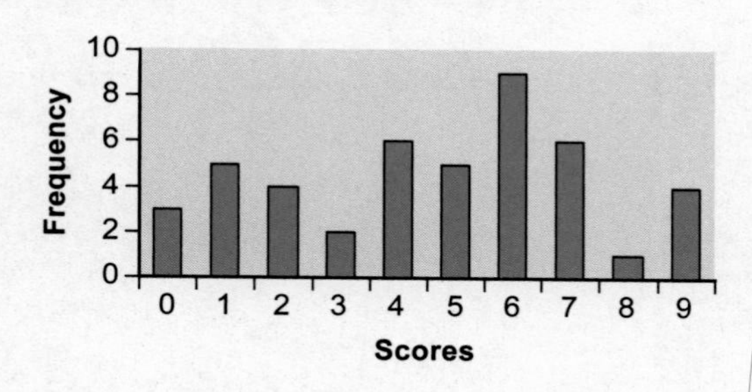

Which was the most frequent score?

Write your answer in the box.

5. Which number is next in this series?

100 97 94 91 ?

○ 90
○ 89
○ 88
○ 87
○ 86
○ 85

6. Add the following amounts together.

$$\begin{array}{r} \$16.75 \\ + \ \$15.25 \\ \hline \end{array}$$

$ [ ]

Write your answer in the box.

7. What is the numeral for 600 000 + 2000 + 300 + 9?

○ 620 309 ○ 602 309 ○ 6 200 309 ○ 6 002 309

8. I toss a coin that shows heads or tails when it lands.

Which of these events is certain?

○ If I toss a coin once, it will land tails.
○ If I toss a coin once, it will land heads.
○ If I toss a coin once, it will land heads or tails.
○ If I toss a coin once, it will land heads and tails.

☞ Answers and explanations on page 175

9. What is the mixed number form of $\frac{9}{2}$?

- ○ 2
- ○ 4
- ○ $4\frac{1}{4}$
- ○ $4\frac{1}{2}$
- ○ $4\frac{3}{4}$
- ○ 41

10. Which of these expressions is true?

- ○ $24634 > 43579$
- ○ $46379 = 97364$
- ○ $89637 < 94362$
- ○ $39369 \neq 39369$

11. What percentage of this figure is coloured?

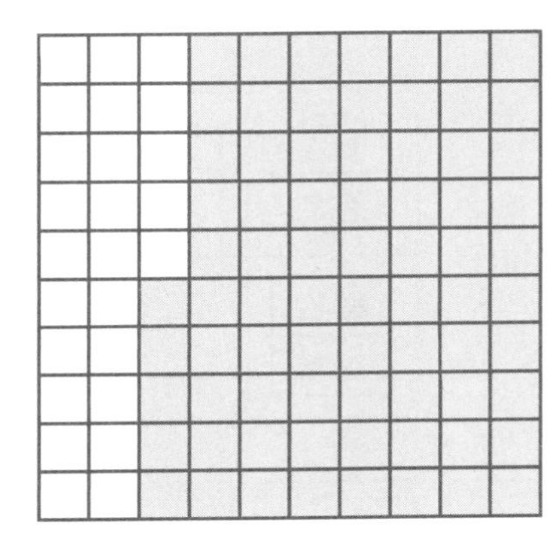

- ○ 25%
- ○ 35%
- ○ 45%
- ○ 55%
- ○ 65%
- ○ 75%
- ○ 85%

12. Here is a pattern of symbols.

Which pattern comes next in the series?

- ○ ✠✠✠✠✠✠
- ○ ☆☆☆☆☆☆☆
- ○ ▲▲▲▲▲▲▲▲▲
- ○ ⌖⌖⌖⌖⌖⌖⌖⌖⌖

13. Here is a shape made up of some blocks.

Which one of the four shapes below is the same as the one above? Is it A, B, C or D?

A

B

C

D

A	B	C	D
○	○	○	○

14. A girl has $25.80 and spends $12.95. How much does she have left?

- ○ $13.85
- ○ $12.15
- ○ $11.85
- ○ $12.85

It would be a good idea to check your answers to questions 1 to 14 before moving on to the other questions.

15. A boy cuts a rope that is 9.95 m long into 1.99 m lengths. How many equal lengths does he cut?

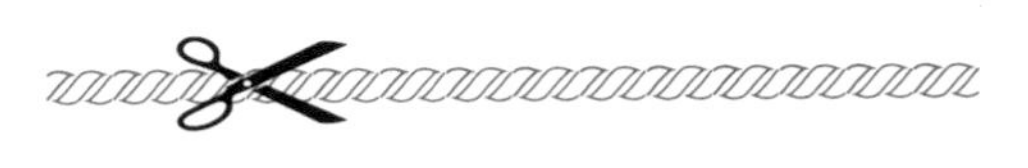

3	4	5	6
○	○	○	○

☞ Answers and explanations on page 175

16. Which two numbers should be added together to give an answer that can be rounded to 240?

○ 143 and 99
○ 99 and 103
○ 2000 and 502
○ 143 and 282

17. Complete this calculation.

$$28 - 6 \times 3 = \square$$

Write your answer in the box.

18. A house uses 1.5 kilolitres of water per day (1000 litres = 1 kilolitre). Last year it used 1200 litres per day.

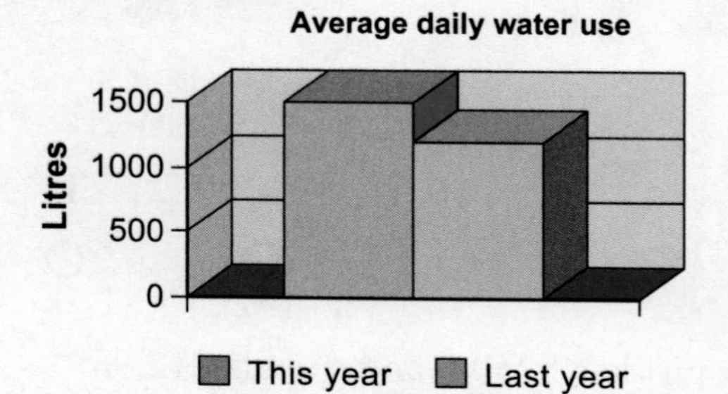

By how much has their water use increased per day?

○ 1500 litres
○ 1200 litres
○ 500 litres
○ 300 litres

19. A dice can land on a 1, 2, 3, 4, 5 or 6. What is the chance it will be an even number?

○ 1 out of 6 chances
○ 3 out of 6 chances
○ 1 out of 3 chances
○ 3 out of 3 chances

20. A shape can be made to flip, slide or turn. Has a flip, slide or a turn (rotate) been done to this coloured shape?

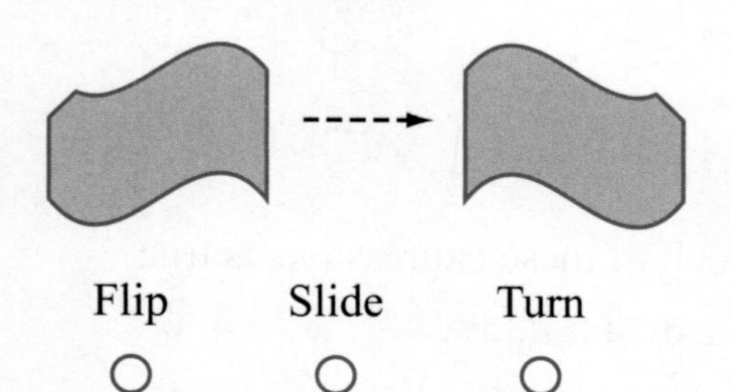

Flip ○   Slide ○   Turn ○

21. Look at this drawing. There is a pattern but one part is missing. This is shown with a question mark (?).

Pick which piece (A, B, C or D) will complete the pattern.

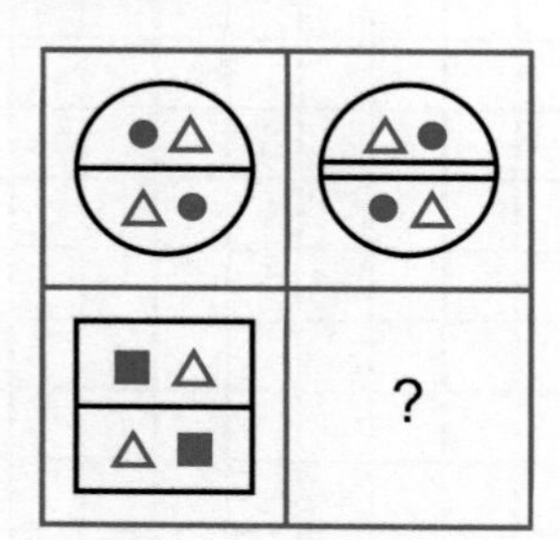

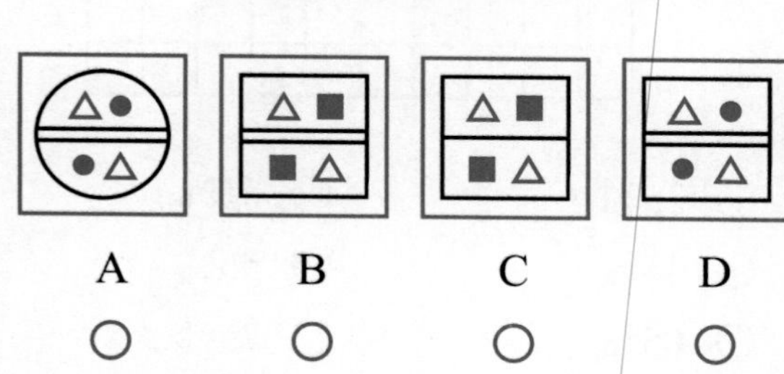

A ○   B ○   C ○   D ○

22. I folded this pattern in half.

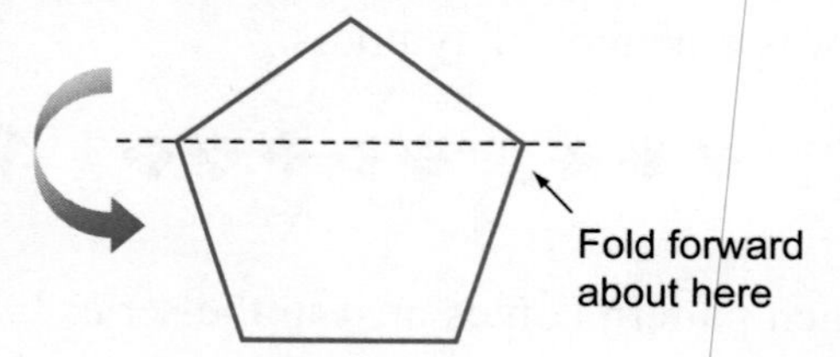

Which shape could I see?

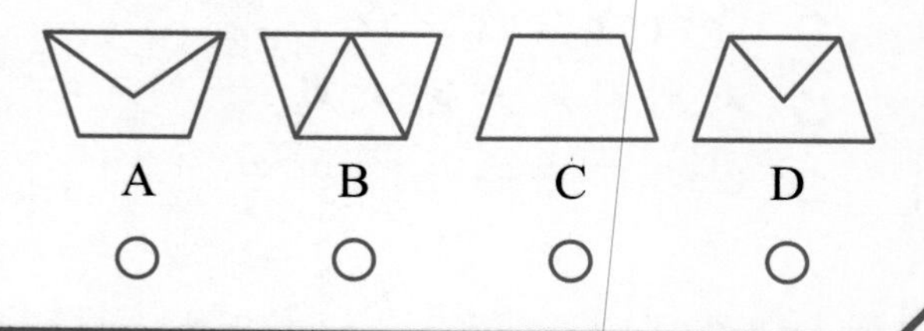

A ○   B ○   C ○   D ○

☞ Answers and explanations on pages 175–176

NUMERACY TEST 4

23. Find the area of the shaded part of this figure.

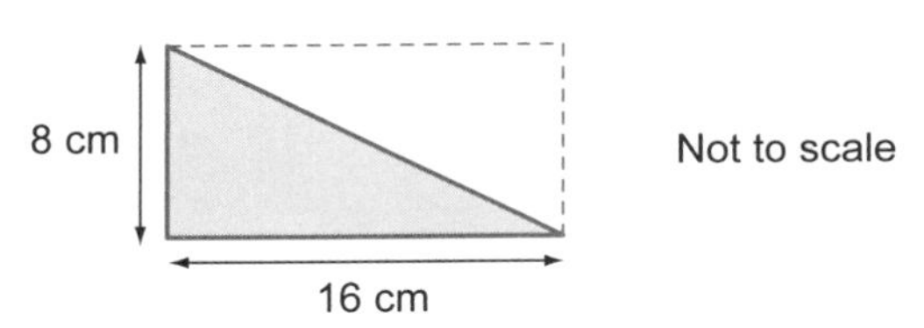

48 cm^2 ○ 64 cm^2 ○ 128 cm^2 ○ 256 cm^2 ○

24. Here is a chart with some symbols.

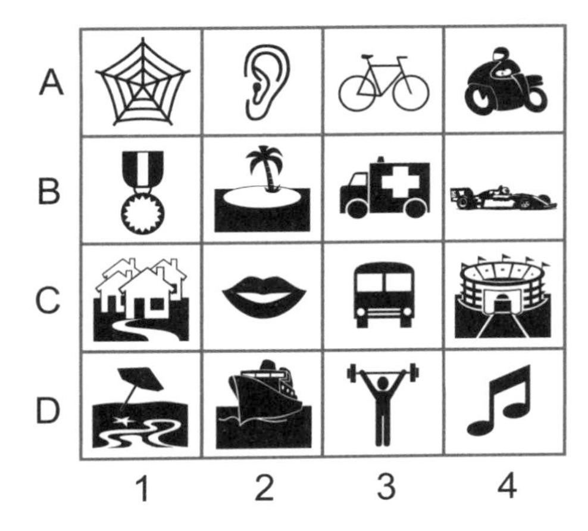

Which symbol is closest or nearest to B3?

25.

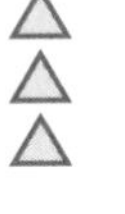 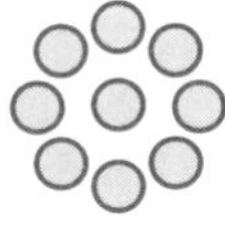  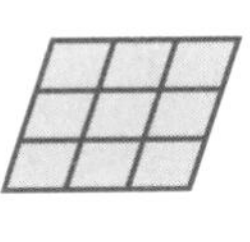 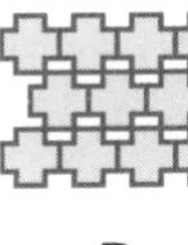

A B C D

Which of the pictures shows a tessellation?

A ○ B ○ C ○ D ○

26. Here is a regular hexagon. Estimate the size of the angle marked with a dot (●) in the figure?

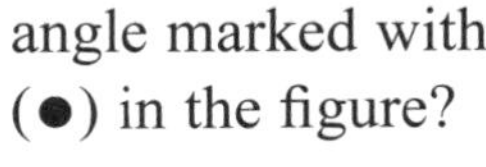

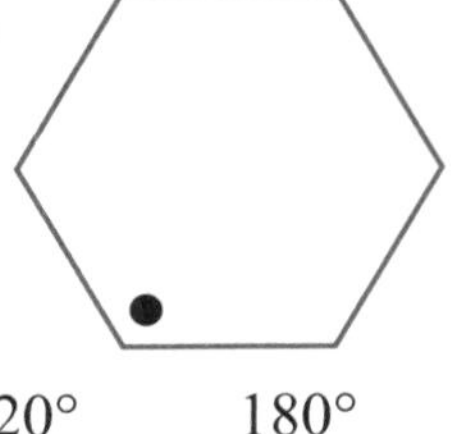

60° ○ 90° ○ 120° ○ 180° ○

27. This pie chart shows the six top vehicle owning countries in the world. They make up almost four-fifths of all vehicles in the world.

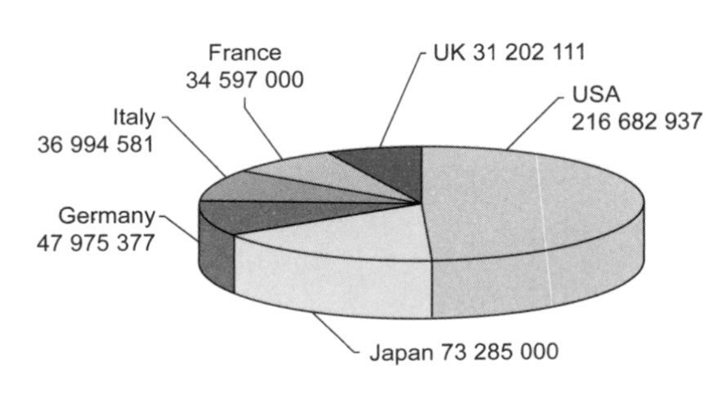

Which is the third largest vehicle owning country?

○ France ○ Japan
○ Germany ○ UK
○ Italy ○ USA

28.

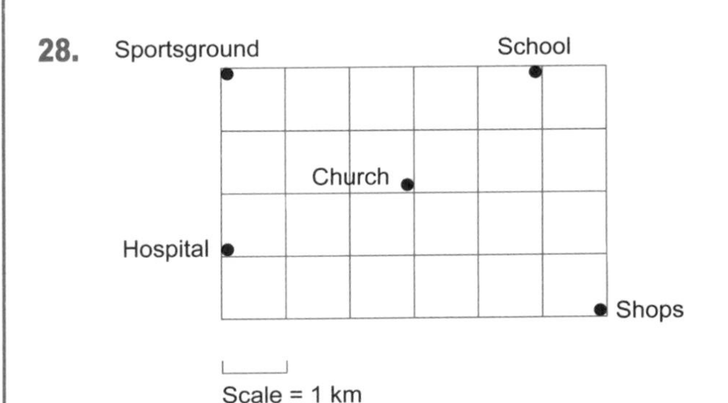

The lines indicate streets and you must walk along these streets.

What is the shortest distance from the shops to the school and then to the sportsground?

[ ] km

Write your answer in the box.

NUMERACY TEST 4

It would be a good idea to check your answers to questions 15 to 28 before moving on to the other questions.

29. This is a rectangular prism.

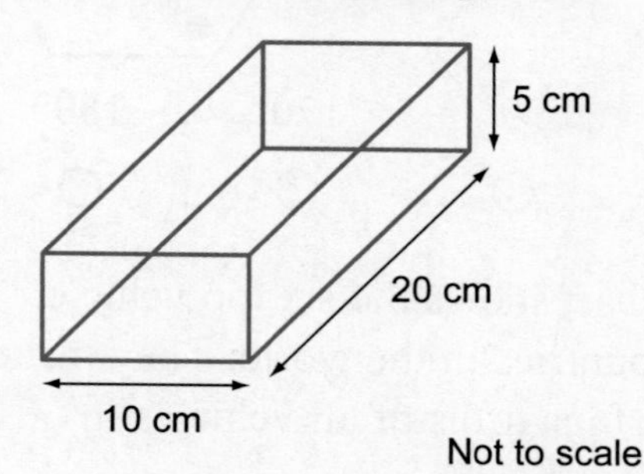

What is the volume of this figure?

- ○ 1000 cm
- ○ 1000 cm^2
- ○ 1000 cm^3
- ○ 2000 cm
- ○ 2000 cm^2
- ○ 2000 cm^3
- ○ 2500 cm
- ○ 2500 cm^2
- ○ 2500 cm^3

30. Australia is a large country and it has three different time zones (in winter). These are Eastern Standard Time, Central Standard Time and Western Standard Time. The time is different across these three areas.

Central Standard Time is half an hour behind Eastern Standard Time.

Western Standard Time is two hours behind Eastern Standard Time.

For instance, when it is 12 noon in Sydney (Eastern Standard Time), it is 11.30 am Central Standard Time and 10 am Western Standard Time.

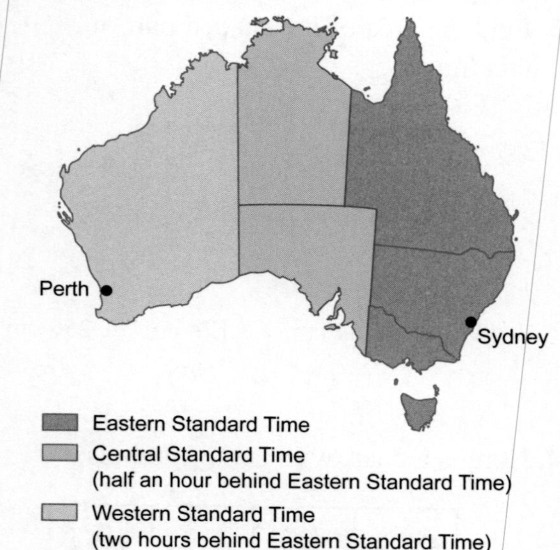

If it is 2 pm in Sydney (Eastern Standard Time), what time will it be in Perth (Western Standard Time)?

- ○ 1.30 pm
- ○ 1.00 pm
- ○ 12.30 pm
- ○ 12 noon
- ○ 11.30 am
- ○ 11.00 am

31. Here is a shape. It contains squares. Some of the squares are all white while some are half coloured and half white.

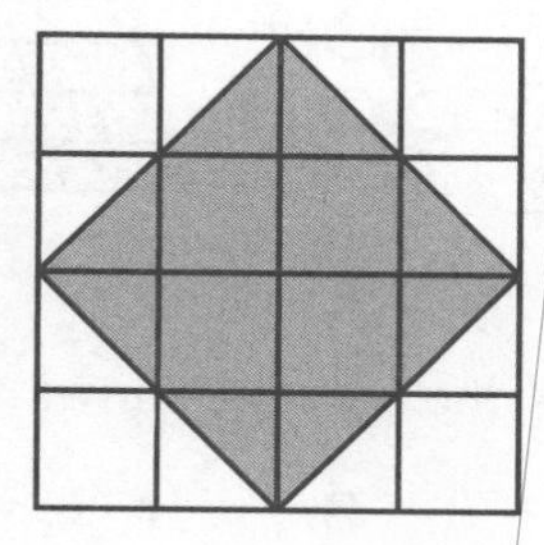

What fraction of the figure is half coloured and half white?

$\frac{1}{2}$	$\frac{1}{3}$	$\frac{1}{4}$	$\frac{2}{3}$	$\frac{3}{4}$
○	○	○	○	○

☞ Answers and explanations on page 176

32. This net is folded to make a solid shape.

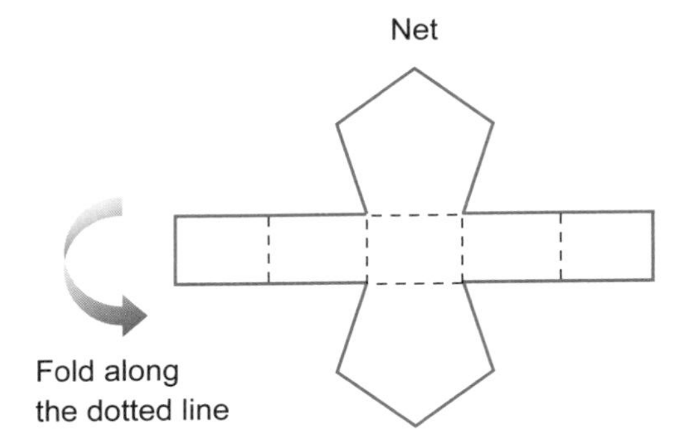

Solid shapes

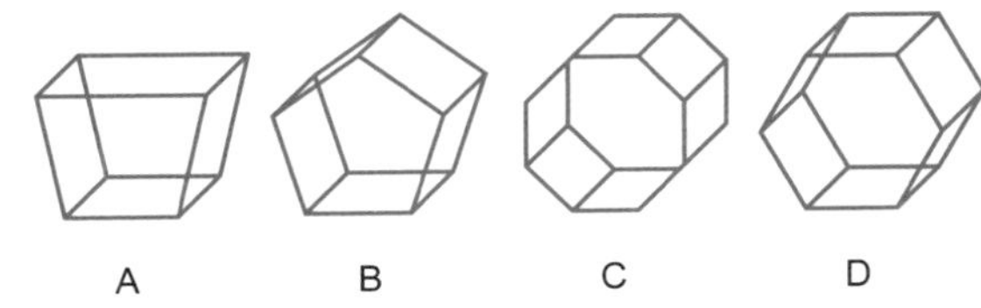

Which solid shape matches the net above?

A ○ B ○ C ○ D ○

33. Form four-digit numbers using the numerals 5, 6, 7 and 8. A digit cannot be used more than once in each number. How many are less than 6875?

○ 9 ○ 10 ○ 11 ○ 12 ○ 13

34. The combined area of the three soccer fields at my school is 13 500 square metres. They are all the same size.

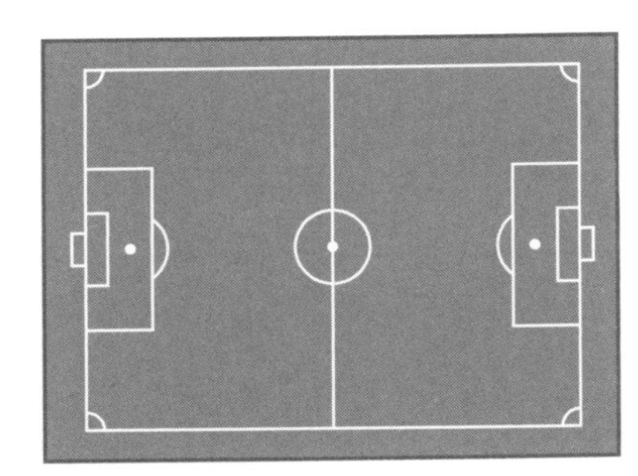

If the width of a soccer field at my school is 45 metres, what is its length?

○ 80 metres ○ 90 metres
○ 100 metres ○ 110 metres

35. What would be the next number in the series 10 000, 8750, 7500, ...?

○ 5500 ○ 5750
○ 6000 ○ 6250
○ 6500 ○ 6750

36. You toss three 50-cent coins at once. What is the chance of throwing three tails?

○ 1 in 3 ○ 3 in 6 ○ 1 in 4 ○ 1 in 2 ○ 1 in 8

37. To relieve famine in a country, 60 000 tonnes of food was sent. If 15% of the food was spoilt or damaged, how much food can be used for famine relief?

○ 41 000 tonnes ○ 45 000 tonnes
○ 47 000 tonnes ○ 49 000 tonnes
○ 51 000 tonnes ○ 53 000 tonnes
○ 55 000 tonnes

38. Here is a water bill for a household. The amount for water usage is not shown.

Nerana
WATER

Water restrictions
Reduce your use!

ACCOUNT FOR RESIDENCE		
Water service		$ 19.00
Sewerage service		$ 120.00
Stormwater drainage		$ 11.00
Water use	113 kilolitres	?
Total amount due		$ 334.00

How much is the water use cost?

$ [ ]

Write your answer in the box.

☞ Answers and explanations on page 176

39. If $\frac{3}{4}$ of a number is 960, what is the number?

- ○ 2880
- ○ 1280
- ○ 3750
- ○ 2160
- ○ 3840
- ○ 750

40. Here are some descriptions.
These chances are numbered from 0 to 1.

1	certain
0.75	quite likely
0.5	an even chance
0.25	unlikely to happen
0	impossible

There are some sentences following. Put a 1 next to the sentence if something is certain; put 0.75 if something is quite likely to happen; put 0.5 next to a sentence if it is an even chance; put 0.25 next to a sentence if it is unlikely to happen; and put a 0 if something is impossible to happen.

Chances	Sentences
	The earth is flat.
	Everyone you know was born on a day of the week ending in *day*.
	A randomly chosen person is male.
	There will be bushfires in the summer in Australia.
	The next person you meet will have been born in Autumn.

Write your answers in these spaces.
Write only the numbers 0, 0.25, 0.5, 0.75 or 1.

41. Here is the map of a large farm. The distance of some sides of the farm are shown below.

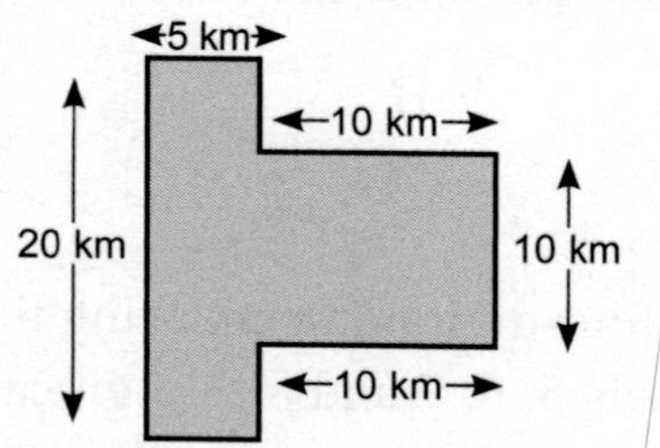

What is the perimeter of this property? (Hint: The length of some sides are not shown and have to be found first.)

- ○ 60 km
- ○ 80 km
- ○ 70 km
- ○ 50 km

42. $\frac{1}{4} + \frac{1}{2} = ?$

- ○ $\frac{2}{6}$
- ○ $\frac{3}{4}$
- ○ $\frac{2}{8}$
- ○ $1\frac{1}{4}$

END OF TEST

Well done! You have completed the final Numeracy Test. It means that you have answered or attempted over 160 Numeracy questions.

How did you go with these test questions? Check to see where you did well and where you had problems. Try to revise the questions that were hard for you.

Use the diagnostic chart on pages 63–64 to see which level of ability you reached. This is only an estimate. Don't be surprised if you answered some difficult questions correctly or even missed some easier questions.

This is the last Numeracy Test. We will start to look at Literacy tasks in the sections that follow. Now take a well-earned rest.

☞ Answers and explanations on page 176

CHECK YOUR SKILLS: NUMERACY TEST 4

Instructions

As you check the answer for each question, mark it as correct (✓) or incorrect (✗). Mark any questions that you omitted or left out as incorrect (✗) for the moment.

Then look at how many you answered correctly in each level. You will be able to see what level you are at by finding the point where you started having consistent difficulty with questions at a certain level. For example, if you answer most questions correctly up to the Intermediate level and then get most questions wrong from then onwards, it is likely your ability is at the Intermediate level. You can ask your parents or your teacher to help you do this if it isn't clear to you.

Am I able to ...

	SKILL	ESTIMATED LEVEL	✓ or ✗
1	Write a numeral of four digits?	Standard	
2	Show a simple fraction of a shape?	Standard	
3	Round a number to the nearest thousand?	Standard	
4	Find the highest frequency from a chart or column graph?	Standard	
5	Realise a number pattern?	Standard	
6	Add two decimal amounts?	Standard	
7	Write a six-digit numeral?	Standard	
8	Determine the likelihood of an event?	Standard	
9	Convert an improper fraction to a mixed number?	Standard	
10	Identify less than in an expression?	Standard	
11	Find a percentage?	Standard	
12	Find a pattern in a series of symbols?	Standard	
13	Recognise a model viewed from a different perspective?	Intermediate	
14	Subtract decimals?	Intermediate	
15	Solve a problem involving division of decimals?	Intermediate	
16	Estimate by rounding off in an addition?	Intermediate	
17	Select the correct order of operations?	Intermediate	
18	Select and apply a change of units from kilolitres to litres?	Intermediate	
19	Estimate the probability of an occurrence?	Intermediate	
20	Recognise a shape that has been flipped horizontally?	Intermediate	
21	Complete an abstract pattern in a matrix?	Intermediate	
22	Visualise a folded shape?	Intermediate	
23	Find the area of a right-angled triangle (half a rectangle)?	Intermediate	
24	Describe the position on a grid?	Intermediate	
25	Identify a tessellation?	Intermediate	
26	Estimate the size of an obtuse angle?	Advanced	
27	Read a pie chart?	Advanced	

CHECK YOUR SKILLS: NUMERACY TEST 4

	SKILL	ESTIMATED LEVEL	✓ or ✗
28	Measure lengths on a chart?	Advanced	
29	Determine the volume of a prism?	Advanced	
30	Find time across time zones of Australia?	Advanced	
31	Find the fraction of a figure that is shaded?	Advanced	
32	Find a solid to match a net?	Advanced	
33	Form four-digit numbers less than a prescribed figure?	Advanced	
34	Find the area of a field?	Advanced	
35	Find the pattern in a series of numbers?	Advanced	
36	Calculate the probability of occurrence?	Advanced	
37	Solve a percentage problem?	Advanced	
38	Calculate a household account?	Advanced	
39	Find a whole number given a fraction?	Advanced	
40	Determine the probability of occurrences?	Advanced	
41	Determine the perimeter of an irregular shape?	Intermediate	
42	Add fractions?	Intermediate	
	TOTAL		

An important note about the NAPLAN Online tests

The NAPLAN Online Reading test will be divided into different sections. Students will only have one opportunity to check their answers at the end of each section before proceeding to the next one. This means that after students have completed a section and moved onto the next they will not be able to check their work again. We have included reminders for students to check their work at specific points in the practice tests from now on so they become familiar with this process.

READING TEST 1

ADAPTED FOR ONLINE FORMAT

This is the first Reading Test. There are 39 questions.

If you aren't sure what to do, ask your teacher or your parents to help you. Don't be afraid to ask if it isn't clear to you.

Allow around 50 minutes for this test. Take a short break if necessary.

In this test you will need to look at a picture or read something first. Then read each question and colour in the circle with the correct answer.

Read the greeting card and answer question 1.

Dear Nicholas,
Seasons greetings!
Love,
Mary-Ellen

1. On which type of card would you find this greeting?
   - ○ You might find it on a Christmas card.
   - ○ You might find it on a birthday card.
   - ○ You might find it on a get-well card.

Read *Abacus* and answer questions 2 to 8.

Abacus

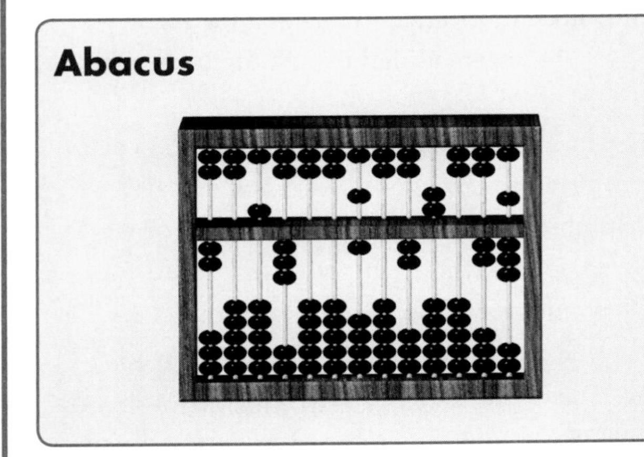

An abacus is a device for counting. The modern abacus uses beads on a wire frame. The abacus was developed by ancient people in the Middle East and used by the Greeks and Romans. They used counters on a board to work out problems. They did this because our number system had not yet been developed.

Hindus and Chinese also used the abacus. Later the counters were moved on wires that were placed in a wooden frame. The abacus was not used much once our number system became popular but it is still used in Asia for quick calculations.

A modern abacus uses counters that are worth five and one. The beads on the left count as one and the beads on the right count as five. Therefore each row adds up to a multiple of 15. Only the beads that are next to the middle bar are counted.

In the figure below, the beads on the abacus add up to 162.

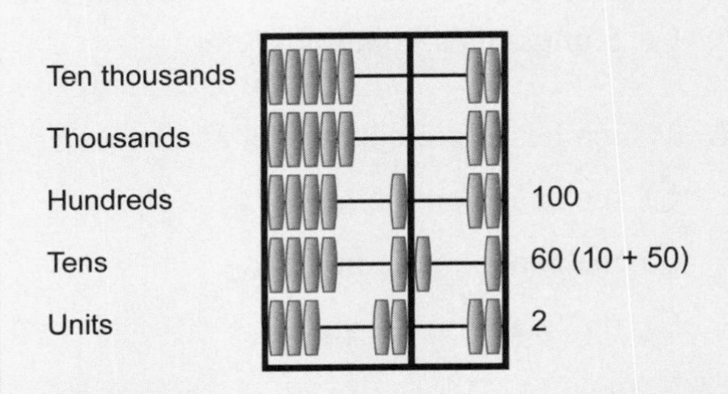

☞ Answers and explanations on page 177

2. What is an abacus?

- ○ It is like a manual calculator.
- ○ It is a Chinese invention.
- ○ It is a wire frame.

3. Who developed the abacus?

- ○ the Ancient Romans
- ○ the Ancient Greeks
- ○ the Hindus
- ○ the Egyptians
- ○ the Chinese
- ○ the Middle-eastern people

4. The abacus was developed

- ○ for working out problems.
- ○ as a number system.
- ○ to count beads.

5. In the article, who is said to have used counters on a board to work out problems?

- ○ the Hindus
- ○ the Greeks
- ○ the Chinese

6. What is the value of each bead on the right?

- ○ 15 units, tens, hundreds, etc.
- ○ 1 unit, ten, hundred, etc.
- ○ 5 units, tens, hundreds, etc.

7. Which beads are counted in an abacus?

- ○ the beads on the left
- ○ the beads in the middle
- ○ the beads on the right

8. Which number is shown in the abacus below?

- ○ 163
- ○ 663
- ○ 113
- ○ 613
- ○ 553

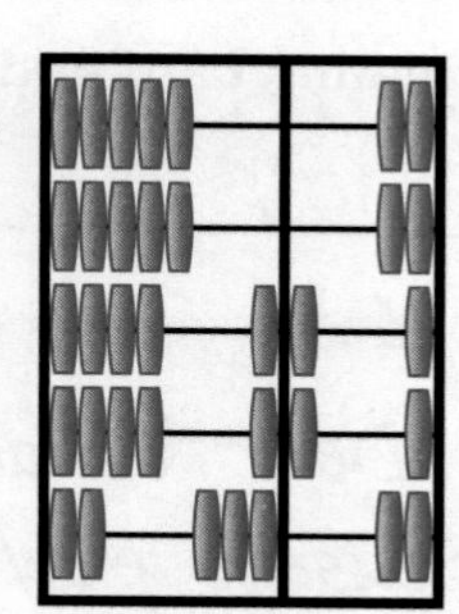

Read the poem and answer questions 9 to 16.

There was one who was famed for the number of things
He forgot when he entered the ship:
His umbrella, his watch, all his jewels and rings,
And the clothes he had bought for the trip.

He had forty-two boxes, all carefully packed,
With his name painted clearly on each:
But, since he omitted to mention the fact,
They were all left behind on the beach.

The loss of his clothes hardly mattered, because
He had seven coats on when he came,
With three pair of boots–but the worst of it was,
He had wholly forgotten his name.
He would answer to 'Hi!' or to any loud cry,
Such as 'Fry me!' or 'Fritter my wig!'
To 'What-you-may-call-um!' or 'What-was-his-name!'
But especially 'Thing-um-a-jig!'

☞ Answers and explanations on page 177

While, for those who preferred a more
forcible word,
He had different names from these:
His intimate friends called him 'Candle-ends,'
And his enemies 'Toasted-cheese.'

'His form is ungainly–his intellect small–'
(So the Bellman would often remark)
'But his courage is perfect! And that, after all,
Is the thing that one needs with a Snark.'

From The Project Gutenberg e-book of *The Hunting of the Snark* by Lewis Carroll

9. What can we say about the person described in the poem?

- ○ This person has a good memory.
- ○ This person has a normal memory.
- ○ This person has a poor memory.

10. How many boxes were packed with his belongings?

- ○ 1
- ○ 3
- ○ 7
- ○ 42

11. Why did it not matter that he forgot his clothes?

- ○ It did not matter because he had an umbrella, his watch and all his jewels and rings.
- ○ It did not matter because he had seven extra coats and three pairs of boots.
- ○ It did not matter because the boxes with his clothes were all carefully packed with his name clearly painted on each.

12. What was the worst problem?

- ○ The worst problem was that he had forgotten his umbrella, his watch and all his jewels and rings.
- ○ The worst problem was that he could not remember his name.
- ○ The worst problem was that he had forgotten to tell someone that all his belongings were still on the beach.

13. In which paragraph or verse are we first told the different names he was called?

- ○ first paragraph
- ○ second paragraph
- ○ third paragraph
- ○ fourth paragraph
- ○ fifth paragraph

14. The phrase *a forcible word* means

- ○ a word that has a powerful effect.
- ○ a loud word.
- ○ a word with a peaceful effect
- ○ a violent action.

15. Which of the following words are opposite in meaning in the poem?

- ○ *intimate friends* and *enemies*
- ○ *form ungainly* and *intellect small*
- ○ *preferred* and *remark*

16. What is needed to hunt for the Snark?

- ○ an ungainly form
- ○ a small intellect
- ○ courage

It would be a good idea to check your answers to questions 1 to 16 before moving on to the other questions.

 ☞ Answers and explanations on page 177

Read *Hand Hygiene* and answer questions 17 to 27.

Hand Hygiene

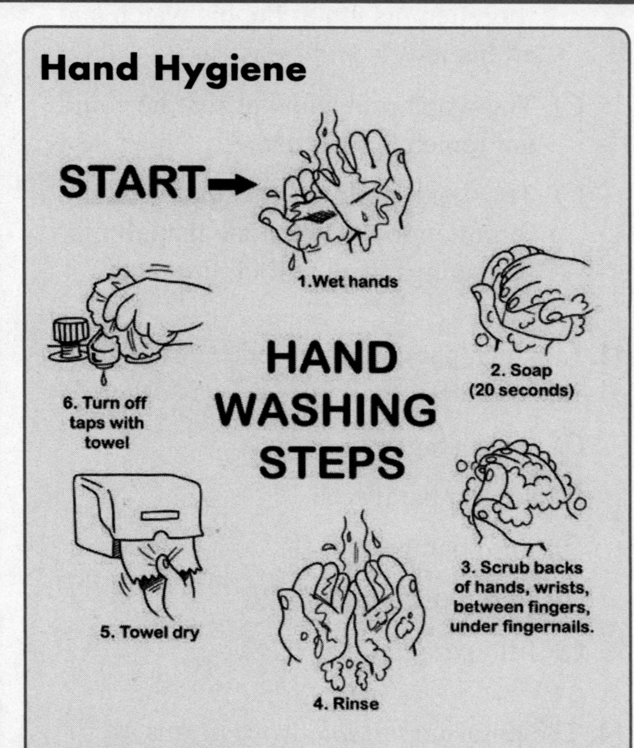

MOST PEOPLE are aware how important it is to wash our hands with water or soap to get rid of dirt and germs. Hand hygiene is vital for people who work in hospitals or who work with food. It is probably one of the best ways for everyone to help in preventing the spread of disease.

The most important times to wash and dry your hands properly is after using a toilet or after changing a baby's nappy, when you are looking after someone who is ill at home or in hospital and before you eat or feed a child or prepare food.

Many people think it is enough just to wash your hands and then maybe to dry them quickly. However, recent research has also shown that it is not only important to wash your hands but it is the way in which you dry them that also helps to make your hands germ free. Even after people wash their hands they can still be contaminated with many thousands of bacteria.

Although most people remember to wash their hands one very big problem is that many people are not really drying their hands properly after washing them. Damp hands contain many thousands of bacteria but after being dried for almost a minute under an electric drier the bacteria reduce to about 500 but they can increase on the finger pads and palms of your hand. Drying with a paper towel can reduce further the bacteria on the finger pads and palms of your hand.

To wash properly, wet your hands and then rub them together separate from the running water for at least 20 seconds until they are nice and soapy. Then rinse your hands and dry them with a clean towel or a disposable paper towel. Paper towels have been shown to be more hygienic than hot air hand dryers. A towel is necessary because washing gets rid of contamination off the skin but does not entirely flush bacteria away from the skin. Some of the contamination that is suspended with the dampness can be removed with a towel. After drying your hands, use a paper towel to turn off the water and to open the door in a washroom.

The best procedure is to get as much of the dampness off with a paper towel and then to hold your hands under a hot air drier. If there is no air drier then it is just as effective to use two separate paper towels.

Unfortunately about half the people using the toilet facilities in places like universities or shopping centres do not wash their hands. Even if they wash their hands, about 30 per cent do not dry them. Even if they dry their hands people only do so for a very short time—you need around 20 seconds under an electric drier.

It is recommended that people preparing food in places like homes, restaurants or cafes at the very least wash their hands and then dry them on a throw-away paper towel.

☞ Answers and explanations on page 177

17. Which sentence is true?

- ○ Many people know that it is important to wash your hands.
- ○ Many people know that it is important to wash and dry your hands.
- ○ Many people know that it is important to be germ free.

18. What problem is identified?

- ○ Many people do not want to be germ free.
- ○ Many people think it is enough to wash their hands.
- ○ Many people wash but don't dry their hands.

19. How many bacteria remain on damp hands?

- ○ hundreds of thousands
- ○ tens of thousands
- ○ several thousand
- ○ hundreds

20. Which word means the same as *bacteria*?

- ○ germ
- ○ poison
- ○ virus
- ○ disease

21. How do we know that bacteria are micro-organisms?

- ○ because they are studied by scientists
- ○ because they cause illness
- ○ because they live in moisture and dampness
- ○ because there can be many thousands on a hand

22. What is the best way to dry hands?

- ○ The best way is to hot air-dry for 20 seconds and then wipe with a towel.
- ○ The best way is to wipe with a paper towel for 20 seconds.
- ○ The best way is to wipe with a paper towel and then hot air-dry for 20 seconds.

23. What is the next best alternative if there is no air-drier?

- ○ The next best alternative is to wipe carefully with a paper towel.
- ○ The next best alternative is to wipe carefully with separate paper towels.
- ○ The next best alternative is to wipe with a paper towel for 10 seconds and then an air-drier for 20 seconds.

24. What could be a major problem in people using facilities?

- ○ About 30 per cent of people do not dry their hands.
- ○ Around half do not even wash their hands.
- ○ About 20 per cent of people do dry their hands for a long enough time.

25. What recommendation is made for people preparing food?

- ○ It is recommended that they wash their hands.
- ○ It is recommended that they wash their hands and use an air-drier.
- ○ It is recommended that they wash and dry their hands and use a paper towel.

26. The word *hygiene* means

- ○ cleanliness.
- ○ medicine.
- ○ antiseptic.
- ○ healthy.

27. Here are four steps for washing hands properly. Number them in order from 1 to 4.

[ ] Rinse your hands.
[ ] Turn off the water.
[ ] Rub your hands together with soap until they are soapy.
[ ] Dry them with a clean towel.

It would be a good idea to check your answers to questions 17 to 27 before moving on to the other questions.

 ☞ **Answers and explanations on page 177**

READING TEST 1

Read *Spooked* and answer questions 28 to 39.

Spooked

At breakfast the next morning, Gerry's father looked at him over his bowl of muesli. 'Gerry … How would you like to go and stay with Auntie Ruth?'

'Auntie Ruth? No thanks! I'm not going to stay with Auntie Ruth.'

'Yes, you are,' said his mother softly. 'Just for a while. I'm going overseas with Dad.'

'No way!' said Gerry. 'I'm not going there.'

'You must,' said his father. 'You can't stay here alone.'

Gerry threw down his spoon and ran from the room. He stamped up the steps to the attic and was about to throw himself on the bed, when he thought of a better idea. He'd show them!

Gerry opened the wardrobe and stepped inside, pulling the doors shut after him.

Yes, he'd show them. Let them watch him suffer! If the spook sliced him to pieces, then they'd be sorry they tried to send him to Auntie Ruth's.

He heard his mother's footsteps on the stairs.

'Come on, Gerry,' she said. 'Don't be silly.' Gerry said nothing. In reply, he opened the wardrobe a chink and threw out a shoe. It was an old black one with the toe worn out.

'Well!' she said. 'If that's all you have to say, I'm leaving.' She went downstairs and left him in the wardrobe.

Gerry was almost too angry to think. How dare they send him to Auntie Ruth's! He was showing them, though. He would stay in the wardrobe with the spook until they changed their minds.

From Spooked! by Errol Broome, HBJ, 1992

28. How many people are mentioned in this story?

- ○ 5
- ○ 4
- ○ 3

29. Who is quoted as saying: 'How would you like to go and stay with Auntie Ruth'?

- ○ Gerry
- ○ the spook
- ○ Gerry's mother
- ○ Gerry's father

30. Which of the following can be said about this piece of writing?

- ○ It aims to describe a family.
- ○ It wants to encourage the reader.
- ○ It shows you how to react when angry.
- ○ It is part of a larger story called Spooked.

31. What was Gerry's answer to his father's question?

- ○ Gerry ignored the question.
- ○ Gerry argued with his father.
- ○ Gerry refused to stay with his aunt.

32. How did Gerry's mother speak to him?

- ○ She insisted quietly.
- ○ She argued with him.
- ○ She let him feel angry.

33. Why does Gerry have to stay with Auntie Ruth?

- ○ because he is an only child
- ○ because the house is spooked
- ○ because he cannot be alone
- ○ because he cannot be trusted

☞ Answers and explanations on page 177

34. What action shows that Gerry was angry?

- ◯ Gerry was angry when he thought of an idea.
- ◯ Gerry was angry when he ran from the room.
- ◯ Gerry was angry when he threw himself on the bed.

35. What is the 'better idea' that Gerry thought of?

- ◯ to step inside the wardrobe
- ◯ to throw himself on the bed
- ◯ to stamp up the steps to the attic
- ◯ to pull the doors shut after him

36. What is Gerry trying to achieve by hiding in the wardrobe?

- ◯ Gerry was trying to scare his parents with the spook.
- ◯ Gerry was trying to hide from his parents in the wardrobe.
- ◯ Gerry was aiming to make his parents sorry if the spook attacked him.

37. The way this passage is written leads the reader to

- ◯ feel jealous of Gerry.
- ◯ feel sorry for Gerry.
- ◯ feel happy for Gerry.
- ◯ feel respect for Gerry.

38. The *spook* that is mentioned in the story is likely to be

- ◯ a ghost.
- ◯ a person.
- ◯ a feeling.
- ◯ an object.

39. His mother left him in the wardrobe to

- ◯ become frightened.
- ◯ soothe his anger.
- ◯ throw out more clothes.
- ◯ have some fun.

END OF TEST

Well done! You have completed the first Reading Test. This test had different types of questions. They are like comprehension passages. You had to look at something or read something and then make a judgement.

How did you find these questions? We hope that you found them interesting. Revise anything that was hard for you. There are further questions in the next Reading Test. The next test contains some different questions. Take a long break before doing any more tests.

Use the diagnostic chart on page 72 to see which level of ability you reached. This is only an estimate. Don't be surprised if you answered some difficult questions correctly or even missed some easier questions.

Please note that multiple interpretations are possible for the levels of difficulty of these tasks. Also, some questions involve skills from different levels. This is only an initial guide to the approximate level of the reading skill assessed.

☞ Answers and explanations on page 177

CHECK YOUR SKILLS: READING TEST 1

Instructions

As you check the answer for each question, mark it as correct (✓) or incorrect (✗). Mark any questions that you omitted or left out as incorrect (✗) for the moment.

Then look at how many you answered correctly in each level. You will be able to see what level you are at by finding the point where you started having consistent difficulty with questions at a certain level. For example, if you answer most questions correctly up to the Intermediate level and then get most questions wrong from then onwards, it is likely your ability is at the Intermediate level. You can ask your parents or your teacher to help you do this if it isn't clear to you.

Am I able to ...

	SKILL	ESTIMATED LEVEL	✓ or ✗
1	Interpret ideas in simple text?	Standard	
2	Find directly stated information?	Standard	
3	Find directly stated information?	Standard	
4	Identify reasons?	Standard	
5	Find directly stated information?	Standard	
6	Find information in a diagram?	Intermediate	
7	Find directly stated information?	Standard	
8	Find information in a diagram?	Intermediate	
9	Understand the general idea of a poem?	Standard	
10	Find a simple fact?	Standard	
11	Find a reason?	Intermediate	
12	Find details?	Standard	
13	Find details?	Standard	
14	Define the effect of an adjective?	Advanced	
15	Select words that are opposite in meaning?	Intermediate	
16	Make a conclusion?	Intermediate	
17	Interpret a statement?	Advanced	
18	Identify a problem?	Intermediate	
19	Discern details from a sentence?	Intermediate	
20	State the meaning of a word?	Standard	
21	Interpret information for an inference?	Advanced	
22	Recognise the sequence of events?	Intermediate	
23	Find an alternative strategy?	Advanced	
24	Find directly stated information?	Standard	
25	Find a recommendation in a text?	Intermediate	
26	Define a word?	Intermediate	
27	Number steps in the order listed?	Intermediate	
28	Find details?	Standard	
29	Find a quotation?	Standard	
30	Analyse reasons?	Advanced	
31	Identify an action?	Standard	
32	Identify an action?	Standard	
33	Explain reasons?	Intermediate	
34	Infer the motivation of a character?	Intermediate	
35	Analyse the details of an event?	Advanced	
36	Infer the purpose of an action?	Advanced	
37	Infer the reader's reaction to a character?	Advanced	
38	Classify an object?	Advanced	
39	Interpret an action?	Intermediate	
	TOTAL		

READING TEST 2

ADAPTED FOR ONLINE FORMAT

This is the second Reading Test. There are 39 questions.

If you aren't sure what to do, ask your teacher or your parents to help you. Don't be afraid to ask if it isn't clear to you.

Allow around 50 minutes for this test. Take a short break if necessary.

In this test you will need to look at a picture or read something first. Then read each question and colour in the circle with the correct answer.

Read the text and answer questions 1 to 2.

In this DIRECTORY you'll see
Just what you never ought to be;
And so, it should Direct your way
To Good Behaviour, every day.
The children of whose faults I tell
Are known by other names, as well,
So see that *you* aren't in this group
Of Naughty Ones. *Don't be a Goop*!

Adapted from The Project Gutenberg e-book of *The Goop Directory Juvenile Offenders Famous for their Misdeeds and Serving as a Salutary Example for all Virtuous Children* by Gelett Burgess, 1913

1. What is the purpose of this text?

- ○ to tell children how to behave
- ○ to make children laugh
- ○ to help children who are lost

2. What is a Goop?

- ○ A Goop is a cartoon character.
- ○ A Goop is a sad character.
- ○ A Goop is a naughty character.
- ○ A Goop is a good character.

Read *The Wolf and the Kid* and answer questions 3 to 5.

The Wolf and the Kid

There was once a little Kid whose growing horns made him think he was a grown-up Billy Goat and able to take care of himself. So one evening when the flock started home from the pasture and his mother called, the Kid paid no heed and kept right on nibbling the tender grass. A little later when he lifted his head, the flock was gone.

 ☞ Answers and explanations on page 177

READING TEST 2

He was all alone. The sun was sinking. Long shadows came creeping over the ground. A chilly little wind came creeping with them making scary noises in the grass. The Kid shivered as he thought of the terrible Wolf. Then he started wildly over the field, bleating for his mother. But not half-way, near a clump of trees, there was the Wolf!

The Kid knew there was little hope for him.

'Please, Mr. Wolf,' he said trembling, 'I know you are going to eat me. But first please pipe me a tune, for I want to dance and be merry as long as I can.'

The Wolf liked the idea of a little music before eating, so he struck up a merry tune and the Kid leaped and frisked gaily.

Meanwhile, the flock was moving slowly homeward. In the still evening air the Wolf's piping carried far. The Shepherd Dogs pricked up their ears. They recognized the song the Wolf sings before a feast, and in a moment they were racing back to the pasture. The Wolf's song ended suddenly, and as he ran, with the Dogs at his heels, he called himself a fool for turning piper to please a Kid, when he should have stuck to his butcher's trade.

From The Project Gutenberg e-book of *The Aesop for Children With Pictures* by Milo Winter, Rand McNally, 1919

3. What message does this passage give the reader?

- ○ The message is not to let anything turn you from your purpose.
- ○ The message is to do something right away.
- ○ The message is that you cannot judge something by the way it looks.
- ○ The message is that something that is bad at first can also be good.

4. Which sentence is true?

- ○ The Kid thought he was an adult because he fooled the Wolf into playing a tune.
- ○ The Kid thought he was an adult because he was able to take care of himself.
- ○ The Kid thought he was an adult because he kept right on nibbling the tender grass.
- ○ The Kid thought he was an adult because he had horns.

5. What is the butcher's trade in the passage? (last paragraph)

- ○ selling meat in a shop
- ○ carving meat for customers
- ○ the killing of animals
- ○ playing some music and enjoying a meal

Look at the pictures and answer question 6.

6. Which picture matches the saying *Where there's a will there's a way?*

○ A

○ B

○ C

○ D

Adapted from The Project Gutenberg e-book of *Dumpy Proverbs* by C Honor and C Appleton, Grant Richards, 1903

☞ Answers and explanations on page 177

Look at the pictures and answer question 7.

7. Which picture matches the saying *A stitch in time saves nine*?

○ A

○ B

○ C

○ D

Adapted from The Project Gutenberg e-book of *Dumpy Proverbs* by C Honor and C Appleton, Grant Richards, 1903

Read *A story from Henry Lawson* and answer questions 8 to 12.

A story from Henry Lawson

Bill and Jim, professional shearers, were coming into Bourke from the Queensland side. They were horsemen and had two packhorses. At the last camp before Bourke Jim's packhorse got disgusted and home-sick during the night and started back for the place where he was foaled. Jim was little more than a new-chum jackaroo; he was no bushman and generally got lost when he went down the next gully. Bill was a bushman, so it was decided that he should go back to look for the horse.

Now Bill was going to sell his packhorse, a well-bred mare, in Bourke, and he was anxious to get her into the yards before the horse sales were over; this was to be the last day of the sales. Jim was the best 'barracker' of the two; he had great imagination; he was a very entertaining story-teller and conversationalist in social life, and a glib and a most impressive liar in business, so it was decided that he should hurry on into Bourke with the mare and sell her for Bill. Seven pounds, reserve.

Next day Bill turned up with the missing horse and saw Jim standing against a veranda-post of the Carriers' Arms, with his hat down over his eyes, and thoughtfully spitting in the dust. Bill rode over to him.

'Ullo, Jim.'

'Ullo, Bill. I see you got him.'

'Yes, I got him.'

Pause.

'Where'd yer find him?'

'Bout ten mile back. Near Ford's Bridge. He was just feedin' along.'

Pause. Jim shifted his feet and spat in the dust.

'Well,' said Bill at last. 'How did you get on, Jim?'

'Oh, all right,' said Jim. 'I sold the mare.'

'That's right,' said Bill. 'How much did she fetch?'

'Eight quid*;' then, rousing himself a little and showing some emotion, 'An' I could 'a' got ten quid for her if I hadn't been a dam' fool.'

'Oh, that's good enough,' said Bill.

'I could 'a' got ten quid if I'd 'a' waited.'

'Well, it's no use cryin'. Eight quid is good enough. Did you get the stuff?'

'Oh, yes. They parted all right. If I hadn't been such a dam' fool an' rushed it, there was a feller that would 'a' given ten quid for that mare.'

'Well, don't break yer back about it,' said Bill. 'Eight is good enough.'

'Yes. But I could 'a' got ten,' said Jim, languidly, putting his hand in his pocket.

Pause. Bill sat waiting for him to hand over the money; but Jim withdrew his hand empty, stretched, and said:

'Ah, well, Bill, I done it in. Lend us a couple o' notes.'

Jim had been drinking and gambling all night and he'd lost the eight pounds as well as his own money.

Bill didn't explode. What was the use? He should have known that Jim wasn't to be trusted with money in town. It was he who had been the fool. He sighed and lent Jim a pound, and they went in to have a drink.

Now it strikes me that if this had happened in a civilized country (like England) Bill would have had Jim arrested and jailed for larceny as a bailee, or embezzlement, or whatever it was. And would Bill or Jim or the world have been any better for it?

**quid—an old monetary unit before the dollar. It was used until 1966: one pound was worth two dollars.*

From The Project Gutenberg e-book of *Children of the Bush* by Henry Lawson. These stories were first published as a collection in 1902. Republished as *Send Round the Hat* and *The Romance of the Swag* in 1907.

8. How much did Bill receive from the sale of the packhorse?

- ○ eight quid
- ○ ten quid
- ○ seven quid
- ○ nothing

9. Why was Bill delayed?

- ○ Bill was delayed because he went back to look for the well-bred mare.
- ○ Bill was delayed because he was drinking and gambling all night.
- ○ Bill was delayed because he was leaning on the veranda post of the Carrier's Arms.
- ○ Bill was delayed because he went back to look for the packhorse.

10. What do we notice about Jim's response to Bill?

- ○ Jim was a most impressive liar.
- ○ Jim was the best 'barracker' of the two.
- ○ Jim was stalling for time.
- ○ Jim was a very entertaining story-teller.

11. What would be a good title for this passage?

- ○ On the Tucker Track: A Steelman Story
- ○ A Sketch of Mateship
- ○ The Shearer's Dream
- ○ The Lost Souls' Hotel

12. What is the message of this story?

- ○ There is no point in seeking revenge; friendship is more important.
- ○ There is no point in getting angry since there is nothing that can be done about it now.
- ○ It is important to have Jim arrested as a thief for stealing Bill's money.
- ○ You should not trust your friends as they can let you down.

It would be a good idea to check your answers to questions 1 to 12 before moving on to the other questions.

☞ **Answers and explanations on page 178**

Read the sentences and answer question 13.

A More than 30 000 walked through the doors at the discount store to cash in on bargains being offered in all departments.

B 'As in previous years, we have many clearance items,' Mr Darwin said.

C The store manager, Mr Charlie Darwin, said people were lined up outside the store when it opened at 9 am.

D Men's and women's clothing were the biggest sellers of the day with strong sales of home appliances.

13. Which is the correct order for these sentences?

- ○ ABCD
- ○ ABDC
- ○ ACDB
- ○ ACBD
- ○ ADBC
- ○ ADCB

Read *Animal Farm* and answer questions 14 to 24.

Animal Farm

Mr. Jones, of the Manor Farm, had locked the hen-houses for the night, but was too drunk to remember to shut the pop-holes. With the ring of light from his lantern dancing from side to side, he lurched across the yard, kicked off his boots at the back door, drew himself a last glass of beer from the barrel in the scullery, and made his way up to bed, where Mrs. Jones was already snoring.

As soon as the light in the bedroom went out there was a stirring and a fluttering all through the farm buildings. Word had gone round during the day that old Major, the prize Middle White boar, had had a strange dream on the previous night and wished to communicate it to the other animals. It had been agreed that they should all meet in the big barn as soon as Mr. Jones was safely out of the way. Old Major (so he was always called, though the name under which he had been exhibited was Willingdon Beauty) was so highly regarded on the farm that everyone was quite ready to lose an hour's sleep in order to hear what he had to say.

At one end of the big barn, on a sort of raised platform, Major was already ensconced on his bed of straw, under a lantern which hung from a beam. He was twelve years old and had lately grown rather stout, but he was still a majestic-looking pig, with a wise and benevolent appearance in spite of the fact that his tushes had never been cut. Before long the other animals began to arrive and make themselves comfortable after their different fashions.

First came the three dogs, Bluebell, Jessie, and Pincher, and then the pigs, who settled down in the straw immediately in front of the platform. The hens perched themselves on the window-sills, the pigeons fluttered up to the rafters, the sheep and cows lay down behind the pigs and began to chew the cud. The two cart-horses, Boxer and Clover, came in together, walking very slowly and setting down their vast hairy hoofs with great care lest there should be some small animal concealed in the straw.

Clover was a stout motherly mare approaching middle life, who had never

☞ Answers and explanations on page 178

READING TEST 2

quite got her figure back after her fourth foal. Boxer was an enormous beast, nearly eighteen hands high, and as strong as any two ordinary horses put together. A white stripe down his nose gave him a somewhat stupid appearance, and in fact he was not of first-rate intelligence, but he was universally respected for his steadiness of character and tremendous powers of work.

After the horses came Muriel, the white goat, and Benjamin, the donkey. Benjamin was the oldest animal on the farm, and the worst tempered. He seldom talked, and when he did, it was usually to make some cynical remark–for instance, he would say that God had given him a tail to keep the flies off, but that he would sooner have had no tail and no flies. Alone among the animals on the farm he never laughed. If asked why, he would say that he saw nothing to laugh at. Nevertheless, without openly admitting it, he was devoted to Boxer; the two of them usually spent their Sundays together in the small paddock beyond the orchard, grazing side by side and never speaking.

From The Project Gutenberg of Australia e-book of *Animal Farm* by George Orwell, 1945

14. Which sentence correctly describes this text?

- ○ This text is near the start of a story.
- ○ This text is near the middle of a story.
- ○ This text is near the end of a story.

15. Why was there stirring and fluttering in the farm buildings?

- ○ because the farmer was too drunk to remember to shut the pop-holes
- ○ because Mrs. Jones was already snoring
- ○ because old Major wanted to tell the animals about his dream
- ○ because old Major, the prize Middle White boar, had had a strange dream on the previous night

16. Who was Willingdon Beauty?

- ○ Manor Farm was Willingdon Beauty.
- ○ Mrs. Jones was Willingdon Beauty.
- ○ Old Major was Willingdon Beauty.
- ○ Mr. Jones was Willingdon Beauty.

17. Which animals came to the big barn first?

- ○ the dogs
- ○ the hens
- ○ the pigeons
- ○ the pigs

18. Who is Muriel?

- ○ Muriel is the farmer's wife.
- ○ Muriel is the goat.
- ○ Muriel is one of the dogs.

19. Why was everyone prepared to lose an hour's sleep?

- ○ because Old Major was respected
- ○ because Mr. Jones, of the Manor Farm, was too drunk
- ○ because Mrs. Jones was safely asleep
- ○ because everyone wanted to hear what Old Major had to say

☞ Answers and explanations on page 178

20. Which sentence is true?

- ○ Boxer and Clover settled down in the straw immediately in front of the sheep and cows.
- ○ Old Major settled down in the straw immediately in front of the sheep and cows.
- ○ The pigs settled down in the straw immediately in front of the sheep and cows.
- ○ Muriel and Benjamin settled down in the straw immediately in front of the sheep and cows.

21. What is the meaning of the word *ensconced* in the third paragraph?

- ○ stood majestically
- ○ went to sleep restfully
- ○ settled down comfortably

22. Who was as strong as two normal horses?

- ○ Boxer
- ○ Clover
- ○ Muriel
- ○ Benjamin

23. Why is a remark from Benjamin described as cynical?

- ○ because Benjamin was not happy with things
- ○ because Benjamin was not respectful
- ○ because Benjamin was not talkative
- ○ because Benjamin was the oldest animal on the farm

24. Imagine that after this scene the animals drove out Mr. Jones and attempted to run the farm themselves. Which statement is correct?

- ○ This passage is from a fable about animals.
- ○ This passage is from a true story about an animal farm.
- ○ This passage is from a children's fairystory.
- ○ This passage is from an adult book on farm life.

It would be a good idea to check your answers to questions 13 to 24 before moving on to the other questions.

Read *Jacques-Yves Cousteau* and answer questions 25 to 33.

Jacques-Yves Cousteau

From www.wylandfoundation.org

Jacques-Yves Cousteau was born in 1910 in Saint-André-de-Cubzac, in France. He was a famous scientist, underwater explorer, French naval officer, author and documentary filmmaker.

As a child he was fascinated with building things and especially with movies. He saved his pocket money and bought himself a movie camera. After he finished school, he joined the French Naval Academy. It was during this time in the French Navy that he began his underwater explorations. He tried to build a machine that would allow people to stay underwater longer.

☞ Answers and explanations on page 178

READING TEST 2

During World War II he worked with French engineer Émile Gagnan as they tried to perfect the aqualung, a cylinder of compressed air connected to a face mask. This now meant that divers could stay underwater for several hours without a heavy diving suit or being connected back to a ship.

In 1950 Cousteau bought the ship *Calypso* to help his explorations. To help pay for these explorations, Cousteau made movies and a number of television films: *The Silent World* (1956) and *World Without Sun* (1966). Each won an Academy Award as the best documentary feature of the year. Cousteau wrote many books, including a series entitled *Undersea Discoveries of Jacques-Yves Cousteau.* One of the world's greatest ocean explorers, Jacques-Yves Cousteau died in June 1997.

25. Who was Jacques Cousteau?

- ○ He was a famous scientist and underwater explorer.
- ○ He was an author and documentary filmmaker.
- ○ He was a French naval officer.
- ○ all of the above

26. When was Jacques Cousteau born?

- ○ 1950
- ○ 1910
- ○ 1956
- ○ 1997

27. Which word below is similar in meaning to *fascinated*?

- ○ bored
- ○ spellbound
- ○ hated
- ○ fed up

28. Which of the following did Jacques Cousteau buy as a child?

○ A

○ B

○ C

○ D

29. What is a documentary?

- ○ a story about real life
- ○ a book about real life
- ○ a film about real life
- ○ a poster about real life

30. Find a rhyming word from the text for these words. Write your answer in the space below.

wavy ______________________

task ______________________

creature ______________________

queries ______________________

clean ______________________

31. Which statements are true about Jacques Cousteau? Colour in more than one response.

- ○ Jacques-Yves Cousteau was born in Brazil.
- ○ He was a famous scientist and explorer.
- ○ He joined the French Naval Academy.
- ○ He invented the aqualung.
- ○ He bought the *Calypso* in 1950.
- ○ He won three Academy Awards for his films.

☞ **Answers and explanations on page 178**

32. What would be considered Jacques Cousteau's greatest diving achievement?

- ○ writing books
- ○ making films
- ○ perfecting the aqualung
- ○ buying the *Calypso*

33. There are many meanings of the word *Calypso*. What does the word *Calypso* mean in this story?

- ○ *Calypso* imprisoned the fabled Greek hero Odysseus on her island.
- ○ *Calypso* is a comic character in the Marvel Universe.
- ○ *Calypso* is the mysterious person who offers competitors a wish if they win.
- ○ *Calypso* is an orchid genus.
- ○ *Calypso* is an oceanographic research ship.
- ○ *Calypso* is a satellite of the planet Saturn.

Read *Marie Curie* and answer questions 34 to 39.

Marie Curie

Marie Curie's Nobel Prize Photograph, 1911 (http://info.med.yale.edu/library/exhibits/curie/marie-nobel-portrait-2.html)

Marie Curie was a Polish-born physicist who was awarded the Nobel Prize for her contribution to science. The Nobel prizes are prestigious awards. They are given yearly to those people who have most helped humanity through: physics, chemistry, medicine or physiology, literature and peace. The physics and chemistry awards are decided by the Royal Swedish Academy of Sciences.

Marie Curie shared the Nobel Prize for physics in 1903 with Antoine Becquerel and Pierre Curie. This was for the discovery of radioactivity.

Marie continued her research into radioactivity after her husband was killed in an accident. She went on to become the first female lecturer at a famous French university, the Sorbonne.

She and her husband had discovered new elements such as polonium and radium. She was awarded a second Nobel Prize in 1911, for chemistry. This was for the discovery of pure radium and polonium and the isolation of metallic radium. She found that radium was much more radioactive than uranium. She died of leukaemia in 1934, caused by exposure to radiation during her work.

34. Why was Marie Curie famous?

- ○ because she was awarded two Nobel prizes
- ○ because she was the first female lecturer at the Sorbonne
- ○ because she first won the Nobel prize in 1903

35. In which fields was Marie Curie awarded a Nobel Prize?

- ○ physics and medicine
- ○ physics and chemistry
- ○ physiology and chemistry
- ○ medicine and chemistry

☞ Answers and explanations on page 178

36. For which discovery was Marie Curie awarded a Nobel Prize in 1911?

- ○ the discovery of pure radium and polonium and isolated metallic radium
- ○ the discovery of pure radium and radioactivity
- ○ the discovery of radioactivity and isolated metallic radium

37. What type of disease is *leukaemia*?

- ○ a lung disease
- ○ a liver disease
- ○ a blood disease

38. Which word best describes 'particles or rays emitted in nuclear decay'?

- ○ polonium
- ○ radium
- ○ radiation
- ○ uranium

39. The Nobel Prize for physics was awarded to Marie Curie

- ○ for her continuing research from 1903 to 1911.
- ○ for helping humanity through science.
- ○ for sacrificing her life in the cause of science.
- ○ for discovering new elements, such as pure radium and pure polonium.

END OF TEST

Well done! You have completed the second Reading Test. This test had different types of questions. They are like comprehension passages. You had to look at something or read something and then make a judgement.

How did you find these questions? We hope that you found them interesting. Revise anything that was hard for you. There are further questions in the next Reading Test. The next test contains some different questions. Now take a long break before doing any more tests.

Use the diagnostic chart on page 83 to see which level of ability you reached. This is only an estimate. Don't be surprised if you answered some difficult questions correctly or even missed some easier questions.

Please note that multiple interpretations are possible for the levels of difficulty of these tasks. Also, some questions involve skills from different levels. This is only an initial guide to the approximate level of the reading skill assessed.

☞ **Answers and explanations on page 178**

CHECK YOUR SKILLS: READING TEST 2

Instructions

As you check the answer for each question, mark it as correct (✓) or incorrect (✗). Mark any questions that you omitted or left out as incorrect (✗) for the moment.

Then look at how many you answered correctly in each level. You will be able to see what level you are at by finding the point where you started having consistent difficulty with questions at a certain level. For example, if you answer most questions correctly up to the Intermediate level and then get most questions wrong from then onwards, it is likely your ability is at the Intermediate level. You can ask your parents or your teacher to help you do this if it isn't clear to you.

Am I able to ...

	SKILL	ESTIMATED LEVEL	✓ or ✗
1	Analyse the purpose of a diagram and text?	Standard	
2	Interpret an idea in a simple text?	Intermediate	
3	State the message of a story?	Advanced	
4	Find the reasons for a character's assumptions?	Advanced	
5	Find details?	Standard	
6	Relate a saying to a picture?	Standard	
7	Relate a proverb to a picture?	Standard	
8	State the outcome of an event?	Intermediate	
9	Find the reason for a delay?	Standard	
10	Interpret a conversation and response?	Advanced	
11	Choose a title for a passage?	Advanced	
12	Find the message of a story?	Advanced	
13	List the correct order for four sentences?	Intermediate	
14	Describe a passage?	Intermediate	
15	Find a reason for an event?	Standard	
16	Find another name for a character in a story?	Standard	
17	Find the sequence of events?	Intermediate	
18	Find the name of a character in a story?	Standard	
19	Indicate a reason for an action?	Intermediate	
20	Make a deduction about location from details in the passage?	Intermediate	
21	Define an infrequent word in context?	Advanced	
22	Find directly stated information?	Standard	
23	Find directly stated information?	Standard	
24	Interpret a complex saying?	Advanced	
25	Find directly stated information?	Standard	
26	Find directly stated information?	Standard	
27	Define a complex word?	Advanced	
28	Find directly stated information?	Standard	
29	Define a term?	Intermediate	
30	Match sounds and words?	Intermediate	
31	Confirm details?	Intermediate	
32	Reason from facts?	Intermediate	
33	Identify a possible meaning?	Advanced	
34	Find information and reasons?	Intermediate	
35	Find information?	Standard	
36	Find information?	Standard	
37	Define the meaning of a word?	Advanced	
38	Define the meaning of a word?	Intermediate	
39	Uncover the reason for an action?	Advanced	
	TOTAL		

READING TEST 3

This is the third Reading Test. There are 39 questions.

If you aren't sure what to do, ask your teacher or your parents to help you. Don't be afraid to ask if it isn't clear to you.

Allow around 50 minutes for this test. Take a short break if necessary.

In this test you will need to look at a picture or read something first. Then read each question and colour in the circle with the correct answer.

Read the sentences and answer questions 1 to 2.

A Further south is Bungara Heads where a headland provides a dramatic backdrop to the beach, local shops and restaurants.

B Follow the signposted tracks to the lookout for stunning views of the southern Blue Coast beaches.

C The headland cliff is backed by hectares of national park.

D Just south of the headland is Nurumbin Beach, a great place for a picnic, otherwise head north to Bungara's sheltered beach and barbecue area where you can picnic under the eucalyptus trees.

1. Which is the correct order for these sentences?

- ○ ABCD
- ○ ABDC
- ○ ACDB
- ○ ACBD
- ○ ADBC
- ○ ADCB

2. What type of information is contained in these sentences?

- ○ information about beaches
- ○ information about holidays
- ○ information about rainforests
- ○ information about where to stay

Read *The Baker* and *The Postman* and answer questions 3 to 9.

The Baker

I'd like to be a baker, and come when morning breaks,
Calling out, 'Beeay-ko!' (that's the sound he makes)—
Riding in a rattle-cart that jogs and jolts and shakes,
Selling all the sweetest things a baker ever bakes;
Currant-buns and brandy-snaps, pastry all in flakes;
But I wouldn't be a baker if …
I couldn't eat the cakes.
Would you?

☞ Answers and explanations on page 178

READING TEST 3

The Postman

I'd like to be a postman, and walk along
the street,
Calling out, 'Good Morning, Sir,' to
gentlemen I meet,
Ringing every door-bell all along my beat,
In my cap and uniform so very nice
and neat.
Perhaps I'd have a parasol in case of rain
or heat;
But I wouldn't be a postman if …
The walking hurt my feet.
Would you?

From The Project Gutenberg Australia e-book of *A Book for Kids* by CJ (Clarence Michael James) Dennis [reissued as *ROUNDABOUT* (1935)]

3. In the poem, which word rhymes with *cakes*?

- ○ pastry
- ○ baker
- ○ that's
- ○ breaks

4. What jolts and shakes?

- ○ the baker's cart
- ○ the morning
- ○ the sound he makes when he is calling out
- ○ the currant-buns, brandy-snaps and pastry

5. Which sentence is true?

- ○ The advantage in being a baker is calling out each morning.
- ○ The advantage in being a baker is riding in a rattle cart.
- ○ The advantage in being a baker is eating the cakes.
- ○ The advantage in being a baker is selling sweet things.

6. How do we know this poem was written some time ago?

- ○ because the cart rattles and shakes
- ○ because he is riding a horse and cart
- ○ because he has to call out loudly each morning
- ○ because he bakes his own bread and cakes

7. What is a *parasol*?

- ○ a sack
- ○ an umbrella
- ○ a cap
- ○ a parachute
- ○ a type of dog

8. What is meant by *beat* in this poem? (line 3)

- ○ to strike
- ○ a rhythm
- ○ a stroke
- ○ a route

☞ Answers and explanations on page 178

9. What do these two short poems have in common?

- ○ Both these poems give reasons for liking and not liking a job.
- ○ These poems are about work that both men and women could do.
- ○ Both these poems are about difficult outdoor jobs.
- ○ These poems are both funny.

Read *Ada Cambridge* and answer questions 10 to 15.

Ada Cambridge (1844–1926)

Ada Cambridge was born in 1844 in Norfolk, England. She was educated by governesses but was not happy with their teaching. She wrote: 'I can truthfully affirm that I never learned anything which would now be considered worth learning until I had done with them all and started foraging for myself. I did have a few months of boarding-school at the end, and a very good school for its day it was, but it left no lasting impression on my mind.' (*The Retrospect*, ch. IV).

In April 1870, she was married to the Rev. George Frederick Cross and a few weeks later sailed for Australia. She arrived in Melbourne and was surprised to find it a well established city. Her husband was sent to Wangaratta. Her best-remembered book is *Thirty Years in Australia*. It describes her busy life as a vicar's wife and the many hardships she endured in the remote bush and a seaside town of a distant land.

Mrs Cross at first was the typical hard-working wife of a country clergyman, taking part in all the activities of the parish and making her own children's clothes. Her health, however, broke down and her activities had to be reduced, but she somehow managed to do a large amount of writing. In 1875 her first novel *Up the Murray* appeared in *The Australasian* newspaper but was not published separately.

In 1893 Mrs Cross and her husband moved to their last parish, Williamstown, near Melbourne, and remained there until 1909. She returned to England after having been away for nearly 40 years. She stayed in England for a few years and then returned to Australia. She died in Melbourne on 19 July 1926. She was survived by a daughter and a son, Dr K Stuart Cross.

From The Project Gutenberg Australia e-book of *Dictionary of Australian Biography* by Percival Serle, Angus and Robertson, 1949

10. Which word means the same as *private teacher*?

- ○ governess
- ○ daughter
- ○ boarding school
- ○ vicar

11. With which instruction was Ada Cambridge most happy?

- ○ Ada Cambridge was happiest with the governesses.
- ○ Ada Cambridge was happiest with the boarding school.
- ○ Ada Cambridge was happiest with learning by herself.

12. Which sentence is true?

- ○ The Rev. George Frederick Cross was first sent to Norfolk.
- ○ The Rev. George Frederick Cross was first sent to Melbourne.
- ○ The Rev. George Frederick Cross was first sent to Wangaratta.
- ○ The Rev. George Frederick Cross was first sent to Williamtown.

13. What is the book for which Ada Cambridge is best remembered?

- ○ Ada Cambridge is best remembered for *The Retrospect*.
- ○ Ada Cambridge is best remembered for *Up the Murray*.
- ○ Ada Cambridge is best remembered for *Thirty Years in Australia*.

14. What is a *hardship*?

- ○ something strong
- ○ something that does not float
- ○ a serious difficulty
- ○ living in a distant land

15. How do we know that life was difficult for Ada Cambridge?

- ○ because she had a busy life as a vicar's wife
- ○ because her health broke down
- ○ because she lived in a seaside town
- ○ because she was taking part in all the activities of the parish

It would be a good idea to check your answers to questions 1 to 15 before moving on to the other questions.

Read *The Ancient Man* and answer questions 16 to 19.

The Ancient Man

ONCE upon a time there was a man named Huang An. He must have been well over eighty and yet he looked like a youth. He lived on cinnabar[1] and wore no clothing. Even in winter he went about without garments. He sat on a tortoise three feet long.

Once he was asked: 'About how old might this tortoise be?' He answered: 'When Fu Hi[2] first invented fish-nets and eel-pots he caught this tortoise[3] and gave it to me. And since then I have worn its shield quite flat sitting on it. The creature dreads the radiance of the sun and moon, so it only sticks its head out of its shell once in two thousand years. Since I have had the beast, it has already stuck its head out five times.'

With these words he took his tortoise on his back and went off. And the legend arose that this man was ten thousand years old.

[1] Cinnabar: a cinnamon to red coloured mineral

[2] Fu Hi is 'the life-breeding breath.'

[3] Tortoises live to a great age.

From The Project Gutenberg e-book of *The Chinese Fairy Book*, edited by R Wilhelm, 1921

16. What type of passage is this?

- ○ history
- ○ non-fiction
- ○ a story
- ○ science-fiction

☞ Answers and explanations on pages 178–179

17. Which sentence is true?

- ○ Huang An looked younger than his age.
- ○ Huang An looked older than his age.
- ○ Huang An looked around his age.

18. Why does the tortoise only stick its head out of its shell once in two thousand years?

- ○ because it can live on cinnabar
- ○ because it is afraid of the light from the sun or the moon
- ○ because it now has a flat shield

19. Why was the man said to be older than 10 000 years?

- ○ because he was compared to the age of Huang An
- ○ because he was compared to the age of the tortoise
- ○ because he was compared to the age of Fu Hi

Read *Daniel* and answer questions 20 to 30.

Daniel

From www.mountephraimpublishing.com

So the king gave his command, and they brought Daniel and threw him into the den of lions. But the king said to Daniel, 'Your God, whom you always serve, will save you.'

Then a stone was brought and laid at the entrance to the den; and the king sealed it with his own seal-ring and with those of his nobles, that no change might be made so as to rescue Daniel. Then the king went to his palace and passed the night fasting.

At dawn, as soon as it was light, the king rose and hurried to the den of lions. When he came near to the den where Daniel was, he cried with a very sad voice, 'O Daniel, servant of the living God, has your God, whom you always serve, been able to save you from the lions?'

Daniel said to the king, 'O king, live forever. My God has sent his angel and has closed the lions' mouths, and they have not hurt me, for I was innocent before him; and also before you, O king, I have done no wrong.'

Then the king was very glad and commanded that they should take Daniel up out of the den. So Daniel was taken up out of the den, and it was found that he was not injured, for he had trusted in his God.

Then the king commanded that those men who had accused Daniel should be brought and thrown into the den of lions.

From The Project Gutenberg e-book of *The Children's Bible* by Henry A Sherman and Charles Foster Kent

20. Who gave the order for the punishment?

- ○ Daniel
- ○ King Darius
- ○ Royal officers
- ○ the men who had accused him

☞ Answers and explanations on page 179

READING TEST 3

21. What is a lions' den?

- ◯ a place for lions to relax and play
- ◯ a cage
- ◯ a cave or a hole

22. Why was a stone put over the opening of the lions' den?

- ◯ so that the lions would not escape
- ◯ so that Daniel could not escape
- ◯ so that the crushing of Daniel would be hidden

23. What is a seal-ring?

- ◯ a stamp held by a round ring
- ◯ a ring with a small seal
- ◯ an ancient pen used for signing

24. Why did King Darius place a special seal on the rock?

- ◯ to ensure that the rock was not moved
- ◯ to decorate the rock
- ◯ to show that it was his rock
- ◯ to protect Daniel

25. For how long was Daniel imprisoned in the lions' den?

- ◯ for one night
- ◯ for 2 days
- ◯ from morning to evening

26. Why couldn't King Darius eat, be entertained or sleep?

- ◯ because the King was keen to see what happened
- ◯ because the King was ill
- ◯ because the King was worried

27. How do you know that Daniel was a religious person?

- ◯ He said that he was innocent.
- ◯ He was prepared to face the lions.
- ◯ He served God all the time.

28. Who saved Daniel from the lions?

- ◯ The servants who lifted Daniel to safety saved him.
- ◯ King Darius, who gave the order to release Daniel from the lions, saved him.
- ◯ An angel who closed the lions' mouths saved Daniel from the lions.

29. What was the king's reaction when Daniel answered from within the lions' den?

- ◯ King Darius was very happy.
- ◯ King Darius was not worried.
- ◯ King Darius was angry with those who accused Daniel.

30. Which statement do you think is correct?

- ◯ There is enough information in the text to decide that the events definitely occurred.
- ◯ There is not enough information in the text to decide whether the events did occur.
- ◯ There is enough information in the text to decide that the events definitely did not occur.

It would be a good idea to check your answers to questions 16 to 30 before moving on to the other questions.

☞ Answers and explanations on page 179

Read *Phar Lap* and answer questions 31 to 39.

Phar Lap

So Tommy became Phar Lap's strapper. He fed him, groomed him and led him out to exercise. Phar Lap would prick his ears and nuzzle Tommy's shoulder. When Tommy was around, the horse was good-natured and gentle. When Tommy was out of sight, Phar Lap was difficult and lazy.

Under Tommy's care, the horse grew into a big two-year-old with a rich, red coat. On one thigh, dark spots formed the sign of the Southern Cross. Phar Lap no longer limped, but he was still awkward and leggy when the time came for his first race. He ran like a no-hoper. People shook their heads and said: 'Phar Lap is no racehorse'.

In nine races, he won only once. Even that was nothing to get excited about because none of the other horses had ever won a race. By the time Phar Lap was three the Melbourne Cup seemed a hopeless dream.

But Mr Telford and Tommy had faith in the horse. They watched his track gallops at 5 o'clock each morning. They saw his giant stride and easy gait. Tommy scolded Phar Lap when he was lazy and gave him lumps of sugar when he worked well. He cuddled the horse, bandaged his legs and put on his blanket after track-work. Phar Lap returned Tommy's love and answered his call to try harder.

Nobody else believed in the horse. It was not until the spring of 1929, when Phar Lap powered into fourth place in a field of good horses that people began to take notice. The word spread: 'This Phar Lap could win the Derby!'

From that day, Phar Lap raced like a smooth powerful machine. On 5 October, he won the Derby in Sydney. Nothing could stop him now. He won another Derby, this time in Melbourne. He won nine races in a row. Sydney, Melbourne, Adelaide—Phar Lap's red, black and white colours blazed their way across Australia.

Crowds streamed to watch him run. They cheered him to victory. They talked about him in the streets. Phar Lap was *theirs*.

From *Bobby Boy* by Errol Broome, HBJ, 1992

31. What is another word for a *stable hand*?

- ○ strapper
- ○ trainer
- ○ jockey

32. What is the meaning of *nuzzle*?

- ○ to press with the nose
- ○ a cover to prevent biting
- ○ the nose or mouth of an animal

33. Which constellation is referred to in the first two paragraphs?

- ○ the racehorse
- ○ Tommy
- ○ Phar Lap
- ○ Southern Cross

34. What was most people's initial impression of Phar Lap?

- ○ Most people thought he was difficult and lazy.
- ○ Most people thought that he was good.
- ○ Most people thought that Phar Lap was not a racehorse.

☞ Answers and explanations on page 179

35. How many races did he win out of nine?

- ○ one
- ○ three
- ○ five
- ○ nine

36. When was winning the Melbourne cup considered only a dream?

- ○ when Phar Lap was aged three
- ○ at five o'clock in the morning
- ○ when Phar Lap was a two-year-old

37. Which sentence is true?

- ○ People started to take notice of Phar Lap on 5 October.
- ○ People started to take notice of Phar Lap in the spring of 1929.
- ○ People started to take notice of Phar Lap when he was three years old.

38. How is Phar Lap's racing style described?

- ○ Phar Lap's racing style is described as winning nine races in a row.
- ○ Phar Lap's racing style is described as red, black and white.
- ○ Phar Lap's racing style is described as smooth and powerful.

39. What does it mean that 'Phar Lap was *theirs*'?

- ○ It means that people began to feel that Phar Lap was like their own horse.
- ○ It means that people began to cheer Phar Lap to victory.
- ○ It means that people began to feel that Phar Lap was worth talking about in the streets.

END OF TEST

Well done! You have completed the third Reading Test. This test had different types of questions. They are like comprehension passages. You had to look at something or read something and then make a judgement.

How did you find these test questions? We hope that you found them interesting. There are further questions in the final Reading Test.

Use the diagnostic chart on page 92 to see which level of ability you reached. This is only an estimate. Don't be surprised if you answered some difficult questions correctly or even missed some easier questions.

Please note that multiple interpretations are possible for the levels of difficulty of these tasks. Also, some questions involve skills from different levels. This is only an initial guide to the approximate level of the reading skill assessed. No claim is made that this will be identical to the scores a student will receive in the actual tests, as the assessors will use a complex scoring system to estimate a student's level of ability.

☞ Answers and explanations on page 179

CHECK YOUR SKILLS: READING TEST 3

Instructions

As you check the answer for each question, mark it as correct (✓) or incorrect (✗). Mark any questions that you omitted or left out as incorrect (✗) for the moment.

Then look at how many you answered correctly in each level. You will be able to see what level you are at by finding the point where you started having consistent difficulty with questions at a certain level. For example, if you answer most questions correctly up to the Intermediate level and then get most questions wrong from then onwards, it is likely your ability is at the Intermediate level. You can ask your parents or your teacher to help you do this if it isn't clear to you.

Am I able to ...

	SKILL	ESTIMATED LEVEL	✓ or ✗
1	Determine the order of paragraphs?	Advanced	
2	Analyse the information?	Standard	
3	Find a rhyming word in a passage?	Standard	
4	Find directly stated information?	Standard	
5	Interpret an advantage?	Intermediate	
6	Make an inference about the time of writing?	Advanced	
7	Define a term not in common use?	Advanced	
8	Define a term that is not in regular use?	Advanced	
9	Compare two short poems for similarity?	Advanced	
10	Define a word?	Intermediate	
11	Outline the reason for a feeling?	Standard	
12	Find a fact?	Standard	
13	Find a fact?	Standard	
14	Decide on the meaning of a less regular word?	Intermediate	
15	Choose from the reasons outlined in the passage?	Intermediate	
16	Identify the type of passage as function?	Standard	
17	Make a judgement based on facts outlined in the passage?	Intermediate	
18	State the reason for an event?	Intermediate	
19	Make a complex inference by analogy?	Advanced	
20	Find details from a story?	Standard	
21	Find details from a story?	Intermediate	
22	State the reasons for an action?	Intermediate	
23	Identify an object?	Advanced	
24	State the reasons for an action?	Intermediate	
25	Find the details in a paragraph?	Standard	
26	Infer the motivation of a person?	Intermediate	
27	Infer the motivation of a person?	Advanced	
28	Find details in a passage?	Intermediate	
29	Find details in a passage?	Intermediate	
30	Make a complex judgement?	Advanced	
31	Define a word?	Advanced	
32	Define a word?	Advanced	
33	Recognise a concept or object?	Standard	
34	Infer a reaction?	Standard	
35	Find a fact?	Standard	
36	Reason from the facts?	Intermediate	
37	Find information?	Intermediate	
38	Find information?	Standard	
39	Infer meaning from a phrase?	Advanced	
	TOTAL		

READING TEST 4

ADAPTED FOR ONLINE FORMAT

This is the final Reading Test. There are 39 questions.

If you aren't sure what to do, ask your teacher or your parents to help you. Don't be afraid to ask if it isn't clear to you.

Allow around 50 minutes for this test. Take a short rest break if necessary.

In this part you will need to look at a picture or read something first. Then read each question and colour in the circle with the correct answer.

Read *Healthy food builds healthy bodies* and answer questions 1 to 5.

Healthy food builds healthy bodies

To eat a healthy, balanced diet we should choose a variety of the following foods each day. These provide plenty of fibre and are low in sugar, salt and fat.

- Fresh fruit
- Fresh vegetables
- Sprouts, nuts and seeds
- Soya beans and lentils
- Cereals and wholegrain products including bread, rice and pasta
- Dairy products like milk, cheese and yoghurt
- Eggs (preferably free-range)
- Cold-pressed oils, spreadable fats like unsalted butter

Only eat meat, fish and poultry occasionally.

Chewing food properly before you swallow it is very important. Even nutritious food can be bad for you if you eat it too quickly or eat too much of it. Always make time to sit down and relax when you eat your food. Eating good food can be lots of fun, especially if you take time to prepare and enjoy your meals.

From *Fun with Food* by Eleanor Parker, HBJ, 1992

1. Why is healthy food important?

- ○ Healthy food makes you stronger.
- ○ Healthy food provides fibre and low sugar.
- ○ Healthy food gives you a diet.

2. Which foods are said to be low in sugar, salt or fat?

- ○ meat
- ○ poultry
- ○ salted butter
- ○ fresh fruit

3. What foods are included with cereals?

- ○ fresh fruit
- ○ meat, fish and poultry
- ○ milk, cheese and yoghurt
- ○ bread, rice and pasta

4. What does *occasionally* mean?

- ○ once every now and then
- ○ once every day
- ○ at every meal
- ○ once a year

5. When is nutritious food bad for you?

- ○ when you chew it properly
- ○ whenever you eat it
- ○ when you eat it too quickly

☞ Answers and explanations on page 179

READING TEST 4

Read *Incredible India* and answer questions 6 to 9.

Incredible India

This time, Amber made a perfect landing right in front of the Taj Mahal. Jeremy landed a few seconds later. Habbibi didn't even question his new form of transport. All he said was, 'This is very handy. One day I hope to be able to travel like this on my own.'

India has many beautiful buildings, but none are more famous than the Taj Mahal. The white marble building glistened in the sun.

'It's so beautiful!' gasped Amber.

Habbibi proudly explained the story behind it. 'It was built many centuries ago by an emperor named Shah Jahan. He was very rich and he loved his wife deeply. When she died he was heart-broken so he built this in her memory. It took 20 000 workers 21 years to build.'

From *SWAT: Incredible India* by Lisa Thompson, Blake Education, 2000

6. A good title for this passage would be

- ○ Amber, Jeremy and Habbibi on their Magical Journey.
- ○ An Emperor Named Shah Jahan.
- ○ The Taj Mahal.
- ○ A Day in India.

7. Who built the Taj Mahal?

- ○ Habbibi
- ○ The Emperor Taj
- ○ Shah Jahan
- ○ Amber

8. How many years did it take to build?

- ○ 20 000 years
- ○ 176 years
- ○ 12 years
- ○ 21 years

9. *Amber said, 'It's so beautiful!'* This is

- ○ a statement.
- ○ a question.
- ○ an exclamation.
- ○ a comment.

Read *Poppy's Punch* and answer questions 10 to 15.

Poppy's Punch

FREE GIFT to you! When you buy a dozen bottles of Poppy's Punch, for just $15, you get a free toy of your choice. Poppy's Punch is a special fruit punch. It is a rare mix of pineapples, strawberries, mint, watermelon, pawpaw and mango, as well as our own secret ingredient to make everyone glow with good health.

Poppy's Punch is all-natural with no preservatives and is great for the kids. Your free toy can be collected from Poppy himself. Hurry, because this offer won't last!

Try Poppy's Punch today; it will put the zip into everyone!

 ☞ Answers and explanations on page 179

10. How many ingredients are there in Poppy's Punch?

○ 5 ○ 6 ○ 7 ○ 8

11. Which word is most similar in meaning to *preservative*?

○ chemical
○ recipe
○ mixture
○ natural

12. Buying a dozen Poppy's Punch is good value because

○ it is all natural.
○ it is a special fruit punch.
○ there is a free gift.
○ it is good for your health.

13. What is the free gift?

○ a dozen bottles of Poppy's Punch
○ a toy
○ Poppy
○ a secret ingredient

14. Why is it necessary to hurry to buy Poppy's Punch?

○ The punch does not last long.
○ The punch will sell out.
○ Poppy didn't make much.
○ The offer will not last long.

15. What word is similar in meaning to *offer*?

○ deal
○ hint
○ trace
○ gentle

It would be a good idea to check your answers to questions 1 to 15 before moving on to the other questions.

Look at the picture and answer question 16.

From *Art Today*, CD2 0081 LIF020

16. What type of illustration is this?

○ a book cover
○ a recruitment poster for army commandos
○ a poster announcing a sale
○ a movie poster

Read the advertisement and answer questions 17 to 18.

The parts of an advertisement are labelled A, B, C, D and E.

From *Art Today*, CD1 0044 LIF052

☞ Answers and explanations on page 179

17. Which section is likely to have a description of the product?

○ A ○ B ○ C ○ D ○ E

18. Which word below rhymes with the word *SAIL* shown in section B of the advertisement?

○ soul
○ sold
○ sell
○ sale

Look at the text and answer question 19.

From *Art Today*, NGC 265D

19. What is the purpose of this illustration?

○ for information
○ for advertising
○ for entertainment
○ only for children

Read *How to play hockey* and answer questions 20 to 25.

How to play hockey

The modern game of hockey is a fast and exciting game for both players and spectators. Each player uses a stick which has a flat side. The ball may only be hit with the flat side of the stick. The head of the stick is made of wood.

Games are played for two periods, each one lasting thirty-five minutes. Hockey requires many skills. Players must learn to use their sticks so that they can run with the ball (dribble), pass the ball from stick to stick with accuracy, dodge past other players, tackle opponents and take the ball from them. Every player needs to be in good physical condition.

There are 11 players in a hockey team. The idea of the game is to score more goals than the opposing side. A goal is scored by hitting the ball past the opposition and shooting it between the goal posts. Each goal is worth one point. Hockey is played on a grass field the same size as a football field or on a synthetic surface. There is also a version of indoor hockey with modified rules.

From *Sport in the Making: a History of Popular Sport in Australia* by Shane Power, HBJ, 1990

20. How many players are there in a hockey team?

○ 35
○ 22
○ 11
○ 7

☞ Answers and explanations on page 179

21. What is the main idea of the game of hockey?

- ○ It is a fast and exciting game.
- ○ Games are played for two periods.
- ○ to score more goals than the opposing side
- ○ Every player needs to be in good physical condition

22. Why does hockey require many skills?

- ○ It is a fast and exciting game that is played on a grass field.
- ○ It is played on a grass field and players need to get the ball.
- ○ There are 11 players on a team and they play on a grass field.
- ○ Players need to get the ball past the opposition and shoot it in the goal post.

23. Which word means the same as *synthetic*?

- ○ artificial
- ○ existing
- ○ authentic
- ○ definite

24. Which sentence is wrong?

- ○ Each period is 35 minutes long.
- ○ A goal in hockey is worth one point.
- ○ The ball is never hit with the flat side of the stick.
- ○ The head of the hockey stick is made of wood.

25. What does the word *modified* mean?

- ○ changed
- ○ optional
- ○ extra
- ○ separate

It would be a good idea to check your answers to questions 16 to 25 before moving on to the other questions.

Read *Achilles* and answer questions 26 to 29.

Achilles

From www.jasharawan.com/images/blogimages/achilles.jpg

You may have heard the expression 'Achilles heel'. This is meant to be a small but fatal weakness that a person might have. We also talk about the Achilles tendon, which is fibrous cord that connects muscles in the calf of your leg to the heel bone. Both the saying and the medical term come from Achilles, who was a person in ancient Greek mythology. He was a famous Greek warrior.

From www.tate.org.uk

When he was born, the Gods told his mother that Achilles would die in battle. In order to protect him, she dipped her baby in the magic waters of a river that flowed from the underworld. Only the heel was untouched by the magic waters because this was the part of the body by which she held him and this was also the only part of his body that was vulnerable.

☞ Answers and explanations on pages 179–180

When the war against Troy began, Achilles joined the battle and set an example of bravery for the other Greek soldiers. Achilles even conquered Hector, the leader of the Trojan army. He became tired of fighting, however, and agreed to ask the Greeks to make peace when Hector's brother shot him with a poisoned arrow in the only vulnerable part of his body, the heel. This story is the beginning of the expression 'Achilles heel', which means a vulnerable or weak point that is fatal.

26. What is meant by the saying *Achilles heel*?

- ○ It is meant to be part of a person's leg.
- ○ It is meant to be a person's weak point.
- ○ It is meant to be an ancient story.

27. Why is the heel the only vulnerable part of Achilles?

- ○ It is the only part of his body that was not dipped into the water.
- ○ It is the only part of his body that was struck by the poison arrow.
- ○ It is the only part of his body that was unprotected by armour.

28. In which battle did Achilles fight?

- ○ Achilles fought in the battle against the Gods.
- ○ Achilles fought in the battle against the Greeks.
- ○ Achilles fought in the battle against Troy.

29. Who shot Achilles with a poisoned arrow?

- ○ Trojan soldiers
- ○ Greeks
- ○ Hector's brother
- ○ Hector

Read *Jabberwocky* and answer questions 30 to 39.

Jabberwocky

by Lewis Carroll

'Twas brillig, and the slithy toves
Did gyre and gimble in the wabe:
All mimsy were the borogoves,
And the mome raths outgrabe.

'Beware the Jabberwock, my son!
The jaws that bite, the claws that catch!
Beware the Jubjub bird, and shun
The frumious Bandersnatch!'

He took his vorpal sword in hand:
Long time the manxome foe he sought –
So rested he by the Tumtum tree,
And stood awhile in thought.

And, as in uffish thought he stood,
The Jabberwock, with eyes of flame,
Came whiffling through the tulgey wood,
And burbled as it came!

One, two! One, two! And through and
through
The vorpal blade went snicker-snack!
He left it dead, and with its head
He went galumphing back.

☞ Answers and explanations on page 180

'And, has thou slain the Jabberwock?
Come to my arms, my beamish boy!
O frabjous day! Callooh! Callay!'
He chortled in his joy.

'Twas brillig, and the slithy toves
Did gyre and gimble in the wabe;
All mimsy were the borogoves,
And the mome raths outgrabe.

From *Through the Looking-Glass and What Alice Found There*, 1871

30. 'Jabberwocky' could be described as a

- ○ serious poem.
- ○ foreign language poem.
- ○ nonsense poem.
- ○ folk poem.

31. A *portmanteau* word is used generally to mean a mixture or blending of words. Which words below are possibly *portmanteau* words? There may be more than one answer.

- ○ beware
- ○ slithy
- ○ sought
- ○ mimsy
- ○ slain
- ○ fumious
- ○ frabjous

Below there are some meanings of words. Each meaning has a letter.

A a grass plot
B a sword
C four o'clock in the afternoon
D to go round and round
E green pigs
F a state of mind
G thick, dense, dark

Here are four words. Match these words with their meanings as shown. Next to each word write the letter of the correct meaning.

32. ______ *brillig*

33. ______ *gyre*

34. ______ *wabe*

35 ______ *raths*

36. The poem appeared in the book *Through the Looking-Glass*. What might Alice have said when she heard the poem?

- ○ 'Poor, poor, me! I have been made to do lessons.'
- ○ 'I have been forced to inflict pain on others.'
- ○ 'It seems to fill my head with ideas.'

37. What does the poem represent?

- ○ a place beyond our world
- ○ a true story
- ○ a world of ghosts
- ○ a myth of heroism

☞ Answers and explanations on page 180

38. Who is narrating the poem?

- ○ The Jabberwock is narrating the poem.
- ○ The son is narrating the poem.
- ○ The beamish boy is narrating the poem.
- ○ An adult is narrating the poem.

39. What emotion is shown with the words '*O frabjous day! Callooh! Callay!*'?

- ○ anxiety
- ○ bravery
- ○ joy

END OF TEST

Well done! You have completed the final Reading Test. It means that you have answered or attempted over 150 Reading questions. Now take a long break before you do any more tests.

How did you find the questions in this test? Were some hard for you? Check to see where you did well and where you had problems.

Use the diagnostic chart on page 101 to see which level of ability you reached. This is only an estimate. Don't be surprised if you answered some difficult questions correctly or even missed some easier questions.

Please note that multiple interpretations are possible for the levels of ability of these tasks. Also, some questions involve skills from different levels. This is only an initial guide to the approximate level of the reading skill assessed. No claim is made that this will be identical to the scores a student will receive in the actual tests, as the assessors will use a complex scoring system to estimate a student's level of ability.

An important note about the NAPLAN Online tests

The NAPLAN Online Conventions of Language test will be divided into different sections. Students will only have one opportunity to check their answers at the end of each section before proceeding to the next one. This means that after students have completed a section and moved onto the next they will not be able to check their work again. We have included reminders for students to check their work at specific points in the practice tests from now on so they become familiar with this process.

☞ Answers and explanations on page 180

CHECK YOUR SKILLS: READING TEST 4

Instructions

As you check the answer for each question, mark it as correct (✓) or incorrect (✗). Mark any questions that you omitted or left out as incorrect (✗) for the moment.

Then look at how many you answered correctly in each level. You will be able to see what level you are at by finding the point where you started having consistent difficulty with questions at a certain level. For example, if you answer most questions correctly up to the Intermediate level and then get most questions wrong from then onwards, it is likely your ability is at the Intermediate level. You can ask your parents or your teacher to help you do this if it isn't clear to you.

Am I able to ...

	SKILL	ESTIMATED LEVEL	✓ or ✗
1	Identify a common idea?	Standard	
2	Interpret an idea in a simple text?	Standard	
3	Find directly stated information?	Standard	
4	Identify the meaning of a word?	Standard	
5	Infer meaning?	Standard	
6	Find a title?	Intermediate	
7	Find information?	Standard	
8	Identify a fact from the text?	Standard	
9	Recognise an exclamation?	Intermediate	
10	Find details from a text?	Standard	
11	Indicate the meaning of a word?	Intermediate	
12	Provide reasons?	Intermediate	
13	Cross-reference a reason to an item in the paragraph?	Intermediate	
14	Determine the reason for an action?	Intermediate	
15	State a synonym?	Intermediate	
16	Identify an illustration as a movie poster?	Intermediate	
17	Find sections of the advertisement?	Intermediate	
18	Find a word to rhyme?	Standard	
19	State the purpose of the text?	Intermediate	
20	Find a basic fact?	Standard	
21	Find directly stated information?	Standard	
22	Find the reason for a situation?	Intermediate	
23	Define an adjective?	Intermediate	
24	Identify a false answer?	Advanced	
25	Define the meaning of a word?	Intermediate	
26	Infer the meaning of an expression?	Intermediate	
27	State the reason?	Intermediate	
28	Find information?	Standard	
29	Find information?	Standard	
30	Identify the type of poem?	Intermediate	
31	State the type of word?	Advanced	
32	Find the meaning of abstract words?	Advanced	
33	Find the meaning of abstract words?	Advanced	
34	Find the meaning of abstract words?	Advanced	
35	Find the meaning of abstract words?	Advanced	
36	Infer a response?	Advanced	
37	Analyse the theme of a text?	Advanced	
38	Identify the narrator?	Advanced	
39	Link an abstract phrase to an emotion?	Advanced	
	TOTAL		

CONVENTIONS OF LANGUAGE TEST 1

This is the first Conventions of Language Test. There are 50 questions.

If you aren't sure what to do, ask your teacher or your parents to help you. Don't be afraid to ask if it isn't clear to you.

Allow around 45 minutes for this test. Take a short break if necessary.

Read the sentences. They have some gaps. Choose the correct word or words to fill each gap.

1. We did not have any rain for the last few months ______ it might rain today.

or	but	since	before
○	○	○	○

2. The teachers were on strike for two days because they wanted a salary ______.

risen	raise	rising	rise
○	○	○	○

3. Parents have a right ______ where their children are.

for knowing	on knowing	to know	to have known
○	○	○	○

4. After losing his passport, Steve did not ______ happy at all.

looks	look	looking	looked
○	○	○	○

5. I should ______ gone to school today, but I was not feeling well.

of	have	an
○	○	○

Did you colour in one of the circles?

6. Flinders Street is the ______ street in this part of the city.

- ○ more narrower
- ○ narrowest
- ○ most narrower

7. I reached into my school bag and found an ______.

- ○ apples
- ○ broken egg
- ○ ruler
- ○ apple

Colour in the circle(s) with the correct answer.

8. Which sentence has the correct punctuation?

- ○ He said what do you mean I lost?
- ○ He said, "What do you mean I lost?"
- ○ He said what do you mean, "I lost."
- ○ He said, "what do you mean I lost?"

9. Which sentence has the correct punctuation?

- ○ Later that day, John finally called, to tell me where he was.
- ○ Later that day, John finally called to tell me where he was.
- ○ Later that day John finally called, to tell me where he was.
- ○ Later, that day, John finally called to tell me where he was.

10. Which sentence has the correct punctuation?

- ○ Gerrys book's were due back at the library on Wednesday.
- ○ Gerry's book's were due back at the library on Wednesday.
- ○ Gerry's books were due back at the library on Wednesday.
- ○ Gerrys books were due back at the library on Wednesday.

Answers and explanations on page 181

11. Which sentence has the correct punctuation?

- ○ The boys bike's were locked up outside the library, but when they went to leave, the bikes were gone.
- ○ The boy's bikes were locked up outside the library, but when they went to leave, the bikes were gone.
- ○ The boys' bikes were locked up outside the library, but when they went to leave, the bikes were gone.
- ○ The boys' bike's were locked up outside the library, but when they went to leave, the bikes were gone.

12. Which sentence correctly uses commas (,)?

- ○ Marc, who hit the tennis ball into the neighbour's window, would now have to go and apologise.
- ○ Marc who hit the tennis ball, into the neighbour's window, would now have to go and apologise.
- ○ Marc who hit the tennis ball into the neighbour's window, would now have to go and apologise.
- ○ Marc, who hit the tennis ball, into the neighbour's window, would now have to go, and apologise.

13. Which word is missing from the sentence below?

My dad, ▬▬▬ knows a lot about soccer, said the referee made a mistake in awarding me a yellow card.

- ○ who
- ○ that
- ○ what

14. Where do the **two** missing speech marks (" and ") go? Colour in two circles.

"Josephine, ○↓ get inside right now, ○↓ said Granny. ○↓ You need to start your ○↓ homework immediately."

15. Where does the missing apostrophe (') go? Colour in one circle only.

○ ○ ○ ○

Mums job was to read books to the twins while Dad helped Samantha and Elli finish their essays.

16. Which words can replace the pronoun *they* in this sentence?

They played until it was time to go.

- ○ My friend
- ○ Evan and him
- ○ The children
- ○ Christopher and me

17. Which type of word is *walked* in this sentence?

The teacher walked slowly around the playground.

- ○ noun
- ○ verb
- ○ adjective
- ○ adverb

18. In which group of words is *close* used as a verb?

- ○ We came to the close of the show.
- ○ Close the door.
- ○ That was a close call.
- ○ He came too close to the edge.

Did you colour in one of the circles?

 ☞ Answers and explanations on page 181

CONVENTIONS OF LANGUAGE TEST 1

Read the sentences. Correct the mistakes and write the correct sentence on the line. Be careful: some sentences have more than one mistake.

19. Our camp was deep in the amazon rainforest.

____

20. We were eating dinner when disaster striked.

____

21. Me and my mother thinks that the newly painted wall looks good.

____

22. Tommy likes his knew school because the children are more kinder to him than at his last.

____

23. Ethan and Chris always likes to play handball during lunch.

____

Colour in the circle(s) with the correct answer.

24. Tom and Julia want to go surfing with ______ friends next Saturday.

there ○ they're ○ their ○

25. As soon as the accident happened I ______ my mother to let her know.

○ rung

○ rang

It would be a good idea to check your answers to questions 1 to 25 before moving on to the other questions.

 ☞ **Answers and explanations on page 181**

CONVENTIONS OF LANGUAGE TEST 1

To the student

Ask your teacher or parent to read the spelling words for you. The words are listed on page 187. Write the spelling words on the lines below.

Test 1 spelling words

26. ____________________

27. ____________________

28. ____________________

29. ____________________

30. ____________________

31. ____________________

32. ____________________

33. ____________________

34. ____________________

35. ____________________

36. ____________________

37. ____________________

38. ____________________

39. ____________________

40. ____________________

Read the sentences. Each sentence has one word that is incorrect. Write the correct spelling of the word in the box.

41. Nothing particuly interesting happened at school today.

42. My youngest brother is especially mishtievous.

43. I found it really hard to consentraite while Dad was mowing the lawn outside my bedroom window.

44. Where is the enterance to the hall?

45. Unfortunately the libary was closed after the fire alarm went off.

The spelling mistakes in these sentences are underlined. Write the correct spelling of each underlined word in the box.

46. When Rascal the dog saw the open gate he shot **threw** it.

47. He then **disapeared** way up the street.

48. On my way home from school, I walked **parst** him.

49. He was **proberly** lost and frightened.

50. He was **heding** for the main road and I was worried about his safety.

END OF TEST

Well done! You have completed the first Conventions of Language Test.

How did you go with these test questions? Some were harder than the sample questions. Check to see where you did well and where you had problems. Try to revise the questions that were hard for you.

Use the diagnostic chart on pages 109–110 to see which level of ability you reached. This is only an estimate. Don't be surprised if you answered some difficult questions correctly or even missed some easier questions.

There are now three more tests, each containing 50 questions. They include many of the same types of questions, plus a few new types.

 ☞ **Answers and explanations on page 181**

Instructions

As you check the answer for each question, mark it as correct (✓) or incorrect (✗). Mark any questions that you omitted or left out as incorrect (✗) for the moment.

Then look at how many you answered correctly in each level. You will be able to see what level you are at by finding the point where you started having consistent difficulty with questions at a certain level. For example, if you answer most questions correctly up to the Intermediate level and then get most questions wrong from then onwards, it is likely your ability is at the Intermediate level. You can ask your parents or your teacher to help you do this if it isn't clear to you.

Am I able to ...

	SKILL	ESTIMATED LEVEL	✓ or ✗
1	Use conjunctions correctly?	Standard	
2	Use compound nouns correctly?	Intermediate	
3	Use the *to*-infinitive correctly to complete a complex verb phrase?	Standard	
4	Use the simple past tense correctly?	Standard	
5	Use the present perfect tense correctly?	Standard	
6	Use comparative adjectives correctly?	Intermediate	
7	Identify the correct word that follows an indefinite article?	Advanced	
8	Use speech marks correctly for direct speech?	Intermediate	
9	Use commas correctly in a complex sentence?	Intermediate	
10	Use apostrophes correctly for possession?	Advanced	
11	Use apostrophes correctly for possession?	Advanced	
12	Use commas correctly in a complex sentence?	Advanced	
13	Use pronouns correctly?	Standard	
14	Use speech marks correctly for direct speech?	Intermediate	
15	Use apostrophes correctly for possession?	Advanced	
16	Recognise the correct use of a pronoun in a sentence?	Intermediate	
17	Recognise the correct use of verb forms in a sentence?	Advanced	
18	Demonstrate the correct use of a verb?	Intermediate	
19	Use capital letters correctly for proper nouns?	Standard	
20	Use the simple past tense correctly?	Intermediate	
21	Match the plural form of the verb to the subject?	Intermediate	
22	Spell *new* and use a comparative adjective correctly?	Intermediate	
23	Match the plural form of the verb to the subject?	Standard	
24	Use possessive adjectives correctly?	Intermediate	
25	Use the simple past tense correctly?	Standard	
26	Spell *great?*	Intermediate	
27	Spell *rain?*	Standard	

CHECK YOUR SKILLS: CONVENTIONS OF LANGUAGE TEST 1

	SKILL	ESTIMATED LEVEL	✓ or ✗
28	Spell *straight?*	Standard	
29	Spell *journey?*	Standard	
30	Spell *friend?*	Advanced	
31	Spell *heart?*	Intermediate	
32	Spell *city?*	Standard	
33	Spell *sweat?*	Intermediate	
34	Spell *dimming?*	Intermediate	
35	Spell *rolling?*	Intermediate	
36	Spell *excellent?*	Standard	
37	Spell *airport?*	Intermediate	
38	Spell *thankful?*	Advanced	
39	Spell *bedroom?*	Advanced	
40	Spell *birthday?*	Advanced	
41	Spell *particularly?*	Advanced	
42	Spell *mischievous?*	Intermediate	
43	Spell *concentrate?*	Intermediate	
44	Spell *entrance?*	Intermediate	
45	Spell *library?*	Advanced	
46	Spell *through?*	Advanced	
47	Spell *disappeared* ?	Advanced	
48	Spell *passed?*	Intermediate	
49	Spell *probably?*	Advanced	
50	Spell *heading?*	Intermediate	
	TOTAL		

CONVENTIONS OF LANGUAGE TEST 2

This is the second Conventions of Language Test. There are 50 questions.

If you aren't sure what to do, ask your teacher or your parents to help you. Don't be afraid to ask if it isn't clear to you.

Allow around 45 minutes for this test. Take a short break if necessary.

Read the sentences. They have some gaps. Choose the correct word or words to fill each gap. Colour in only one circle for each answer.

1. I forgot to bring the batteries for my torch ______ I had to borrow some.

○ and ○ but ○ so ○ or

2. The McGuinness family have been living at number 24 ______ 1952.

○ until ○ by ○ since

3. I approached Nicolette, but she denied ______.

○ doing it ○ done it ○ do it

Colour in the circle with the correct answer.

4. Which sentence has the correct punctuation?

○ I wonder if Connor will arrive on time?

○ I wonder if Connor will arrive on time.

○ I wonder, "if Connor will arrive on time?"

○ I wonder, "If Connor will arrive on time."

Did you colour in one of the circles?

5. Which word or words correctly completes the sentence?

The youngest son plays violin ______ than his eldest brother.

○ more better ○ better ○ best ○ more best

☞ Answers and explanations on page 182

CONVENTIONS OF LANGUAGE TEST 2

Read the advertisement. The text has some gaps. Colour in the circle with the correct missing word to complete the text.

MARK CAMPBELL
PERFORMING LIVE AT THE STATE THEATRE!

The finest entertainer ____6____ the country!
Mark Campbell is back with his new show.

FOR ONE NIGHT ONLY! Price: $95

Tickets on sale ____7____ Monday 28 September, 9 am ____8____ the Box Office ____9____ the theatre.

Bookings ____10____ phone 123 405 or see the website www.markcampbellconcert.com

6. from ○ at ○ by ○ in ○

7. from ○ across ○ by ○ in ○

8. from ○ on ○ at ○ since ○

9. from ○ before ○ in ○ by ○

10. from ○ at ○ by ○ through ○

Read the sentences. They have some gaps. Choose the correct word or words to fill each gap. Colour in only one circle for each answer.

11. I love summer time ________ the heat and humidity.

despite ○ although ○ whereas ○ even though ○

12. George had ________ to visit to his grandmother in hospital when I phoned him.

went ○ gone ○ goed ○ going ○

☞ Answers and explanations on page 182

13. Dion was driving at 100 km/h when he crashed ________ a traffic light.

into ○ at ○ around ○ in ○

14. No student will go without a laptop ________ I am Headmaster.

while ○ until ○ because ○ since ○

15. It was so hot yesterday that I ________ 5 litres of water.

drink ○ drank ○ drinked ○ drunk ○

16. We are planning ________ with the court case.

on proceed ○ to proceed ○ in proceeding ○ to proceeding ○

Colour in the circle(s) with the correct answer.

17. Which underlined words can be replaced with *we're*?

I asked the driver, "Where ○ is the town?" I thought we were ○ almost there but he said, "We are ○ nearly there."

18. Which words does the pronoun *they* refer to in this sentence?

When they went to the stable, the boy showed them the young pony.

Sam and Mary ○ the jockey ○ the boy and me ○ the visitor ○

19. What type of word is *courage* in this sentence?

When everyone disagreed with him today, he showed courage and proved them wrong.

verb ○ adverb ○ noun ○ adjective ○

Answers and explanations on page 182

20. In which sentence is the word *better* used as an adverb?

- ○ This is a change for the better.
- ○ She will better her record in this race.
- ○ This is a better car.
- ○ He is better suited to drawing than writing.

21. Some people say Jack is ▬▬▬ than Jessica, but really they are the same height.

tallest	taller	more tallest	more taller
○	○	○	○

22. Which sentence correctly uses commas (,)?

- ○ The customer rather angry, and impatient, left the store.
- ○ The customer, rather angry, and impatient, left the store.
- ○ The customer rather angry and impatient, left the store.
- ○ The customer, rather angry and impatient, left the store.

Did you colour in one of the circles?

23. Where does the missing apostrophe (') go? Colour in only one circle.

The students were preparing for exams when the fire alarm went off in the principals office.

24. Where do the **two** missing speech marks (" and ") go?

Michele asked Has the mail arrived yet ?

25. Amelia read the newspaper while she <u>am</u> waiting for the train to arrive.

○ was ○ is ○ were

It would be a good idea to check your answers to questions 1 to 25 before moving on to the other questions.

 ☞ **Answers and explanations on page 182**

CONVENTIONS OF LANGUAGE TEST 2

To the student

Ask your teacher or parent to read the spelling words for you. The words are listed on page 187. Write the spelling words on the lines below.

Test 2 spelling words

26. ______________________
27. ______________________
28. ______________________
29. ______________________
30. ______________________
31. ______________________
32. ______________________
33. ______________________
34. ______________________
35. ______________________
36. ______________________
37. ______________________
38. ______________________
39. ______________________
40. ______________________

Read *Boy caught in bath drain*. The spelling mistakes have been underlined. Write the correct spelling for each underlined word in the box.

Boy caught in bath drain

A <u>todler</u> [41] was <u>ingered</u> [42] when he had his fingers trapped down a bath drain on Saturday night.

41. ☐

42. ☐

The Glebe boy, aged 3, was having a bath when <u>too</u> [43] of his fingers became trapped.

43. ☐

The Police <u>Resque</u> [44] unit was called, but they could not free the boy, so the bathtub had to be removed.

44. ☐

He was taken by <u>amboolence</u> [45] to St Henry's Childrens Hospital, still attached to the drain.

45. ☐

CONVENTIONS OF LANGUAGE TEST 2

There is an incorrectly spelled word on each line below. Write the correct spelling of the word in the box.

46. People need to take dog safety seriosly.

47. After the incident occured the whole

48. nayborhood was saddened. The owner of the dog was

49. embarassed and preferred to stay indoors until everyone forgot

50. about the vishious attack.

END OF TEST

Well done! You have completed the second Conventions of Language Test. We really mean this as there were many questions to answer.

How did you go with these test questions? Some were harder than the last test. Check to see where you did well and where you had problems. Try to revise the questions that were hard for you.

Use the diagnostic chart on pages 117–118 to see which level of ability you reached. Again, we remind you that this is only an estimate. Don't be surprised if you answered some difficult questions correctly or even missed some easier questions.

There are now two more tests, each containing 50 questions. They include many of the same types of questions, plus a few new types.

☞ **Answers and explanations on page 183**

CHECK YOUR SKILLS: CONVENTIONS OF LANGUAGE TEST 2

Instructions

As you check the answer for each question, mark it as correct (✓) or incorrect (✗). Mark any questions that you omitted or left out as incorrect (✗) for the moment.

Then look at how many you answered correctly in each level. You will be able to see what level you are at by finding the point where you started having consistent difficulty with questions at a certain level. For example, if you answer most questions correctly up to the Intermediate level and then get most questions wrong from then onwards, it is likely your ability is at the Intermediate level. You can ask your parents or your teacher to help you do this if it isn't clear to you.

Am I able to ...

	SKILL	ESTIMATED LEVEL	✓ or ✗
1	Use conjunctions correctly?	Standard	
2	Use prepositions correctly?	Intermediate	
3	Choose the correct form and tense of a verb to complete a verb phrase?	Intermediate	
4	Use indirect speech correctly?	Advanced	
5	Use a comparative adverb correctly?	Intermediate	
6	Use prepositions correctly?	Standard	
7	Use prepositions correctly?	Standard	
8	Use prepositions correctly?	Standard	
9	Use prepositions correctly?	Intermediate	
10	Use prepositions correctly?	Intermediate	
11	Use conjunctions correctly?	Intermediate	
12	Use the past perfect tense correctly?	Intermediate	
13	Use prepositions correctly?	Intermediate	
14	Use conjunctions correctly?	Standard	
15	Use the simple past tense correctly?	Standard	
16	Use the *to*-infinitive correctly to complete a complex verb phrase?	Intermediate	
17	Find a suitable contraction?	Intermediate	
18	Recognise the correct use of a pronoun in a sentence?	Intermediate	
19	Recognise parts of speech in a sentence?	Intermediate	
20	Demonstrate the correct use of an adverb?	Advanced	
21	Use comparative adjectives correctly?	Intermediate	
22	Use commas correctly in a complex sentence?	Advanced	
23	Use apostrophes correctly for possession?	Advanced	
23	Use speech marks correctly for direct speech?	Intermediate	
25	Use the correct form of the past tense?	Intermediate	
26	Spell *squid?*	Standard	
27	Spell *hoe?*	Standard	

CHECK YOUR SKILLS: CONVENTIONS OF LANGUAGE TEST 2

	SKILL	ESTIMATED LEVEL	✓ or ✗
28	Spell *through?*	Intermediate	
29	Spell *chief?*	Standard	
30	Spell *glove?*	Standard	
31	Spell *dwelling?*	Standard	
32	Spell *boring?*	Standard	
33	Spell *hopping?*	Advanced	
34	Spell *disguising?*	Standard	
35	Spell *confusing?*	Standard	
36	Spell *permitting?*	Standard	
37	Spell *rabbit?*	Intermediate	
38	Spell *telescope?*	Standard	
39	Spell *cushion?*	Intermediate	
40	Spell *xylophone?*	Intermediate	
41	Spell *toddler?*	Intermediate	
42	Spell *injured?*	Advanced	
43	Identify the difference between *too* and *two*?	Intermediate	
44	Spell *rescue*?	Advanced	
45	Spell *ambulance?*	Intermediate	
46	Spell *seriously*?	Advanced	
47	Spell *occurred*?	Advanced	
48	Spell *neighbourhood*?	Advanced	
49	Spell *embarrassed*?	Advanced	
50	Spell *vicious*?	Advanced	
	TOTAL		

CONVENTIONS OF LANGUAGE TEST 3

This is the third Conventions of Language Test. There are 50 questions.

If you aren't sure what to do, ask your teacher or your parents to help you. Don't be afraid to ask if it isn't clear to you.

Allow around 45 minutes for this test. Take a short break if necessary.

Read the sentences. They have some gaps. Choose the correct word or words to fill each gap. Colour in only one circle for each answer.

1. I ate my lunch ______ Tommy played handball.

while ○ during ○ for ○ although ○

2. Myra goes to school ______ car, but I prefer to catch the bus.

on ○ by ○ at ○ in ○

3. Our television ______ to be fixed because it is still broken.

have ○ has ○ is ○ will ○

4. The school reports ______ on the last day of term.

went out ○ goed out ○ gone out ○ going out ○

Read the sentence. There are two words missing. Colour in the circle with the words that complete the sentence. Colour in only one circle.

5. ______ and ______ ride our skateboards to school every day.

Him/I ○ Him/me ○ He/I ○ He/me ○

☞ Answers and explanations on page 183

CONVENTIONS OF LANGUAGE TEST 3

Colour in the circle with the correct answer.

6. Which sentence has the correct punctuation?

- ○ We can get to Brisbane more quickly can't we? If we take the freeway.
- ○ We can get to Brisbane more quickly can't we if we take the freeway?
- ○ We can get to Brisbane more quickly, can't we? if we take the freeway.
- ○ We can get to Brisbane more quickly, can't we, if we take the freeway?

7. Where does the missing question mark (**?**) go?

"It's nearly the school holidays ○ I hope you will able to visit us soon ○ When will you next be in Perth ○ ○ "

Read the sentence. There is a word missing. Choose the correct word to fill the gap.

8. I ▬▬▬ the envelope containing money that I hid.

found	finded	founded	find
○	○	○	○

Colour in the circle with the correct answer.

9. Which sentence is correct?

- ○ Nick doesn't like brussels sprouts. Neither do I.
- ○ Nick doesn't like brussels sprouts. Either do I.
- ○ Nick doesn't like brussels sprouts. Or do I.

10. Which sentence has the correct punctuation?

- ○ Chrissy said to meet with Amy this afternoon, so we went.
- ○ Chrissy said "to meet with Amy this afternoon, so we went."
- ○ Chrissy said to "meet with Amy this afternoon, so we went."
- ○ Chrissy said "To meet with Amy this afternoon, so we went."

☞ Answers and explanations on page 183

CONVENTIONS OF LANGUAGE TEST 3

11. Which of these sentences has the correct punctuation? Colour in only one circle.

- ○ Many companies, make sugar-free soft drinks which contain less sugar but do not quite taste the same.
- ○ Many companies, make sugar-free soft drinks, which contain less sugar but do not quite taste the same.
- ○ Many companies make sugar-free soft drinks, which contain less sugar, but do not quite taste the same.
- ○ Many companies, make sugar-free soft drinks, which contain less sugar, but do not quite taste the same.

Read the sentence. There is a word missing. Choose the correct word or words to fill the gap. Colour in only one circle.

12. Pedro is the ______ person I have ever met.

clumsiest	clumsier	most clumsiest	most clumsier
○	○	○	○

Colour in the circle(s) with the correct answer.

13. Which sentence has the correct punctuation?

- ○ Yvette said Time for our piano lesson.
- ○ "Yvette said time for our piano lesson."
- ○ Yvette said, "time for our piano lesson."
- ○ Yvette said, "Time for our piano lesson."

Did you colour in one of the circles?

14. Where does the missing apostrophe (') go?

The womens handbags were stolen and their credit cards were never found.

15. Where do the **two** missing speech marks (" and ") go?

"Hey, Theo, what do you think? said Christian. Do we have time for another game?"

☞ Answers and explanations on page 183

16. Which sentence has the correct punctuation?

- ○ You can come back on Wednesday said Peter.
- ○ "You can come back on Wednesday" said Peter.
- ○ "you can come back on Wednesday," said Peter.
- ○ "You can come back on Wednesday," said Peter.

Read the sentences. They have some gaps. Choose the correct word or words to fill each gap. Colour in only one circle for each answer.

17. Evaporation is when the sun heats the water in oceans, rivers, plants, lakes and soil ______ turn it into vapour or steam.

so that	in order to	because	while
○	○	○	○

18. As the water vapours rise, they cool and change back ______ liquid, forming clouds.

into	in	to	from
○	○	○	○

19. Precipitation occurs ______ so much water has condensed that the air cannot hold it anymore and it falls back to the earth in the form of rain, hail or snow.

into	when	for	before
○	○	○	○

20. Some water falls ______ into the oceans, lakes or rivers or the soil where plants may take it up.

back	in	because	up
○	○	○	○

21. Sarah advised me ______ music lessons.

to have	for having	had	in having
○	○	○	○

22. Lara said the purple dress was ______ than the pink one.

prettier	more prettier	prettiest	most prettiest
○	○	○	○

☞ Answers and explanations on pages 183–184

CONVENTIONS OF LANGUAGE TEST 3

23. ______ Tony left, Marie made sure he had his keys with him.

Before ○ During ○ Where ○

24. Jamie eats apples more often than ______.

they ○ them ○ themselves ○

Did you colour in one of the circles?

Colour in the circle(s) with the correct answer.

25. Where do the **two** missing commas (,) go?

Aaron's history book ○ which weighs ○ about 3 kg ○ fell ○ out of his locker ○ and onto my foot.

It would be a good idea to check your answers to questions 1 to 25 before moving on to the other questions.

To the student

Ask your teacher or parent to read the spelling words for you. The words are listed on page 188. Write the spelling words on the lines below.

Test 3 spelling words

26. ______________

27. ______________

28. ______________

29. ______________

30. ______________

31. ______________

32. ______________

33. ______________

34. ______________

35. ______________

36. ______________

37. ______________

38. ______________

39. ______________

40. ______________

Answers and explanations on page 184

CONVENTIONS OF LANGUAGE TEST 3

The spelling mistakes in these sentences are underlined. Write the correct spelling of each word in the box.

41. Our resturant is advertising for staff.

42. We need an expirienced chef.

43. The applicent must meet all our needs.

44. They must have previously worked in a busy kichen.

45. Also they must have an interess in cooking seafood.

Read the sentences. Each sentence has one word that is incorrect. Write the correct spelling of the word in the box.

46. The successful person will have excelent skills in looking after other staff.

47. They must pay atenshun to detail.

48. They must also be able to deliva great guest service.

49. Send your application to the maniger.

50. The last date for applications is 3 Janury.

END OF TEST

Well done! You have completed the third Conventions of Language Test.

How did you go with these test questions? Some were harder than the last test. Check to see where you did well and where you had problems. Try to revise the questions that were hard for you.

Use the diagnostic chart on pages 125–126 to see which level of ability you reached. Again, we remind you that this is only an estimate. Don't be surprised if you answered some difficult questions correctly or even missed some easier questions.

There is now only one more test to complete. It contains 50 questions. They include many of the same types of questions, plus a few new types.

☞ Answers and explanations on page 184

Instructions

As you check the answer for each question, mark it as correct (✓) or incorrect (✗). Mark any questions that you omitted or left out as incorrect (✗) for the moment.

Then look at how many you answered correctly in each level. You will be able to see what level you are at by finding the point where you started having consistent difficulty with questions at a certain level. For example, if you answer most questions correctly up to the Intermediate level and then get most questions wrong from then onwards, it is likely your ability is at the Intermediate level. You can ask your parents or your teacher to help you do this if it isn't clear to you.

Am I able to ...

	SKILL	ESTIMATED LEVEL	✓ or ✗
1	Use conjunctions correctly?	Standard	
2	Use prepositions correctly?	Intermediate	
3	Match the singular form of the verb to the subject?	Standard	
4	Use the simple past tense correctly?	Intermediate	
5	Use pronouns correctly?	Standard	
6	Use question marks and commas correctly in a complex sentence?	Intermediate	
7	Use question marks correctly?	Intermediate	
8	Use the simple past tense correctly?	Intermediate	
9	Use conjunctions correctly?	Intermediate	
10	Recognise that indirect speech does not require speech marks?	Advanced	
11	Use commas correctly in a complex sentence?	Advanced	
12	Use superlative adjectives correctly?	Intermediate	
13	Use speech marks correctly for direct speech?	Intermediate	
14	Use apostrophes correctly for possession?	Advanced	
15	Use speech marks correctly for direct speech?	Intermediate	
16	Use speech marks correctly for direct speech and capital letters at the start of sentences?	Intermediate	
17	Identify the correct conjunction?	Intermediate	
18	Identify the correct preposition?	Intermediate	
19	Identify the correct preposition?	Advanced	
20	Identify the correct preposition?	Advanced	
21	Use the *to*-infinitive correctly to complete a complex verb phrase?	Intermediate	
22	Use comparative adjectives correctly?	Intermediate	
23	Use conjunctions correctly?	Standard	
24	Use pronouns correctly?	Standard	
25	Use commas correctly in a complex sentence?	Intermediate	
26	Spell *height?*	Standard	

CHECK YOUR SKILLS: CONVENTIONS OF LANGUAGE TEST 3

	SKILL	ESTIMATED LEVEL	✓ or ✗
27	Spell *wheat?*	Standard	
28	Spell *soul?*	Intermediate	
29	Spell *asked?*	Intermediate	
30	Spell *month?*	Intermediate	
31	Spell *hoping?*	Intermediate	
32	Spell *making?*	Advanced	
33	Spell *village?*	Advanced	
34	Spell *mistaking?*	Standard	
35	Spell *buttoning?*	Standard	
36	Spell *translating?*	Standard	
37	Spell *bargain?*	Advanced	
38	Spell *coffee?*	Advanced	
39	Spell *tomorrow?*	Advanced	
40	Spell *recommend?*	Advanced	
41	Spell *restaurant?*	Advanced	
42	Spell *experienced?*	Intermediate	
43	Spell *applicant?*	Advanced	
44	Spell *kitchen?*	Advanced	
45	Spell *interest?*	Advanced	
46	Spell *excellent?*	Standard	
47	Spell *attention?*	Intermediate	
48	Spell *deliver?*	Intermediate	
49	Spell *manager?*	Intermediate	
50	Spell *January?*	Advanced	
	TOTAL		

CONVENTIONS OF LANGUAGE TEST 4

ADAPTED FOR ONLINE FORMAT

This is the last Conventions of Language Test. There are 50 questions.

If you aren't sure what to do, ask your teacher or your parents to help you. Don't be afraid to ask if it isn't clear to you.

Allow around 45 minutes for this test. Take a short break if necessary.

Read the sentences. They have some gaps. Choose the correct word or words to fill each gap. Colour in only one circle for each answer.

1. I pulled the book ______ the top shelf and put it on my desk.

from ○ of ○ with ○ into ○

2. Matilda recognised me at once ______ I had not seen her for many years.

in case ○ although ○ while ○ since ○

3. Mum and I ______ leaving tomorrow.

am ○ is ○ are ○ will ○

4. Many parents are going out ______ mobile phones for their children.

and buying ○ for buying ○ to buyed ○ to buying ○

5. I am as old as ______ .

they ○ their ○ them ○ theirselves ○

Colour in the circle(s) with the correct answer.

6. Which word **can** be used as a plural?

sheep ○ ewe ○ lamb ○ flock ○

☞ Answers and explanations on page 184

7. Where do the **two** missing apostrophes (’) go?

First floor is womens footwear and formal dresses, and mens shoes are on the fourth floor.

8. Where do the **two** missing speech marks (“ and ”) go?

Brett said, Neil, please show Andrea to her new office.

9. Which sentence has the correct punctuation?

- ○ The teacher asked what they were doing.
- ○ “The teacher asked what they were doing.”
- ○ The teacher asked, “what they were doing?”
- ○ The teacher asked, “What they were doing?”

10. Which sentence has the correct punctuation?

- ○ We will still be able to play football won’t we? Even if it is raining.
- ○ We will still be able to play football won’t we even if it is raining?
- ○ We will still be able to play football, won’t we? even if it is raining.
- ○ We will still be able to play football, won’t we, even if it is raining?

11. Which sentence is correct?

- ○ I was not aware that the science project was due today. Neither was Ross.
- ○ I was not aware that the science project was due today. Either was Ross.
- ○ I was not aware that the science project was due today. Or was Ross.
- ○ I was not aware that the science project was due today. Nor did Ross.

☞ Answers and explanations on page 184

12. Which sentence has the correct punctuation?

- ○ Max, who has applied for entry to several local high schools really wants to go to Varity College.
- ○ Max, who has applied for entry, to several local high schools really wants to go to Varity College.
- ○ Max who has applied for entry, to several local high schools, really wants to go to Varity College.
- ○ Max, who has applied for entry to several local high schools, really wants to go to Varity College.

13. Where do the **four** missing speech marks (“ and ”) go?

○ No, ○ Luke, ○ Mum called out, ○ ○ the call was not for you. ○

Read the sentences. They have some gaps. Choose the correct word or words to fill each gap.

14. We wanted good seats for the football ______ we booked in advance.

so	since	so that	whereas
○	○	○	○

15. The council will determine whether to ______ with the approval of the plans to build a new house.

going ahead	on going ahead	go ahead	in going ahead
○	○	○	○

Did you colour in one of the circles?

Answers and explanations on page 184

CONVENTIONS OF LANGUAGE TEST 4

Read the text *Delta Electrical* which has some gaps. Choose the correct words to complete the text.

Delta Electrical

Tired of waiting all day for [16]

Delta Electrical can service all your electrical problems 24 hrs a day, 7 days a week.

Don't wait days for a repair you [17] today.

Call Delta Electrical NOW on 1800 494 567 for immediate service.

[18] offer fixed prices so you get an upfront price before we start.

> "Previously, I had to wait days before we had electricity [19]. It would take ages to get someone [20] fix the problem. Now I get immediate service."
>
> *TW, Cronulla*

16. ○ service!
○ service.
○ service?
○ service;

17. ○ require
○ required
○ requiring

18. ○ Us
○ We
○ He
○ She

19. ○ in
○ back
○ after
○ through

20. ○ as
○ when
○ for
○ to

☞ **Answers and explanations on page 184**

CONVENTIONS OF LANGUAGE TEST 4

Read the sentences. Choose the correct word or words, or punctuation, to complete each sentence. Colour in only one circle for each answer.

21. George and Ahmed ______ kebabs for lunch.

- ○ is eating
- ○ are eating
- ○ will eating

22. Anthony is ______ father.

- ○ Michaels
- ○ Michael's
- ○ Michaels'

23. Gerry, who is a first-grade footballer ______ used to live in my street.

- ○ ,
- ○ .
- ○ ?
- ○ !

24. John said that his new bike is ______ than his old one.

- ○ better
- ○ gooder
- ○ best

25. Nick is the ______ in the family.

- ○ youngest
- ○ most young
- ○ more youngest

Did you colour in one of the circles?

It would be a good idea to check your answers to questions 1 to 25 before moving on to the other questions.

☞ Answers and explanations on pages 184–185

CONVENTIONS OF LANGUAGE TEST 4

To the student

Ask your teacher or parent to read the spelling words for you. The words are listed on page 188. Write the spelling words on the lines below.

Test 4 spelling words

26. ______________________

27. ______________________

28. ______________________

29. ______________________

30. ______________________

31. ______________________

32. ______________________

33. ______________________

34. ______________________

35. ______________________

36. ______________________

37. ______________________

38. ______________________

39. ______________________

40. ______________________

The spelling mistakes in these sentences are underlined. Write the correct spelling of each underlined word in the box.

41. There were many stares from the ground floor to level three.

42. Customer service is an important part of our busyness.

43. This shopping centre is were you would expect to see many people that you know.

44. Celine was among the fourty people seated in the bus for two hours.

45. Clement enquired about becomming an Australian citizen.

☞ Answers and explanations on page 185

CONVENTIONS OF LANGUAGE TEST 4

Read the sentences. Each sentence has one word that is incorrect. Write the correct spelling of the word in the box provided.

46. I was beginning to see that his actions were a bit wierd towards me.

47. The staff made the decision to offer relligion as a subject for next year.

48. I guarentee you that it will all be all right.

49. I preferred to vaccum instead of cleaning the laundry.

50. Celine began to critisize her sister, then an argument followed.

END OF TEST

Well done! You have completed the final Conventions of Language Test. It means that you have answered or attempted 200 Conventions of Language questions.

How did you go with the questions in this test? Were some harder for you? Check to see where you did well and where you had problems.

Use the diagnostic chart on pages 134–135 to see which level of ability you reached. Again, we remind you that this is only an estimate. Don't be surprised if you answered some difficult questions correctly or even missed some easier questions.

Instructions

As you check the answer for each question, mark it as correct (✓) or incorrect (✗). Mark any questions that you omitted or left out as incorrect (✗) for the moment.

Then look at how many you answered correctly in each level. You will be able to see what level you are at by finding the point where you started having consistent difficulty with questions at a certain level. For example, if you answer most questions correctly up to the Intermediate level and then get most questions wrong from then onwards, it is likely your ability is at the Intermediate level. You can ask your parents or your teacher to help you do this if it isn't clear to you.

Am I able to ...

	SKILL	ESTIMATED LEVEL	✓ or ✗
1	Use prepositions correctly?	Standard	
2	Use conjunctions correctly?	Standard	
3	Match the plural form of the verb to the subject?	Standard	
4	Use conjunctions correctly with verbs?	Intermediate	
5	Use object pronouns correctly?	Standard	
6	Identify a word without a plural?	Advanced	
7	Use apostrophes correctly for possession?	Advanced	
8	Use speech marks correctly for direct speech?	Intermediate	
9	Recognise that indirect speech does not require speech marks?	Advanced	
10	Use question marks and commas correctly?	Intermediate	
11	Use conjunctions correctly?	Intermediate	
12	Locate a pair of commas in a complex sentence?	Advanced	
13	Use speech marks for direct speech?	Intermediate	
14	Recognise a common grammatical convention (conjunction)?	Standard	
15	Use the correct word to complete a complex verb phrase?	Advanced	
16	Use question marks correctly?	Standard	
17	Use the simple present tense correctly?	Intermediate	
18	Use pronouns correctly?	Intermediate	
19	Recognise a common grammatical convention (conjunction)?	Intermediate	
20	Use the *to* infinitive correctly?	Advanced	
21	Match the plural form of the verb to the subject and use the present continuous tense correctly?	Intermediate	
22	Use apostrophes correctly for possession?	Standard	
23	Use commas correctly in a complex sentence?	Intermediate	
24	Use comparative adjectives correctly?	Intermediate	
25	Use superlative adjectives correctly?	Intermediate	
26	Spell *weak*?	Intermediate	

CHECK YOUR SKILLS: CONVENTIONS OF LANGUAGE TEST 4

	SKILL	ESTIMATED LEVEL	✓ or ✗
27	Spell *shoe*?	Standard	
28	Spell *blue*?	Standard	
29	Spell *cries*?	Standard	
30	Spell *choice*?	Standard	
31	Spell *dance*?	Standard	
32	Spell *soar*?	Intermediate	
33	Spell *aunt*?	Standard	
34	Spell *batting*?	Intermediate	
35	Spell *padding*?	Intermediate	
36	Spell *stripping*?	Intermediate	
37	Spell *seaweed*?	Standard	
38	Spell *explain*?	Advanced	
39	Spell *chemist*?	Advanced	
40	Spell *asthma*?	Advanced	
41	Spell *stairs*?	Standard	
42	Spell *business?*	Standard	
43	Spell *where*?	Standard	
44	Spell *forty?*	Advanced	
45	Spell *becoming*?	Intermediate	
46	Spell *weird*?	Intermediate	
47	Spell *religion*?	Intermediate	
48	Spell *guarantee*?	Advanced	
49	Spell *vacuum*?	Advanced	
50	Spell *criticise*?	Advanced	
	TOTAL		

Check the Writing section (www.nap.edu.au/naplan/writing) **of the official NAPLAN website for up-to-date and important information on the Writing Test.** Sample Writing Tests and marking guidelines that outline the criteria markers use when assessing your writing are also provided. Please note that, to date in NAPLAN, the types of texts that students have been tested on have been narrative and persuasive writing.

The Australian Curriculum for English requires students to be taught three main types of texts:

- imaginative writing (including narratives and descriptions)
- informative writing (including procedures and reports)
- persuasive writing (expositions).

Informative writing has not yet been tested by NAPLAN. The best preparation for writing is for students to read a range of texts and to get lots of practice in writing different types of texts. We have included information on all types of texts in this book.

About the test

The NAPLAN Writing test examines a student's ability to write effectively in a specific type of text. Students will come across a number of types of texts at school. These can be factual (real) or literary (imaginary). Although we provide you with some graded sample answers on pages 140–142 and 155–157, we do not provide any others because grading writing is a time-consuming task which can be very subjective. It's more important that you focus on improving the standard of your writing.

Usually there is only one Writing question in the NAPLAN Writing Test. You will be provided with some stimulus material that acts as a prompt to writing: something to read or a picture to look at.

The NAPLAN Online Writing Test

For the Year 5 NAPLAN Writing Test students will use a digital device (a computer or tablet) to answer the question. It is a good idea for students to practise typing their writing on a digital device. Students can take a NAPLAN-style Online Writing Test on the Excel Test Zone site at www.exceltestzone.com.au to familiarise themselves with the keyboard functions that will be available.

Marking the Writing Test

When the markers of the NAPLAN Writing Test assess your writing they will mark it according to various criteria. Knowing what they look for will help you understand what to look out for in your own child's writing. These are very complex criteria and teachers receive special training for this marking.

The emphasis is on the quality of expression and what the student has to say. Some features that may be emphasised are:

- the quality of the content
- what the student thinks about the topic
- what feelings are developed
- how it is structured
- whether the writing is organised clearly, using paragraphs and appropriate sequencing
- whether the writing is cohesive
- the quality of the spelling and punctuation/ grammar.

Advice for parents and teachers

If students aren't sure how to write a persuasive or narrative text then use the practice tests to develop these skills. It may not be easy for them at first. One way to start is to ask them to talk about the topic and to state their views on the subject. Next you could show them how to plan their writing. Then they can start to write.

Give plenty of praise and encouragement. Remember that Year 5 students are still quite young. Emphasise whatever is good and overlook any errors at first. Space out the time between the writing tasks. Do not attempt one immediately after the other as this does not allow time for development, Come back to these errors at a much later stage, perhaps a little before you start the next practice test.

In this book we look at persuasive and narrative writing. We start with writing a persuasive text on the following page.

WRITING: PERSUASIVE TEXTS

In this section of the Writing Test we start with a sample of a persuasive text. First we give some details about this type of writing, then there is a sample question with answers, and finally there are two practice Writing Tests for persuasive texts.

About persuasive texts

- A persuasive text is designed to convince. It states one side of a case and expresses a point of view. The first step is to decide on your opinion: are you for or against?
- You don't need to list reasons for and reasons against. Support your point of view with facts, examples and evidence.
- Persuasive texts can be posters, advertisements, letters, debates or reports.
- Their main purpose is to persuade the reader to see an issue from the author's point of view. The writing aims to persuade the reader to change his or her mind, and to win the support of the reader on a specific issue. To do this the author uses persuasive devices.

Examples of persuasive devices

- You can speak to the reader. For example:

  The government should give money to countries that suffer from famine and disasters. This will show that Australia cares for all people that suffer. It is important that we all donate to foreign aid charities.
- You can ask a question that leads to the answer you want. For example:

  Students are able to judge just as fairly as adults. So isn't it right to let them have a say in some matters?
- You can give facts and support your ideas with findings. For example:

  The majority of scientists at the world conference agreed on climate change.
- You can use descriptive persuasive words. For example:

  true, fair, honest, essential, best.
- You can use persuasive words to influence the reader. For example:

  naturally, obviously, definitely, probably, certainly.
- You can use strong modal verbs. For example:

  can, might, should, could, would.
- You can use words that make the reader think. Thinking words can include persuasive statistics. For example:

  The medical research cautioned parents that 90% of primary school children are not exercising half an hour a day.
- You can include emotional language. For example:

  Many people consider that we must protect the environment, Certainly we must try ..., I am absolutely appalled that we provide so little help to countries in times of disaster.
- You can use emotional adjectives. For example:

  important, significant and invaluable.
- You can use rhetorical questions. A rhetorical question asks the reader a question but does not expect an answer. It is used for its persuasive effect. It makes the reader think and tries to emphasise one likely answer. For example:

  Are we to think that ...?

Structure of a persuasive text

Introduction

- The first paragraph introduces the topic. Make this a statement of your opinion.
- It should be a short paragraph of approximately one to two sentences. It should include a strong sentence which captures the reader's interest.

The body

The main part of your writing should consist of arguments. In a persuasive text an argument shows how you think by listing the reasons for your opinion. It is the case that you are putting forward, just like a lawyer puts forward a case in court. Focus on the main points and elaborate on them.

- Use a new paragraph for each new point or idea. Include reasons, evidence and examples to support your opinion.
- Try to include at least three paragraphs with at least two sentences in each paragraph. Avoid using paragraphs of one sentence only.
- State your arguments or ideas in order, one after the other. They should be logical, i.e. they should make sense. Start with the strongest argument.
- Express your point of view clearly. Use strong, persuasive language. Back up each idea, opinion or argument with evidence.
- Use linking words. Linking words are sometimes called connectives. Connectives are words that improve the flow of your writing and are used to join ideas. For example:

  firstly, secondly, thirdly, another reason, finally, because, next, then, when, after, so, therefore, however, even though, for this reason, although, pay attention to, another point of view, on the other hand, alternatively.
- Use the present tense to explain ideas or arguments. For example:

  I believe that ...
- Use the past tense to give examples. For example:

  I have heard that ..., People have tried to ...
- Remember to acknowledge your sources when you use information or statistics. In other words, give the reader an idea of where the facts were obtained.

Conclusion

The conclusion is a strong, convincing statement used to repeat your position and summarise all your key points.

For example:

In conclusion, it is evident that ...

It does not contain any new information or points. The conclusion should be about three sentences in length.

On the following page we have provided a Sample Writing question for a persuasive text. In the persuasive text you will be required to:

- express an opinion
- include facts to support your opinion
- make sure that the first sentence of each paragraph is the key to what follows
- write in an easy-to-understand way
- persuade the reader
- use a new paragraph for each new idea.

We have also provided six sample answers to the sample question. We have grouped them into the three levels of ability used throughout this book. Please note that these are approximate guidelines only.

In this part you will be doing some writing. Each Writing Test should take you 42 minutes. Write your answer on separate sheets of paper. Use the top part of the first sheet or the persuasive text planning page to plan your ideas.

When you have finished, hand in your writing to your teacher, parents or another adult to mark it for you. If it is convenient and possible for you, then you may wish to type your answer directly on a computer.

Topic: Hunting is a good sport.

Today you are going to write a persuasive text. The topic for your writing is whether hunting is a good sport.

Write an answer that shows your opinion and ideas.

- Begin with a clear opening paragraph: tell the reader what you are going to write.
- Then write your opinions.
- Give your reasons: be convincing.
- Explain so that someone else can understand easily.
- At the end give a short summary of your ideas.

Remember to:

- think about your views on the topic
- include a clear opening and concluding statement
- plan your writing, thinking about arguments for and against
- use paragraphs
- write in sentences
- check your spelling and punctuation
- write at least two pages.

Hunting is a good sport

STANDARD LEVEL 1

Hunting as a sport is a really silly idea.

The first reason is that you distroy animals and make them excteenct.

The second reason is that it gets rid of other animals food.

Another reason is that it can hurt them

Remember animals belong safely in the bush let thewm live there

STANDARD LEVEL 2

Hunting would not be good as a sport. Animals should be left alone where they belong.

Firstly, hunting makes lots of animals excteenct. We need to help them grow and not distroy them and kill them off and kidnapp them.

Secondly, hunting gets rid of other animals food. If they do not eat other animals they can't sirvive.

Thirdly, hunting is cruel. How would you like it if you are minding youre own bisness and you get shot for nothing. It's mean so don't distroy animals for you're fun.

In conclusion I believe that hunting for sport should be banned.

INTERMEDIATE LEVEL 1

I think that hunting as a sport would not make a good idea. There are lots of reasons why.

Firstly, hunting makes many speshes of animals excteenct. Taking them from their homes is not a good idea. Lots of animals like the dodo are already excteenct and others will soon be too.

Next, hunting interrupts the food chain and kills many animals that other animals need to survive off. They won't produce so numbers of animals will go down or disapeer.

Finally, hunting is not a sport it is just shooting for fun. Hunters should maybe play video games that is a much safer sport and no one gets murdered for real.

Therefore I believe that hunting should not be allowed as a sport. Hunters should stay in their homes and pretend to shoot so animals stay safe.

INTERMEDIATE LEVEL 2

I disagree with the topic statement that hunting is a good sport. Hunting endangers our wildlife; it interrupts the food chain and is nothing more than mindless target practice for cowards.

Firstly, hunting threatens many species with extinction and has already made many species extinct, e.g. the dodo, the tasmanian tiger and others are well on their way. Experts believe that if hunting is allowed to continue, it will endanger many other species such as the panda, and the great white shark.

Please note: Spelling, punctuation and grammar errors have been included to replicate the likely response of a Year 5 student.

Secondly, hunting interrupts the food chain and kills many animals that other animals need to survive off, leaving the predator animals starving and will die. If we did not eat animals would we be able to survive? How will certain animals survive if they don't eat animals?

Finally, hunting is mindless target practise that only cruel or starving people take part in. If hunters want target practice, they should fire at an archery target. Why fire at animals? People always fire at animals because they can't fight back. It is murder, plain, cruel murder.

In conclusion, I strongly disagree with hunting. Hunters should think about what they do before they do it. If the hunters realised they were putting animals at risk, they would certainly stop. If they realised they were shooting their food, they would also stop. If they realised they could shoot something else, they would stop. This is to any hunters that might read this. STOP HUNTING!

ADVANCED LEVEL 1

Animals should not be hunted. Hunting is the cruel cold murder of unprotected animals. It is dangerous and shows a plain lack of respect for animals.

Firstly, hunting threatens many species with extinction. Bloodthirsty hunters who have no respect for the hunted animals have already made many species of animals extinct. Scientists believe 3 species of animals are made extinct every hour! Some examples are the dodo and the Siberian Tiger, and others are well on their way. Hunters kill for sport, for fun, for body parts or fur, and for that trophy on the wall, without thinking of the consequences of their actions. Many years ago hunting was for survival for food, but that is no longer the case. Hunting endangers species by reducing the animal population. Obviously, if everyone killed as they pleased, the animal population could never get the chance to recover. It can be said that setting limits is a solution, but in my view this would be very difficult to monitor.

Secondly, hunting interrupts the food chain. Many animals that others need to eat to survive are killed off, leaving other predator animals starving. Many hunters believe they can step in here and control things by hunting. How are animals meant to survive if they can't eat certain animals? By hunting down these predator animals, we are not giving animals in the food chain a fair chance of survival.

Furthermore, hunting is mindless target practise that only cruel or starving people take part in. If hunters want target practise, they should fire at an archery target. Why fire at defenceless animals? Animals have rights too! They have the right to remain safe from human beings. They naturally protect themselves from other animals, but are not ever taught to deal with armed human beings. How can they compete against a gun? What chance do they have? Hunters fire at animals because animals can't fight back. It's murder - plain, cruel murder.

In addition, hunting should not be allowed as a sport because it is dangerous. Dangerous for hunters and for animals. Weapons owned for hunting have fallen into the wrong hands and been used for crimes. Also when animals see hunters, this causes them to get frightened and run out

Please note: Spelling, punctuation and grammar errors have been included to replicate the likely response of a Year 5 student.

of the bush onto the road, where they get killed by passing cars.

In conclusion, there is no need for hunting as a sport. Animals need to be protected and treated with respect. They should not be tortured or mistreated before being used as trophies or food. There is no reason for hunting.

ADVANCED LEVEL 2

Hunting should not be allowed as a sport. We should not harm defenceless animals. They experience pain just like we do and have the right to safety. We should treat them as we would want to be treated.

Firstly, hunting threatens many species with extinction. Hunters who have no respect for animals have already made many species of animals extinct. Some examples are the golden toad and the Rodrigues pigeon, which we or our children will never know anything about. If everyone killed as they pleased, the animal population would never increase. Limiting how much each hunter can collect would not work, because this is very hard to check.

Secondly, hunting interrupts the food chain. Many animals are killed, that others need to eat to survive. This leaves other predator animals starving. How are animals meant to survive if they can't eat certain animals? By hunting down these predator animals, we are not giving animals in the food chain a fair chance of survival.

Furthermore, hunting is mindless target practise that only cruel or starving people take part in. If hunters want target practise, they should fire at an archery target.

Animals definitely have rights too! They have the right to remain safe from human beings. How can they compete against a gun? Coward hunters fire at animals because animals can't fight back. It's murder - plain, cruel murder.

Another reason why hunting should not be allowed as a sport is that it is dangerous. It is dangerous for hunters to own guns and it is also dangerous for animals. Weapons used for hunting have been misused for crimes. Also when animals run away from hunters they run out onto the road, where they'll get injured or killed.

In conclusion, hunting should not be allowed as a sport. Animals need to be protected and remain safe. They certainly should not be killed for sport. Hunters should definitely think about what they do before they do it. There is absolutely no need for hunting.

Please note: Spelling, punctuation and grammar errors have been included to replicate the likely response of a Year 5 student.

WRITING TEST 1

In this part you will be doing some writing. Each Writing Test should take you 42 minutes. Write your answer on separate sheets of paper. Use the top part of the first sheet or the persuasive text planning page to plan your ideas.

When you have finished, hand in your writing to your teacher, parents or another adult to mark it for you. If it is convenient and possible for you, then you may wish to type your answer directly on a computer.

Topic: Have computers helped students learn more than in the past?

Today you are going to write a persuasive text. The topic for your writing is whether computers have helped students learn more than in the past.

Write an answer that shows your opinion and ideas.

- Begin with a clear opening paragraph: tell the reader what you are going to write.
- Then write your opinions.
- Give your reasons: be convincing.
- Explain so that someone else can understand easily.
- At the end give a short summary of your ideas.

Remember to:

- think about your views on the topic
- include a clear opening and concluding statement
- plan your writing, thinking about arguments for and against
- use paragraphs
- write in sentences
- check your spelling and punctuation
- write at least two pages.

Here is a persuasive text planning page to start you off. Use this page to plan your ideas.

PERSUASIVE TEXT

INTRODUCTION

Introduce the topic and state your opinion. What do you think about the issue? Are you for or against? (1–2 sentences)

ARGUMENTS

List the reasons that support your opinion. (3–4 paragraphs)

REASON 1

List points and give examples to back up your reasons.

REASON 2

List points and give examples to back up your reasons.

REASON 3

List points and give examples to back up your reasons.

LINKING WORDS

although ... even though ... however ... on the other hand ... at the same time ...

MODAL VERBS

must ... can ... might ... should ... could ... would

PERSUASIVE WORDS

naturally ... obviously ... definitely ... probably ... certainly ... possibly ... always ... it ... unless ... sometimes ... unlikely ... hopefully ... perhaps ... absolutely ...

THINKING WORDS

Experts believe that ... It can be said that ... In my view ... Another point of view is ... The evidence supports ... In my opinion ... Some people feel ... On the other hand ... Surely ...

CONCLUSION

Repeat your opinion and summarise the main points of the argument. (3 sentences)

In conclusion ... Therefore ... I believe that ... It's evident that ... Overall ... Although there are many benefits to/in ... As a result ... In considering these arguments ...

CHECK YOUR SKILLS: WRITING TEST 1

Use this chart to evaluate your writing.

GUIDELINES FOR WRITING A PERSUASIVE TEXT	✓ or ✗
Have you clearly expressed your point of view on the specific issue?	
Have you made at least three points with strong arguments and solid supporting points?	
Have you backed up each argument with evidence?	
Have you used the simple present tense to give views, e.g. *We must try …*?	
Have you used the present perfect tense to give examples, e.g. *I have heard that …, People have tried to …*?	
Have you used a variety of correct sentence structures—including simple, compound and complex sentences—to develop arguments?	
Have you linked arguments by using a variety of time connectives, e.g. *firstly, secondly, thirdly, finally, because, in addition, next, then, when, after, consequently, so, therefore, furthermore, however, even though, for this reason, although, pay attention to, in contrast, another point of view, in spite of this, on the other hand, alternatively, the evidence supports a different point of view …*?	
Have you used clear, descriptive and persuasive words?	
Have you used modal verbs/conditionals, e.g. (high) *always, undoubtedly, certainly, absolutely, definitely, obviously, never, must*; (medium) *probably, maybe, apparently, often, can, might, should, could, would, if, unless*; (low) *unlikely, hopefully, perhaps, sometimes, possibly*?	
Have you used persuasive devices such as statistics (e.g. 75% *of students in my class have a mobile phone and believe that …*), emotive language (e.g. *Many people consider that …, We must protect …, Certainly we must try …, I am absolutely appalled that …, important, significant, invaluable*) and rhetorical questions (e.g. *Are we to think that ...?*)?	
Have you considered the audience and purpose of the text?	
Have you organised your writing into new paragraphs for each separate idea or argument?	
Have you used thinking and action verbs to build arguments, e.g. *In my opinion …, Some people feel …, On the other hand …, Probably …, It is certain …, Surely …*?	
Have you used a variety of conjunctions, e.g. *when, because, so, if, but*?	
Have you used reported speech, e.g. *'I've noticed that …', 'I've heard that …'*)?	
Have you punctuated sentences correctly with capital letters, full stops, commas, exclamation marks and question marks?	
Have you used the following correctly most of the time: speech marks, possessive apostrophes, dashes, colons, semicolons and parentheses?	
Have you used the correct spelling of common words?	
Have you used the correct spelling of unusual or difficult words?	
Have you provided an effective and convincing concluding statement that summarises your opinion, introduced by an appropriate phrase, e.g. *Consequently …, Admittedly …, In conclusion …, It's evident that …, Overall …, In considering these arguments …*?	

WRITING TEST 2

In this part you will be doing some writing. Each Writing Test should take you 42 minutes. Write your answer on separate sheets of paper. Use the top part of the first sheet or the persuasive text planning page to plan your ideas.

When you have finished, hand in your writing to your teacher, parents or another adult to mark it for you. If it is convenient and possible for you, then you may wish to type your answer directly on a computer.

Topic: Should students learn a second language at school?

Today you are going to write a persuasive text. The topic for your writing is whether you think students should learn a second language at school.

Write an answer that shows your opinion and ideas.

- Begin with a clear opening paragraph: tell the reader what you are going to write.
- Then write your opinions.
- Give your reasons: be convincing.
- Explain so that someone else can understand easily.
- At the end give a short summary of your ideas.

Remember to:

- think about your views on the topic
- include a clear opening and concluding statement
- plan your writing, thinking about arguments for and against
- use paragraphs
- write in sentences
- check your spelling and punctuation
- write at least two pages.

Use this persuasive text planning page to plan your ideas.

PERSUASIVE TEXT

INTRODUCTION

Introduce the topic and state your opinion. What do you think about the issue? Are you for or against? (1–2 sentences)

ARGUMENTS

List the reasons that support your opinion. (3–4 paragraphs)

REASON 1

List points and give examples to back up your reasons.

REASON 2

List points and give examples to back up your reasons.

REASON 3

List points and give examples to back up your reasons.

LINKING WORDS

although … even though … however … on the other hand … at the same time …

MODAL VERBS

must … can … might … should … could … would

PERSUASIVE WORDS

naturally … obviously … definitely … probably … certainly … possibly … always … it … unless … sometimes … unlikely … hopefully … perhaps … absolutely …

THINKING WORDS

Experts believe that … It can be said that … In my view … Another point of view is … The evidence supports … In my opinion … Some people feel … On the other hand … Surely …

CONCLUSION

Repeat your opinion and summarise the main points of the argument. (3 sentences)

In conclusion … Therefore … I believe that … It's evident that … Overall … Although there are many benefits to/in … As a result … In considering these arguments …

CHECK YOUR SKILLS: WRITING TEST 2

Use this chart to evaluate your writing.

GUIDELINES FOR WRITING A PERSUASIVE TEXT	✓ or ✗
Have you clearly expressed your point of view on the specific issue?	
Have you made at least three points with strong arguments and solid supporting points?	
Have you backed up each argument with evidence?	
Have you used the simple present tense to give views, e.g. *We must try …*?	
Have you used the present perfect tense to give examples, e.g. *I have heard that …, People have tried to …*?	
Have you used a variety of correct sentence structures—including simple, compound and complex sentences—to develop arguments?	
Have you linked arguments by using a variety of time connectives, e.g. *firstly, secondly, thirdly, finally, because, in addition, next, then, when, after, consequently, so, therefore, furthermore, however, even though, for this reason, although, pay attention to, in contrast, another point of view, in spite of this, on the other hand, alternatively, the evidence supports a different point of view …*?	
Have you used clear, descriptive and persuasive words?	
Have you used modal verbs/conditionals, e.g. (high) *always, undoubtedly, certainly, absolutely, definitely, obviously, never, must*; (medium) *probably, maybe, apparently, often, can, might, should, could, would, if, unless*; (low) *unlikely, hopefully, perhaps, sometimes, possibly*?	
Have you used persuasive devices such as statistics (e.g. 75% *of students in my class have a mobile phone and believe that …*), emotive language (e.g. *Many people consider that …, We must protect …, Certainly we must try …, I am absolutely appalled that …, important, significant, invaluable*) and rhetorical questions (e.g. *Are we to think that ...?*)?	
Have you considered the audience and purpose of the text?	
Have you organised your writing into new paragraphs for each separate idea or argument?	
Have you used thinking and action verbs to build arguments, e.g. *In my opinion …, Some people feel …, On the other hand …, Probably …, It is certain …, Surely …*?	
Have you used a variety of conjunctions, e.g. *when, because, so, if, but*?	
Have you used reported speech, e.g. *'I've noticed that …', 'I've heard that …'*)?	
Have you punctuated sentences correctly with capital letters, full stops, commas, exclamation marks and question marks?	
Have you used the following correctly most of the time: speech marks, possessive apostrophes, dashes, colons, semicolons and parentheses?	
Have you used the correct spelling of common words?	
Have you used the correct spelling of unusual or difficult words?	
Have you provided an effective and convincing concluding statement that summarises your opinion, introduced by an appropriate phrase, e.g. *Consequently …, Admittedly …, In conclusion …, It's evident that …, Overall …, In considering these arguments …*?	

WRITING: NARRATIVE TEXTS

In this section of the Writing Test we start with a sample of a narrative text. First we give some details about this type of writing, then there is a sample question with answers, and finally there are two practice Writing Tests for narrative texts.

Improving your narrative writing

For the Writing Test you might be asked to write a narrative. If you are, try to write in a way that is a true response and that indicates your interests.

Don't just write in a formal and rehearsed manner or by simply repeating something that is known to you. Look at the task and consider the following:

- Does it want me to set out a conversation?
- Does it want me to describe something?
- Does it want me to say how something happened?
- Does it want my point of view?
- Does it want me to write a poem?

When people are doing something that interests them, they achieve at a higher level. Try to include something that interests you in your writing.

Below are some ways to help you improve your writing and make it more interesting to read.

Tips for writing a narrative

- Always try to make the opening of a narrative interesting or exciting for the reader. Start with dialogue, suspenseful action or description.

  For example:
  "Where am I?" I yelled, to no one in particular, OR *Smoke started eerily moving throughout the house, creeping under doors, choking me with every movement.*
- Take a look at the beginnings of some of your favourite books to see how the authors started their narratives.
- Try to make the characters in your narrative sound realistic and convincing. Give them appropriate names.
- Remember to describe what the characters look like and how they act and feel, using plenty of adjectives and adverbs.

  For example:
  relieved, grumpy, terrified, politely, mad, immature, fearlessly, angrily, daring, persuasive.
- Try to show their personalities in the things they do, say and think. Here are some examples:
  - *talkative*—someone who is friendly and chatty, someone who is inclined to talk a great deal, someone who is not quiet or shy or someone who might interrupt other people
  - *clumsy*—someone awkward, someone without skill or someone who is always breaking things
  - *confident*—someone sure of themselves or someone who is not shy or insecure.

  What type of character in your story (a talkative, clumsy or confident person) would be likely to say the following:
  "I was sure I would be able to climb over the wall to escape"?
- Build descriptions by using
  - alliteration (words starting with the same letter).

    For example:
    the rising river rushed

- rhyme.

  For example:
  hustle and bustle
- onomatopoeia (words that sound like the thing they describe).

  For example:
  crashed and banged
- similes and metaphors.

- Imagine that you are photographing everything you see happening.
- Expand sentences to explain who, what, how, where, when and why something happened.

  For example:
  The frightened boy collapsed wearily to the floor, then slowly grabbed the old, wrinkled and itchy blanket and pulled it over his shaking body.
- Write sentences of different lengths.
- Base your narrative on an unexpected chain of events, a catastrophe or a problem that needs to be solved. Narratives may even consist of more than one problem. They become exciting when things don't go as planned, when an accident has occurred or when someone or something gets lost or stolen. Suspense is also built up by slowly leading up to events. Instead of writing *The house collapsed*, use speech, description and action to build up to the event: *The wind was howling and the sound of thunder became louder and louder. We heard an almighty crash. "What was that?" I asked my brother Michael, with a shaky voice. "Just the wind," he replied, not too confidently. As bits of the ceiling crumbled all around us, I huddled up against Michael. "No, it's not just the wind," I replied, looking at the fearful look on his face. The house started to tremble and things were crashing and banging all around us. We ran, not looking behind us at all as the roof caved in and then everything went black.*
- Include dialogue between descriptions.
- Use questions.
- Start sentences in different ways.
- Think about the final sentence of your narrative. This is just as important as the opening sentence. Remember: this is the last thing that will be read, and this image is the one that will stay with the reader. The ending will need to explain how the problem was solved or the event resolved.

Alternative descriptive words

Make your writing more interesting by using alternatives for these common words.

BIG: large, huge, enormous, gigantic, vast, massive, colossal, immense, bulky, hefty, significant

GOT/GET: obtain, acquire, find, get hold of, gain, achieve, take, retrieve, reach, get back, recover, bring

WENT/GO: leave, reach, go away, depart, exit, move, quit, scramble, crawl, trudge, tread, trample, skip, march, shuffle, swagger, prance, stride, strut

GOOD: decent, enjoyable, superior, fine, excellent, pleasant, lovely, exquisite, brilliant, superb, tremendous

NICE: pleasant, good, kind, polite, fine, lovely

SAW/SEE: glimpse, notice, spot, witness, observe, watch, view, consider, regard, perceive, detect

SMALL: little, minute, short, tiny, miniature, petite, minor, unimportant, microscopic, minuscule, puny

HAPPY: content, pleased, glad, joyful, cheerful, in high spirits, ecstatic, delighted, cheery, jovial, satisfied, thrilled

SAD: depressed, gloomy, miserable, distressed, dismal, disappointed

BAD: awful, terrible, horrific, horrifying, horrendous, evil, naughty, serious, regretful, rotten, appalling, shocking, ghastly, dire, unpleasant, poor, frightening, inexcusable, atrocious, abysmal, sickening, gruesome, unspeakable, outrageous, disgusting, deplorable

GOING: leaving, departing, disappearing, separating, exiting

RUN: sprint, jog, scuttle, scamper, dart, dash, scurry, rush, hurry, trot

WALK: stroll, march, stride, pace, hike, stagger, move, wander, step, tread

SAID:	boasted	exclaimed	mumbled	replied	stammered
acknowledged	boomed	explained	murmured	requested	stated
added	bragged	expressed	nagged	responded	stormed
admitted	called	feared	noted	revealed	stuttered
advised	claimed	giggled	objected	roared	suggested
agreed	commanded	grinned	observed	screamed	taunted
alerted	commented	grunted	ordered	screeched	thought
announced	complained	indicated	pleaded	shouted	told
answered	cried	insisted	pointed out	shrieked	urged
argued	decided	instructed	questioned	snapped	uttered
asked	declared	laughed	rambled	sneered	wailed
babbled	demanded	lied	reassured	sobbed	warned
began	denied	mentioned	remarked	spoke	whined
blurted	emphasised	moaned	repeated	squealed	whispered

Useful adjectives

Using a variety of adjectives will add interest to your story.

A

able, absolute, active, adorable, adventurous, affectionate, alert, alive, almighty, amazing, amusing, ancient, angelic, angry, annoying, awful, awkward

B

babyish, bad, bald, bare, beautiful, bending, big, bitter, blunt, boastful, bold, boring, brainless, brainy, brave, brilliant, broken, brutal, busy

C

careful, caring, cautious, charming, chatty, childlike, chilly, chirpy, choosy, clean, clever, clumsy, cold, colourful, complete, confident, considerate, cool, correct, courageous, crazy, crooked, curious, cute

D

damaged, dangerous, daring, dazzling, deadly, delicate, delicious, desperate, determined, difficult, dirty, diseased, disgraceful, dishonest, disobedient, dreamy, dried, drowsy, dull, dusty

E

eager, easy, elderly, elegant, enchanting, energetic, enormous, entertaining, envious, excellent, exciting, experienced, expert, extreme

F

fabulous, faint, fair, faithful, false, fancy, fashionable, faultless, fearful, fearless, feeble, ferocious, fierce, fiery, fine, firm, fit, flabby, flashy, floppy, fluffy, foggy, foolish, forgetful, fortunate, fragrant, freaky, fresh, friendly, frightening, frightful, frosty, funny, fuzzy

G

generous, gentle, genuine, ghostly, gifted, glamorous, gloomy, glossy, good, gorgeous, graceful, great, greedy, grubby, grumpy

H

hairy, handsome, handy, happy, hard, harmless, hazy, healthy, heavenly, heavy, helpful, helpless, heroic, honest, hopeful, hopeless, horrible, horrific, hot, huge, humble, humorous, hungry, hurtful

I

icy, ignorant, immature, important, incredible, indescribable, inquisitive, invisible, irritable, itchy

J

jealous, jittery, joyful, juicy, jumpy

K

keen, kind

L

large, lazy, light, likeable, little, lively, loaded, lonely, long, loud, lousy, lovely, lucky, luxurious

M

mad, magical, magnificent, marvellous, massive, masterful, mature, mean, mighty, mindless, miniature, modern, modest, monstrous, muddy, musical, mysterious

N

nasty, natural, naughty, neat, nervous, new, nice, noisy, nosy, numb, nutritious, nutty

O

obedient, observant, occasional, odd, old, organised, original, outrageous, outstanding, overgrown

P

pale, paralysed, peaceful, peculiar, perfect, persistent, persuasive, picky, piercing, pimply, plain, playful, pleasant, pleasing, poisonous, polite, poor, popular, precious, pretty, priceless, prickly, proper, protective, proud, puffy, pushy, puzzling

Q

quarrelsome, queer, questionable, quick, quiet, quirky

R

radiant, rare, rattled, raw, reasonable, reckless, refreshing, relaxed, relieved, remarkable, respectable, restless, revolting, rich, rigid, rosy, rotten, round, rowdy, royal, rubbery, rude, rusty

S

sad, saggy, savage, scary, scheming, scrappy, scrawny, scruffy, scrumptious, secretive, selfish, sensible, serious, shaky, shapeless, shattered, shiny, shocking, short, shy, silent, sincere, skilful, skinny, sleek, sleepy, slimy, slippery, sloppy, slow, small, smart, smelly, smooth, snappy, sneaky, soapy, soft, solid, sorrowful, sour, sparkly, special, speedy, spellbound, spicy, spiky, spoilt, spooky, sporty, spotty, squeaky, stainless, sticky, stranded, strange, streaky, strong, stupid, stylish, sudden, sulky, sunny, super, sweet, swift

T

talkative, tall, tame, tearful, tedious, tempting, tender, terrible, terrifying, thirsty, thorny, thoughtful, thoughtless, thrilling, ticklish, tidy, timid, tiny, tiresome, traditional, trendy, tricky, troublesome, trusting, truthful, trying

U

ugly, unexpected, unfair, unfortunate, unkind, unknown, unsteady, unwell, unwilling

V

vain, valued, venomous, vicious, victorious, vigorous, violent, vulgar

W

wacky, warm, wasteful, weak, wealthy, weary, weird, well, wet, whimpering, wicked, wide, wiggly, wild, wise, wishful, witty, wobbly, wonderful, woolly, worthy, wrecked, wrinkly, wrongful

Y

young, youthful

Z

zany, zealous

SAMPLE QUESTION: NARRATIVE WRITING

Here is a Sample Writing question for a narrative text.

Topic: Grandma's attic

Today you are going to write a narrative or story. The idea for your story is *Grandma's attic*.

Remember to:

- think about the characters
- make sure there is a complication or problem to be solved
- plan your writing
- use paragraphs
- write in sentences
- check your spelling and punctuation
- write at least two pages.

SAMPLE ANSWERS: NARRATIVE WRITING

We have provided six sample answers to the sample question. We have grouped them into the six levels of ability used throughout this book. Please note that these are approximate guidelines only.

Grandma's attic

STANDARD LEVEL 1

I went in grandmas attic I didn't feele anything strang. I was scaird I didn't know waht to do I looked around and found lots of old furnitar I opened some draws and they was full of money. I ran to find grandma and show her i thort she woldn't beleiv me she asked me where did all this money come from i don't know i said but now we are rich.

STANDARD LEVEL 2

I was on holidays and staying with grandma. grandma is busy so I sneeked up to her attic to have a peek inside. I opened the door and saw a magical fairytle land with all my favourite storybook characters like cindarella, goldilocks, and little red riding hood. I heard a noise and a witch apeared who took me hostige and locked me in her magic wardrobe. I was very scared and could not yell for help. I wanted to run back downstairs and i wish i had never opened grandmas attic door.

INTERMEDIATE LEVEL 1

Last year I stayed with Grandma for a week while my parents were overseas. There was lots to do at Grandma's and I really liked going to stay with her. One thing I was not allowed to do was go into her attic, but I didn't know why. One day while Grandma was destructed I thought I would sneak up to her attic just for a quick peek.

I opened the attic door and nearly chocked on all the stinky dust that blew everywhere. I could hardly see. It was very dark up there and the light didn't work. Suddenly I heard a knock at the front door. I heard a man whispering something to grandma. They both then rushed upstairs. What was I going to do now? I heard him say that a crazy driver drove straight towards him, but he managed to run away and he came straight here. Then the attic door opened and they both came in quickly saying we need to find it now. Grandma was angry to see me in the attic and asked me what I was doing there. I didn't like this man so I tried to run downstairs to go and call the police, but the man said he wouldn't let me leave. He looked at grandma and said that I already know too much and I would have to stay in the attic. I was really scared. What would happen next?

INTERMEDIATE LEVEL 2

I had lived with Granny for seven years now. In that time I was never allowed to go into her attic, and I really didn't know why. It didn't really bother me until my adventurous friend Anthony decided that we should go and take a look, while Granny was outside looking after her vegetable garden.

'Anthony, I don't think it's a good idea. I don't want to get into any trouble.' I said to him. 'Ah, come on, Leo, what are you, chicken?' he teased me. 'I suppose a quick look won't hurt,' I mumbled. But I didn't feel good about it. So off we went, up those squeaky wooden stairs, slowly hanging onto the railing, taking little steps at a time.

Please note: Spelling, punctuation and grammar errors have been included to replicate the likely response of a Year 5 student.

The door was locked. 'What do we do now, genius?' I asked Anthony. 'Don't worry, I've done this before,' he replied.

And so Anthony took a pin out of his jeans pocket and opened the lock. We tiptoed inside and saw a room full of dust and lots of sheets covering furniture and things.

We pulled one of the sheets off and underneath it was a freezer. We slowly opened the freezer door, and a man's body popped out! We both screamed, pushed it back in and quickly shut the door. We ran all the way back downstairs as fast as we could only to meet Granny at the bottom. She had a smile as big as anything I had ever seen. 'So, you found it I see,' Granny cackled with laughter, 'I guess now, you'll have to be next!' I grabbed Anthony's sweaty hand with all my might. Was this it? Was I going to die just because of the silly attic? ...

ADVANCED LEVEL 1

I was so excited when my parents said we would be flying to Paris to see Grandma. I hadn't seen her for a few years.

Grandma had a beautiful old charming cottage with many rooms. The only room we were not allowed in was the attic. I had no idea why, and yes, I was a teeny bit curious.

One day when the others were outside enjoying tea and coissants, I decided I would finally go exploring, and see what all the fuss was about with the attic. Just one little peek surely wouldn't hurt!

As I climbed the creaky stairs, trying not to make any noise, I wondered what Grandma was hiding up there. I got to the door and reached for the dirty doorknob. I tried turning it and surprisingly it was unlocked!

Amazingly, the attic was full of paintings, paints, brushes and easils. 'Grandma? An artist? I mumbled in shock'. And a good one too! The paintings were incredible. There was one in the middle of the room that Grandma must have still been working on. I took a step closer to get a better look, and tripped on a brush. As I went to balance myself I knocked some jars of paint onto Grandma's painting! 'Oh no!' I said, 'What will I do now?' There was paint everywhere. The painting was ruined. I knew there was no way to get out of this. I had to go downstairs and admit to it.

So, down I went to find Grandma to tell her what I did. She was quite upset that I would disobey her and she was also disapointed about the painting. It was supposed to be a surprise gift for us to take back home. Now I ruined everything! I apologised, offered to clean everything up and realised that next time I need to listen when I am told to do something. I should never have been anywhere near Grandma's attic.

Please note: Spelling, punctuation and grammar errors have been included to replicate the likely response of a Year 5 student.

ADVANCED LEVEL 2

It was early evening, and outside the wind howled angrily. Thunder roared, and rain had just began to hit the rusty corrugated roof. I was so scared, I began to tremble and wished that Grandma was back from her doctors appointment. I ran around the house making sure all the windows and doors were properly shut. Just when I was about to shut the very last one, a lightning bolt struck just in front of me, and shattered the window into smitherines.

I reached down to tidy up the broken glass, when under the desk, a rolled up piece of paper caught my eye. It was wedged between the back of the desk and the drawer. 'Hello, what do we have here?' I questioned, in utter wonder. I stuck my hand in to pull it out. Curiously, I unravelled the yellowing piece of paper. It was a map! I turned it around until it was clear; it was an old map of Grandma's house! There was a large red 'X' in the right top hand corner. I examined it closely and then realised the 'X' was where Grandma's attic was. 'What is hidden here?' I murmured. There was only one way to find out.

The rain had now stopped (but it was still eerily quiet). With my map in hand, I slowly began to rummage through the attic. I crawled behind a bookshelf. Nothing! Dust came flying at me, irritating my eyes and making me sneeze.

I searched and searched, turning over every item in the attic. Still nothing! I could not seem to find any hint of a so-called treasure. I was feeling frustrated and thought it may be someone's bad idea of a joke. Should I give up? Just when I was going to, I stumbled on a loose floorboard and excitedly, I lifted it up. Underneath, I could see the corner of a wooden, gold decorated box. Finally, the treasure! I bent down to pull the box up when I heard a loud BANG! Suddenly pieces of wood came flying past me from above. The floor started shaking, furniture came tumbling down with books being hurled at me like cannons. It felt like an earthquake. What had I done? What had I disturbed by removing this box?

Panic came over me, as I couldn't feel my left leg anymore. All I wanted to do was put the box back before anything else went wrong. I wanted to scream for help, but then I remembered that Grandma was probably still at the doctor's. I sobbed in desperation, and looked around at the mess surrounding me. I was still somehow grapsing the box. How much worse could things get? Hands shaking, I slowly opened it, and then everything went black …

Please note: Spelling, punctuation and grammar errors have been included to replicate the likely response of a Year 5 student.

WRITING TEST 3

In this part you will be doing some writing. Each Writing Test should take you 42 minutes. Use the top part of the first sheet or the narrative text planning page to plan your ideas.

When you have finished, hand in your writing to your teacher or parents, another adult to mark it for you. If it is convenient and possible for you, then you may wish to type your answer directly on a computer.

Topic: Please!!

Look at the picture below.

Write about what has happened. Think about what is happening and why.

Remember to:

- use paragraphs in your writing
- write in sentences
- check your spelling and punctuation
- write at least two pages.

WRITING TEST 3

Here is a narrative text planning page to start you off. Use this page to plan your ideas.

NARRATIVE TEXT

INTRODUCTION/ORIENTATION: introduction of the main characters and setting

WHO?

WHAT?

WHEN?

WHERE?

COMPLICATION (PROBLEM): what triggered the problem
(There may be more than one.)

SEQUENCE OF EVENTS: what happens

BEGINNING

Connectives: *First(ly), next, later, after, afterwards, while, as, meanwhile, eventually, when, so, because, soon, consequently, immediately, previously, however, on the other hand, similarly, finally, despite this, otherwise ...*

MIDDLE

END

RESOLUTION: how the characters resolved the problem

CONCLUSION: the final outcome
Does it end with a question; a mystery; a statement; or with a coda (a moral or lesson learnt from the experience)?

CHECK YOUR SKILLS: WRITING TEST 3

Use this chart to evaluate your writing.

GUIDELINES FOR WRITING A NARRATIVE TEXT	✓ or ✗
Is there a clear beginning, middle and end?	
Is there a clear introduction stating who/what/where/when?	
Is the writing organised into paragraphs that focus on one idea?	
Does the writing develop a complication: create a problem, or trigger a surprising or unexpected chain of events?	
Have you added expression: feelings, thoughts, actions, what is seen, heard or felt?	
Have you used a variety of correct sentence structures including simple, compound and complex sentences?	
Have you used good adjectives/adverbs to build description and add information to your writing?	
Have you used imagery effectively, such as a simile or metaphor? e.g. *The sky lit up like fireworks …*	
Have you used past/present/future tense accurately?	
Have you used pronouns correctly?	
Have you used verbs correctly: accurate tense and number, e.g. *he is*, *they are*?	
Have you used a variety of time connectives, e.g. *firstly*, *next*, *later*?	
Have you used a variety of conjunctions, e.g. *when*, *because*, *so*, *if*, *but*?	
Have you included dialogue?	
Have you punctuated sentences correctly with capital letters, full stops, commas, exclamation marks and question marks?	
Have you used the following correctly most of the time: speech marks, possessive apostrophes, dashes, colons, semicolons and parentheses?	
Have you used the correct spelling of common words?	
Have you used the correct spelling of unusual or difficult words?	
Does the writing end in an interesting way?	

WRITING TEST 4

In this part you will be doing some writing. Each Writing Test should take you 42 minutes. Use the top part of the first sheet or the narrative text planning page to plan your ideas.

When you have finished, hand in your writing to your teacher, parents or another adult to mark it for you. If it is convenient and possible for you, then you may wish to type your answer directly on a computer.

Topic: Water

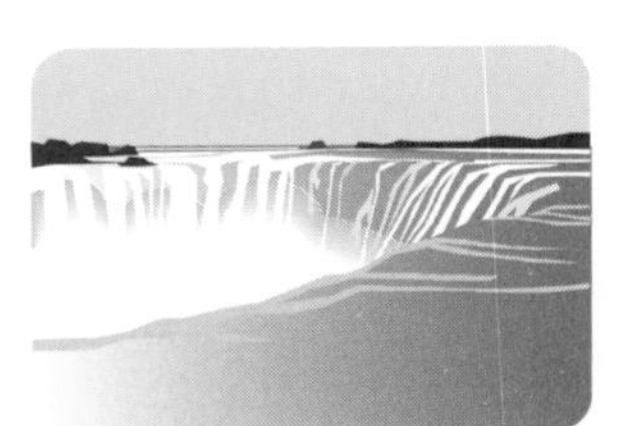

Today you are going to write a narrative or story. The idea for your topic is *Water*. Describe the adventure/incident you had involving water. Use the pictures above for ideas.

Remember to:

- use paragraphs in your writing
- write in sentences
- check your spelling and punctuation
- write at least two pages.

Use this narrative text planning page to plan your ideas.

NARRATIVE TEXT

INTRODUCTION/ORIENTATION: introduction of the main characters and setting

WHO?

WHAT?

WHEN?

WHERE?

COMPLICATION (PROBLEM): what triggered the problem
(There may be more than one.)

SEQUENCE OF EVENTS: what happens

BEGINNING

Connectives: *First(ly), next, later, after, afterwards, while, as, meanwhile, eventually, when, so, because, soon, consequently, immediately, previously, however, on the other hand, similarly, finally, despite this, otherwise ...*

MIDDLE

END

RESOLUTION: how the characters resolved the problem

CONCLUSION: the final outcome
Does it end with a question; a mystery; a statement; or with a coda (a moral or lesson learnt from the experience)?

CHECK YOUR SKILLS: WRITING TEST 4

Use this chart to evaluate your writing.

GUIDELINES FOR WRITING A NARRATIVE TEXT	✓ or ✗
Is there a clear beginning, middle and end?	
Is there a clear introduction stating who/what/where/when?	
Is the writing organised into paragraphs that focus on one idea?	
Does the writing develop a complication: create a problem, or trigger a surprising or unexpected chain of events?	
Have you added expression: feelings, thoughts, actions, what is seen, heard or felt?	
Have you used a variety of correct sentence structures including simple, compound and complex sentences?	
Have you used good adjectives/adverbs to build description and add information to your writing?	
Have you used imagery effectively, such as a simile or metaphor? e.g. *The sky lit up like fireworks …*	
Have you used past/present/future tense accurately?	
Have you used pronouns correctly?	
Have you used verbs correctly: accurate tense and number, e.g. *he is*, *they are*?	
Have you used a variety of time connectives, e.g. *firstly*, *next*, *later*?	
Have you used a variety of conjunctions, e.g. *when*, *because*, *so*, *if*, *but*?	
Have you included dialogue?	
Have you punctuated sentences correctly with capital letters, full stops, commas, exclamation marks and question marks?	
Have you used the following correctly most of the time: speech marks, possessive apostrophes, dashes, colons, semicolons and parentheses?	
Have you used the correct spelling of common words?	
Have you used the correct spelling of unusual or difficult words?	
Does the writing end in an interesting way?	

Adjectival clause

An adjectival clause provides further information about the person or thing named. It functions as an adjective, describing a noun and answering the questions What? Who? How many? or Which?

This is the bike <u>that was given to me by Dad</u>.

An adjectival clause contains a subject and verb and usually begins with a relative pronoun (*who*, *whom*, *whose*, *which* or *that*).

Adjectival phrase

An adjectival phrase is a group of words, usually beginning with a preposition or a participle, that acts as an adjective, giving more information about a noun.

The man <u>in the blue jumper</u> is my uncle. (preposition)

The man <u>wearing the blue jumper</u> is my uncle. (participle)

Adjective

An adjective is a word used to describe and give more information about a noun.

Some examples include *<u>multiple</u> books*, *a <u>delicious</u> cake*, *my <u>gorgeous</u> friend.*

Adverb

An adverb is a word used to describe or give more information about a verb, an adjective or another adverb, to tell us how, when or where the action happened. Adverbs often end in *-ly*.

The flag flapped <u>wildly</u> in the wind. (how)

I <u>always</u> brush my teeth in the morning. (when)

He slid <u>downwards</u> towards the side of the boat. (where)

Adverbial clause

An adverbial clause acts like an adverb. It functions as an adverb, giving more information about the verb, usually telling when, where or how. It indicates manner, place or time, condition, reason, purpose or result.

Water is important <u>because plant and animal communities depend on water for food, water and shelter</u>. (reason)

Adverbial phrase

An adverbial phrase is a group of words, usually beginning with a preposition, that acts as an adverb, giving more information about the time, manner or place of the verb, telling us where, when, how far, how long, with what, with whom, and about what.

Chloe hit Ava <u>with the old broom</u>.

Apostrophe

An apostrophe is a form of punctuation used to show:

1. a contraction (missing letters in a word), e.g. *can't = cannot*
2. possession, e.g. *David's book*, *the boys'* (plural) *mother*

Brackets ( )

Brackets are a form of punctuation used to include an explanatory word, phrase or sentence.

He took the book from his friend <u>(Anthony)</u> but never returned it.

Capital letter

Capital letters are used at the beginning of sentences, as well as for proper nouns, e.g. the names of people, places, titles, countries and days of the week.

Colon (:)

A colon is a form of punctuation used to introduce information, such as a list, or further information to explain the sentence.

The following should be taken on the trip: a warm jacket, socks, jeans, shirts and shoes.

The warning read: "Give up now or else!"

GLOSSARY OF GRAMMAR AND PUNCTUATION TERMS

Comma (,)

A comma is a form of punctuation used to break up the parts of a sentence, or to separate words or phrases in a list.

The children, who have not completed their homework, will be punished.

My brother likes to eat peanuts, steaks, oranges and cherries.

Conjunction/connective

A conjunction or connective is a word joining parts of a sentence or whole sentences.

Conjunctions: *and*, *but*, *where*, *wherever*, *after*, *since*, *whenever*, *before*, *while*, *until*, *as*, *by*, *like*, *as if*, *though*, *because*, *so that*, *in order to*, *if*, *unless*, *in case*, *although*, *despite*, *whereas*, *even though*

My button fell off <u>because</u> it was not sewn on properly.

Connectives: *in other words*, *for example*, *therefore*, *then*, *next*, *previously*, *finally*, *firstly*, *to conclude*, *in that case*, *however*, *despite this*, *otherwise*

<u>First</u> we do our homework, and <u>then</u> we go out to play.

Dash (—)

A dash is a form of punctuation used to indicate a break or pause in a sentence.

Life is like giving a concert while you are learning to play the instrument—now that is really living.

We really hoped that he would stay—maybe next time.

Exclamation mark (!)

An exclamation mark is a form of punctuation used to mark the end of a sentence where strong emotions or reactions are expressed.

Ouch! I cut my finger.

I listened at the door. Nothing!

Full stop (.)

A full stop is a form of punctuation used to indicate the end of a sentence. Full stops are used before the closing of quotation marks.

David sat under the tree.

Nicholas said, "Come with me, James."

Imagery

Imagery includes:

Metaphor is when one thing is compared to another by referring to it as *being* something else, e.g. *The thief looked at her <u>with a vulture's eye</u>.*

Simile is comparing two different things using the words *as* or *like*, e.g. *The hail pelted down <u>like bullets</u>. He was <u>as brave as a lion</u>.*

Personification is giving human qualities or characteristics to non-human things, e.g. *<u>Trees were dancing</u> in the wind.*

Alliteration is the repetition of consonant sounds at the beginning of successive words for effect, e.g. *The <u>sun sizzled softly</u> on the sand. The <u>rising river rushed</u>.*

Onomatopoeia is the formation of words to imitate the sound a certain thing or action might make, e.g. *banged*, *crashed*, *hissed*, *sizzled*.

Repetition is repeating words or phrases for effect, e.g. *Indeed there will be time, time to relax, time to enjoy the sun and surf, time to be oneself once more.*

Modality

Modality is the range of words used to express different degrees of probability, inclination or obligation. Modality can be expressed in a number of ways:

- Verbs: *can*, *could*, *should*, *might*, *must*, *will*, *it seems*, *it appears*
- Adverbs: *perhaps*, *possibly*, *generally*, *presumably*, *apparently*, *sometimes*, *always*, *never*, *undoubtedly*, *certainly*, *absolutely*, *definitely*

GLOSSARY OF GRAMMAR AND PUNCTUATION TERMS

- Nouns: *possibility*, *opportunity*, *necessity*
- Adjectives: *possible*, *promising*, *expected*, *likely*, *probable*.

Noun

Nouns are words used to represent a person, place or thing. There are different types of nouns:

Common nouns are nouns that represent things in general, e.g. *boy*, *desk*, *bike*.

Proper nouns take a capital letter. They represent a particular thing, rather than just a general thing. Proper nouns are used to name a place, person, title, day of the week, month and city/country, e.g. *Michaela*, *November*, *Monday*, *Madagascar.*

Abstract nouns are things we cannot see but can often feel, e.g. *sadness*, *honesty*, *pride*, *love*, *hate*, *issue*, *advantages*.

Collective nouns are nouns that name a group of things, e.g. *herd*, *litter*, *team*, *flock*.

Preposition

Prepositions are words that connect a noun or pronoun to another word in the sentence. They also indicate time, space, manner or circumstance.

I am sitting <u>between</u> my brother and sister.

Some common prepositions are *in*, *at*, *on*, *to*, *by*, *into*, *onto*, *inside*, *out*, *under*, *below*, *before*, *after*, *from*, *since*, *during*, *until*, *after*, *off*, *above*, *over*, *across*, *among*, *around*, *beside*, *between*, *down*, *past*, *near*, *through*, *without*.

Pronoun

A pronoun is a word that is used in place of a noun. Pronouns refer to something that has already been named, e.g. *My brother is 10 years old. <u>He</u> is taller than me.*

Be careful of repetition and ambiguous use of pronouns: *<u>He</u> went to the shops with <u>his friend</u> and <u>he</u> told <u>him</u> to wait outside.*

The pronouns are *I*, *you*, *me*, *he*, *she*, *it*, *we*, *they*, *mine*, *yours*, *his*, *hers*, *ours*, *theirs*, *myself*, *ourselves*, *herself*, *himself*, *themselves*, *yourself*, *this*, *that*, *these*, *those*, *each*, *any*, *some*, *all*, *one*, *who*, *which*, *what*, *whose*, *whom*.

Question mark (?)

Question marks are needed at the end of any sentence that asks something, e.g. *What did you say?*

If a question is asked in an indirect way it does not have a question mark, e.g. *I asked him what he said.*

Quotation marks (" ")

Quotation marks have several uses.

- They are used to show the exact words of the speaker:

  John said, "I prefer the colour blue."

  "What are you doing?" asked Marie.

  "I like cats," said Sophia, "but I like dogs too."

  When there is more than one speaker, a new line should be used when the new person begins to speak:

  "What should we do now?" asked Ellen.

  "I'm not too sure," whispered Jonathan.
- They are used when writing the names of books and movies.
- They are used when quoting exact words or phrases from a text.

Semicolon (;)

A semicolon is a form of punctuation used to separate clauses. It is stronger than a comma but not as final as a full stop.

Eighteen people started on the team; only twelve remain.

In our class we have people from Melbourne, Victoria; Sydney, New South Wales; and Brisbane, Queensland.

Sentence

A sentence is a group of words consisting of one or more clauses. It will begin with a capital letter and end with a full stop, question mark or exclamation mark.

Simple sentence: *I caught the bus.*

Compound sentence: *I caught the bus and arrived at school on time.*

Complex sentence: *Since I managed to get up early, I caught the bus.*

Tense

Tense is the form of the verb (a doing word) that tells us when something is happening in time—present, past or future.

I look, I am looking (present)

I will look (future)

I looked, I was looking (past)

Auxiliary verbs (e.g. *be*, *have* and *do*) help change the verb to express time, e.g. *I have looked, I have been looking, I had looked, I had been looking, I will have looked, I will have been looking.*

Verb

A verb is a word that expresses an action, e.g. I ran, he forgot, she went, Mary shouted. It can also express a state, e.g. *the boys are laughing, he is clever, he was all smiles, I know my spelling words.*

Active verb: The verb is in the active voice when the subject of the sentence does the action, e.g. *James broke the glass.* (*James* is the subject of this sentence.)

Passive verb: The passive voice tells you what happens to or what is being done to the subject, e.g. *The glass was broken by James.* (Here *the glass* is the subject of the sentence.)

The passive is often used in informative writing, where it is not always necessary to state the doer of an action, or the doer is not known, or it is not relevant.

Congratulations!

You have now finished all of the practice tests. This was a considerable effort and you deserve a reward for all this hard work! We hope that these tests were of some help to you. We wish you every success in your schooling.

Reader comments

Thank you for using this guide to the NAPLAN Tests. We hope that you found the practice tests helpful for your students or your child. If you have any comments or questions, we would be pleased to respond. Also let us know if you found any errors or omissions. We benefit from this feedback as it often highlights matters we have overlooked.

NUMERACY TEST 1 (pp. 25–32)

1. **39.** The numbers increase by three. They start with 3 then 6, 9, 12, 15, 18, 21, 24, 27, 30, 33, 36 then 39. You may have also noted a visual sloping pattern in the shading. It's important to stress again, that with all of these questions, have a guess if you aren't sure as there is no penalty for guessing incorrectly.
2. The **second clock**, **,** shows 8:00. The time is eight o'clock. (This question is taken from our Year 3 NAPLAN Numeracy Test 1 and so are 7 other questions but with some changes. This may help you see if there has been some improvement from Year 3 to Year 5. The comparable questions from Year 3 to Year 5 are: 13-2; 29-3; 19-7; 8-8; 6-9; 28-10; 22-11; 23-13.)
3. There are **6** triangular prisms. The diagram below shows the triangular prisms.

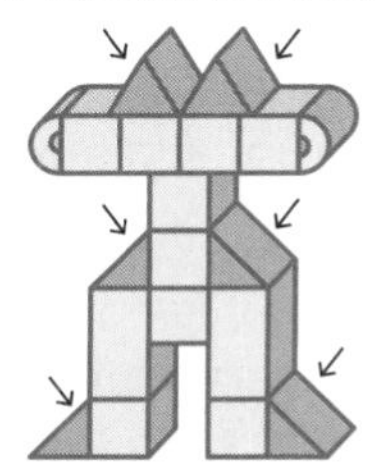

4. **4 hundreds**
5. The **first answer** is correct. It's the largest angle. The space between the lines is widest. Don't let the length of the lines confuse you. It's the size of the opening that's important.
6. **45 minutes.** This is because 11 + 18 + 16 = 45.
7. **480.** The numbers increase by 100. You start with 280 then add 100 to make 380. Then you add 100 to 380 to make 480. Did you write your answer in the box?
8. **35.** There are 19 Magpies and 16 Pigeons (19 + 16 = 35).
9. $1.35. There is $3.85 in coins less $2.50 leaves $1.35.
10. **B.** This has only two out of the eight spaces coloured.
11. **B.** This is H-shaped with five blocks. The others are quite different. It may help if you try to draw the shape and then rotate it.
12. **1963–1898.** You may wish to read some of the other books in the Narnia series by CS Lewis.
13. **3 × $3.50 = $10.50.** Each football costs $3.50 so three footballs will be three times $3.50. Did you write your answers in the spaces?
14. **$4 + $3 + $15.** You need to round the numbers up or down before adding them to estimate the answer quickly. So $3.70 becomes roughly $4.00 (it is closest to $4.00); $3.20 becomes $3.00 (it is closest to $3.00); and $15.10 becomes $15.00 (it is closest to $15.00). If the number ends in 50 cents or more then round it up, otherwise round it down.
15. **My book and phone together are the same length as my computer.** The computer is 30 cm; the book is 20 cm and the phone is 10 cm. Do you understand how to read the chart?
16. **1 out of 6 chances.** When you spin the arrow it could land anywhere. There are six sections so the chance of landing in one of them is called one-in-six. It's the same when you throw a dice. Sometimes it will be a five and sometimes it will not. Overall you should expect that it will be the number that you want about one in every six times.
17. **14.** The front and back are only one face each.
18. **515.** 784 − 269 = 515. Make sure that you know how to do these types of sums.
19. **10.4** (4.6 + 5.8 = 10.4)
20. **238.** 1904 ÷ 8 = 238.
21. The missing numbers are **5 and 9** and the sum is 354 + 59 = 413.
22. **40 cm.** The wood starts at 15 cm and finishes at 55 cm which makes 40 cm.
23. **B** is correct. We have tried to show this for you (it isn't drawn to scale).
24. **South-east.** After one space the arrow points to East then after another space it points to South-east.
25. $\mathbf{\frac{5}{4}}$. This is an improper fraction because the numerator (5) is larger than the denominator (4).
26. **40 km per hour.** Speed is distance divided by time. So if the speed is 160 and the time is 4, then the speed must be 40 because 40 = 160 ÷ 4. This calculation is actually easy but understanding what to do may have been unclear to you.

27. **C.** This number is 0.13 and is closest to 0.1
28. **Papua New Guinea.** Papua New Guinea is 461 601 sq km and is the second largest nation in area and population after Australia. Many of the countries in Oceania are quite small and the pie chart may have been hard for you to read.
29. **16 cm.** You need to guess the parts that are not indicated. You know that each side is 4 cm so that is a helpful start. You also know that part of the side is 2 cm. This is also helpful. The best way to proceed is to subtract the 2 cm length from the 4 cm; this leaves 2 cm for the corner areas. It's a little hard to explain in words, so we have also drawn it for you.

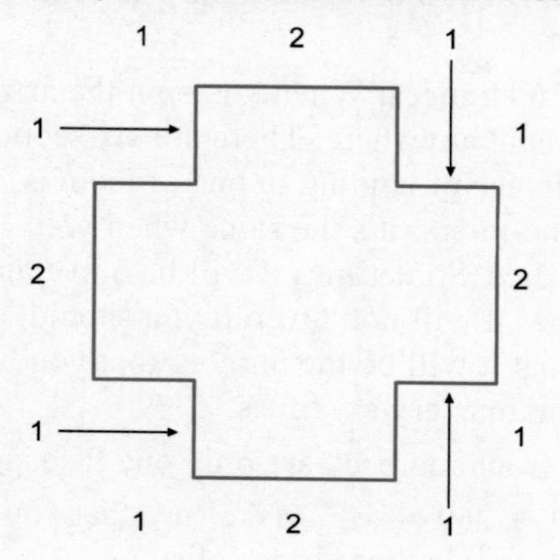

30. **18 km.** You need to count the squares. The six squares from Tuggerah to The Entrance equal 18 km, so each square is 3 km. There are six squares from The Entrance to Erina, which means that this distance is also 18 km.
31. **15 out of 25 parts.** There are 25 triangles and 15 are coloured.
32. 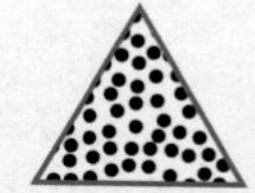

    The pattern shown above completes the picture. You have to imagine how it will look when each part is folded.
33. **2.5 litres**
34. **one-quarter.** The bottle holds 10 litres and only contains 2.5 litres currently so this is one-quarter.
35. $\mathbf{\frac{1}{4}}$. This is because 3 out of the 12 were dogs and three-twelfths is one-quarter.
36. **15.** The first number is $1 + 2 = 3$, then the next number is $1 + 2 + 3 = 6$, then the next number is $1 + 2 + 3 + 4 = 10$ and the next number is $1 + 2 + 3 + 4 + 5 = 15$.
    The last row of the triangle increases by one. So the series is 3, 6, 10 then 15. This is something you might not have been taught in school.
37. **3 in 9.** After you picked the first shoe there are nine left altogether. There are also three black shoes. So the chances are 3 in 9 of picking a black shoe.
38. **6.5 kg.** The average weight of a cat is 5 kg ($15 \div 3 = 5$) and the average weight of a dog is 8 kg ($32 \div 4 = 8$). So if a cat weighs 5 kg and a dog weighs 8 kg, their combined weight is 13 kg. Divide this number by 2 to get the average. Therefore the average weight of a cat and a dog is 6.5 kg. This is a little tricky.
39. **4 cm; 9 cm.** The perimeter is $4 + 4 + 9 + 9 = 26$ and the area is $4 \times 9 = 36$. One way to start is with the area. Find out the factors of 36 (that is 1 and 36; 2 and 18; 3 and 12; 4 and 9; 6 and 6). Then check whether each of these factors would give a perimeter of 26 cm.
40. **120.** You start with one-quarter and you add 60 to give you three-quarters. So that means that the 60 balls are half the box (because $\frac{3}{4} - \frac{1}{4} = \frac{1}{2}$) and $\frac{1}{2}$ in this case is equal to 60. Again this could be a little tricky or perhaps easy if you see the main point straightaway.
41. **A = 16 B = 18.** If you insert the numbers in the puzzle and follow the arrows then this should make sense. The other answers are not correct.
42. **8.** There are five whole squares and six half-squares.

NUMERACY TEST 2 (pp. 36–43)

1. **7; 8; 9.** The numbers increase by 1. They are also four more than the numbers in the first row.
2. The **second clock** shows which is 10:00 am. The time is ten o'clock in the morning. The other clocks show 4 am, 8 am and 9 am. All of these are earlier than 10 am. It's important to stress again, that with all of these questions have a guess if you are not sure as there is no penalty for guessing incorrectly. (This question is taken from our

Year 3 NAPLAN Numeracy Test 2 and so are 9 other questions but with some changes. This may help you see if there has been some improvement from Year 3 to Year 5. The comparable questions from Year 3 to Year 5 are: 13-2; 11-13; 23-11; 24-17; 26-15; 28-14; 29-16; 32-31; 33-26; 35-21.)

3. **Rectangle.** Both faces will be rectangles. See if you can imagine it.
4. **25 549**
5. **B.** B is the right angle. A right angle is 90° and is like a corner.
6. **126 animals.** This is because 45 + 35 + 9 + 10 + 27 = 126.
7. **320.** The numbers increase by 200. You start with 120 then add 200 to make 320. Then you add 200 to 320 to make 520. Or you can work backwards from 520. Did you write your answer in the rectangle?
8. The column should be at **150 litres**.

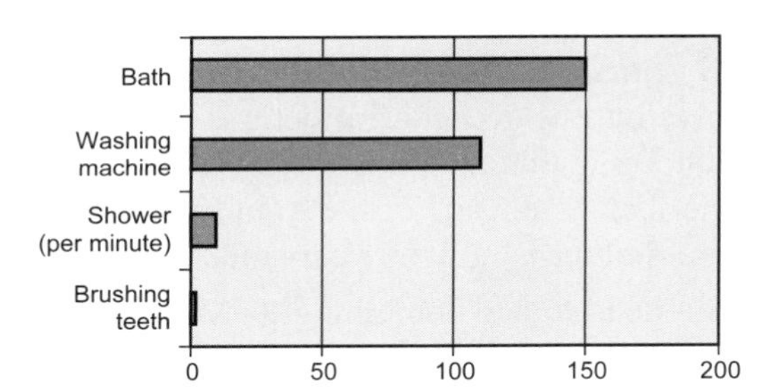

9. **11 dots.** There were 45 dots and there are 34 remaining, so 11 must be covered. This is the easy way to answer the question. A harder way is to imagine the dots behind the figure.

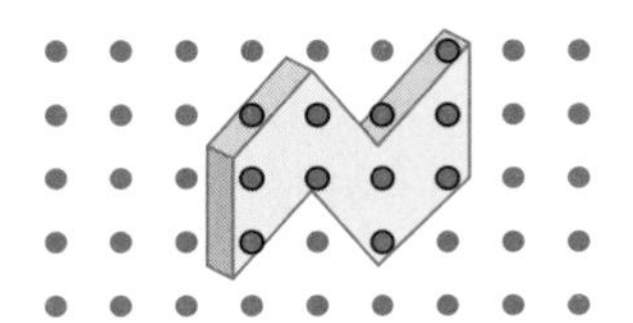

10. **11.** The grid has 28 squares and there are 17 uncovered which means that 11 must be coloured. This is a little like the earlier question.
11. **B.** The others are quite different. It may help if you try to draw the shape and then rotate it.
12. **1 600 000 − 502 000**
13. **60 ÷ 10 = 6 pieces.** The wood is 60 centimetres. Each piece will be 10 cm, so the sum is 60 ÷ 10 = 6. Did you write your answers in the boxes?
14. **60.** The answer to the sum is 59 because 31 + 28 = 59 but the estimate is 30 + 30 = 60. We take the number in the sum and change it to an estimated number that ends in zero. We choose the estimate that is closest to it. The 31 becomes a 30 estimate and the 28 is closest to 30.
15. **The temperature in Adelaide is now more than the predicted high for the day**. This must seem a little strange at first. You may be asking yourself how the temperature can now be higher than the high. This is because the high temperature is what the weather bureau thinks the temperature will be. It can change. I hope that this was not too tricky for you. Ask someone to explain this if it isn't clear.
16. **Top.** It's 1 out of 2 chances for the top row. The middle row is 1 out of 3 chances and the bottom row is 1 out of 4 chances. 1 out of 4 is worse than 1 out of 3 and both are worse than 1 out of 2. You have a better chance of picking the glasses or spectacles in the top row.
17. **Flip.** The coloured shape has been flipped over.

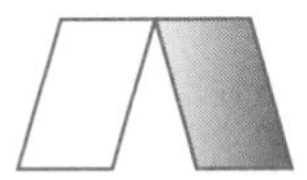

18. **485.** 764 − 279 = 485. Make sure that you know how to do these types of sums.
19. **$12.60**
20. **321.** 2568 ÷ 8 = 321.
21. **6.** You start with 8 then add 7 to give 15. Three get off so that leaves 15 − 3 = 12. Half get off and half of 12 is 6 so that leaves 12 − 6 = 6.
22. **35 m.** The house starts at around 15 m and finishes at 50 m which makes 35 m.
23. The **first answer** is correct. We have tried to show this below (it isn't drawn to scale).

24. **North-west.** After one space the arrow points to North then after another space it points to North-west.
25. $\mathbf{1\frac{3}{4}}$

ANSWERS TO NUMERACY TESTS

26. The correct answer is shown below. The big trick is to find the 6 or the 7 first then the other numbers are easy.

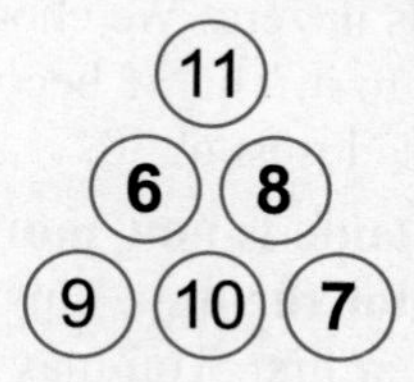

27. **20 August.** One week is 6 August, two weeks is 13 August and three weeks will be 20 August.

28. **New York.** New York has 184 skyscrapers.

29. **30 cm.** You need to guess the parts that are not indicated. It's a little hard to explain in words, so we have also drawn it for you.

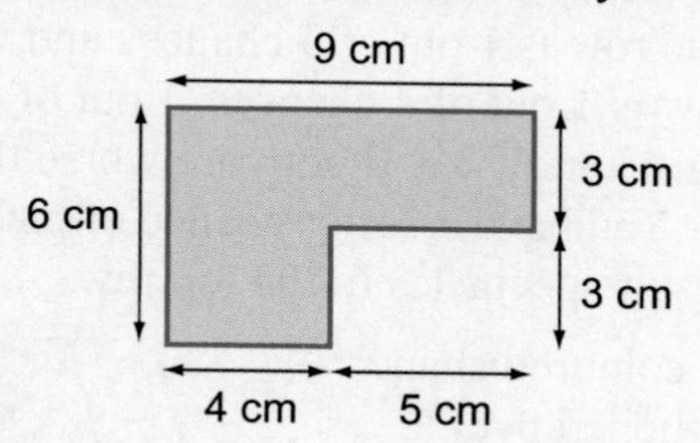

30. **100 km.** You need to count the squares or sections. The five sections from Madaba to Quneitra equal 100 km, because each square is 20 km.

31. **It is more likely you will score a number from 1 to 4 rather than a 5 or 6.** Any number from 1 to 6 is possible. When you throw the die it is more likely that the number will be from 1 to 4 than a 5 or 6. This is because there are four chances out of six of throwing a 1 to 4 and only two chances out of six of throwing a 5 or 6.

32. The **third shape** is correct.

The pattern shown above completes the picture. You have to imagine how it will look when each part is folded.

33. **three-fifths.** There are 10 litres in the bottle and only 6 litres are full so this is six tenths or three fifths.

34. **16.** The first square number is 2×2, then 3×3, then 4×4 and then 5×5.

35. $\frac{1}{3}$. This is because 5 out of the 15 were bicycles and five-fifteenths is one-third.

36. **South-west.** The final symbol is ☯. You go down and to the left, which is south-west to get back to where you started. The steps have been numbered for you.

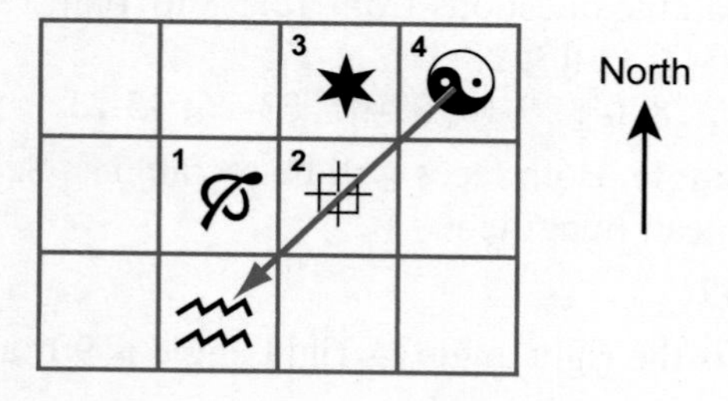

37. **7 out of 19.** There are 20 socks. One blue sock is chosen leaving 19 socks and seven of the 19 are blue socks.

38. **9 days.** Three workers take 15 days so the job will take 45 man-days of work altogether. If five workers are hired then they can do 45 man-days of work in nine days.

39. **3 cm; 6 cm.** The perimeter is $3 + 3 + 6 + 6 = 18$ and the area is $3 \times 6 = 18$.

40. **48 years.** This is not an easy question to solve but the actual arithmetic is very simple. You know that the child is 12 years old and one-fifth of the age of the grandfather. So the grandfather is now 60 years old.

You need to add something to 12 and to add the same amount to 60 so that one answer will be half of the other.

The really easy way to answer this is to try all the answers and see which one fits.

Start with 48 years. The child is now 12 so this will be 36 more years and if you add 36 to the age of 60 for the grandfather this is 96. Of course, 48 is half of 96.

There is another way to solve this but it's even more complicated.

41. **247.** Check your answer by multiplying 8 by 247 and this gives 1976.

42. **9.1.** This is the largest number.

NUMERACY TEST 3 (pp. 46–53)

1. **9 pentagons**
2. The **second clock** is closest to 7:30. (This question is taken from our Year 3 NAPLAN Numeracy Test 3 and so are 8 other questions but with some changes. This may help you see if there has been some improvement from Year 3 to Year 5. The comparable questions from Year 3 to Year 5 are: 13-2; 19-7; 22-10; 23-11; 24-17; 29-13; 30-21; 31-25; 35-22.)
3. **They are all parallelograms.**
4. **8026**
5. **8.** There are six small right-angled triangles, an internal triangle in the top half and the larger one that contains all of them.
6. **$31.00.** This is because $18.50 + $12.50 = $31.00.
7. **47.** The numbers decrease by 3. You start with 50 then subtract 3 to make 47. Then you subtract another 3 from 47 to make 44. Did you write your answer in the box?
8. **24 countries.** There are 57 English-speaking countries and 33 French-speaking countries so the difference is 24 countries. The number of countries does not really indicate how many people speak the language. The most spoken language is actually Chinese (Mandarin) followed by Spanish, English, then Arabic.
9. There are 10 trapeziums and you should have coloured **any two**.
10. **4.** The 10 cents is twice as much as the 5 cents: the 20 cents is twice as much as the 10 cents; the $1 is twice as much as the 50 cents; and the $2 is twice as much as the $1.
11. **C.** The others are slightly different. Here is the original and the copy. The copy is turned over.

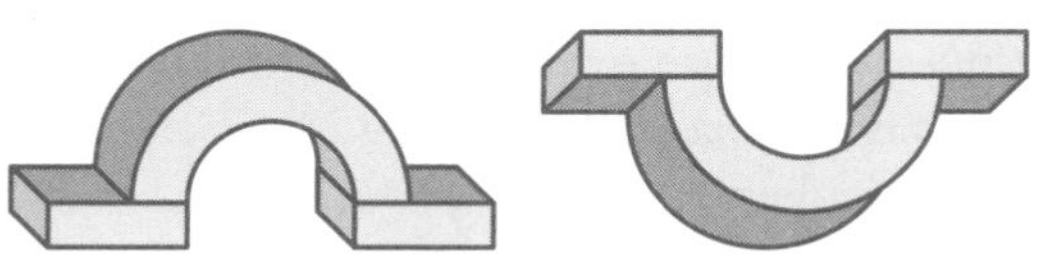

12. **Last block = 900 − 300 − 200.** If you start with 900 hectares then take away the first block of 300 hectares and then the next block of 200 hectares you are left with 400 hectares.
13. **There is one even number which is a prime number.** The number is 2. The reason it is the only one is that all other even numbers can be divided by two, so none of them can be a prime number. The prime numbers from 1 to 20 are: 2, 3, 5, 7, 11, 13, 17, 19.
14. **$4 + $1 + $3 + $4 + $2.** You need to round the numbers up or down before adding them to estimate the answer quickly. So $4.29 becomes roughly $4 (it is closest to $4); $0.99 becomes $1 (it is closest to $1.00); $2.82 becomes $3 (it is closest to $3), $4.29 becomes $4 (it is closest to $4) and $1.63 becomes $2 (it is closest to $2). If the number ends in 50 cents or more then round it up otherwise round it down.
15. **Lotus has about twice as many wins as Brabham.** Lotus has 79 wins compared with Brabham which has 35 wins. It is slightly more than twice as many but far closer than any of the other options. Do you understand how to read the chart?

Company	Wins
Benetton	27
Brabham	35
Ferrari	184
Lotus	79
McLaren	148
Renault	25
Williams	113

16. **1 out of 4 chances.** If you toss two coins then you can end up with four arrangements:
    Head, Head
    Head, Tail
    Tail, Head
    Tail, Tail.
17. **Turn.** The coloured shape has been turned or rotated.
18. **359.** 946 − 587 = 359.
19. **$20.40.** First estimate the answer. $6.80 is almost $7 and if you multiply it by three, the answer will be close to $21. Then multiply but remember to place the decimal point two numbers from the end of your answer. Practise these types of sums if you are not sure.
20. **The last answer is correct.** It is the smallest angle. The space between the lines is narrowest. Do not let the length of the lines confuse you. It is the size of the opening that is important.
21. **7 × (10 − 4) = 7 × 6 = 42**

22. **B.** Here is the complete pattern.

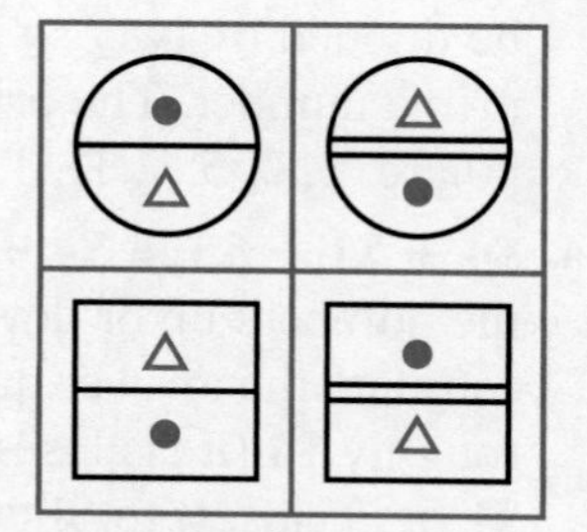

Notice that there are circles across the top row and only rectangles in the bottom row. Next the first column has one line in the middle but the second column has two lines in the middle.

Thirdly the pattern of the blue circle and the triangle change from the first column to the second column. So there are three things happening at once. Don't worry if this was too hard for you. It wasn't an easy question.

23. **A.** The **first answer** is correct.

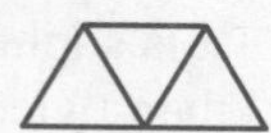

24. **130 cm².** The shaded figure is a triangle and the way you find the area of a triangle is to take half the length of the base and multiply it by the height (Area = $\frac{1}{2}$Base × Height). The base of the triangle is 26 cm and the height is 10 cm.

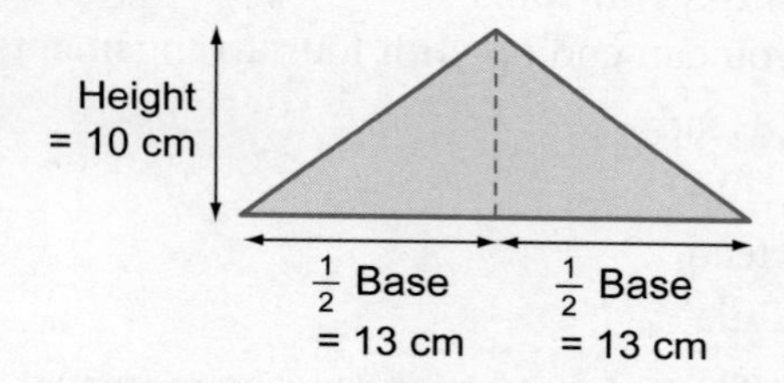

Even if you didn't know this you can find it because the triangle is part of the rectangle. In fact, if you look closely it is half the rectangle.

25. **The answer to the addition is always four times the first number plus six.** This is because the second number is always one more than the first number; the third number is always two more; and the fourth number is always three more than the first number.

26. Here are two different versions of the completed diagram. Both are correct. Each row, column and diagonal adds up to 15.

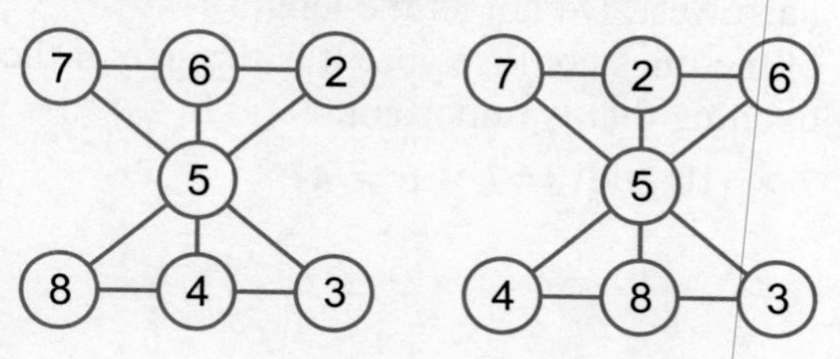

27. **A.** A is 0 and is closest to 0.02. B is 0.05 and is further away.

28. **Hindus.** Hindus are the third-largest major world religious belief with 870 000 000 followers.

29. **5 cm.** The volume is 650 cm³. The breadth is 10 cm and the length of the prism is 13 cm so that is also a helpful start.

The volume of a rectangular prism is length times breadth times height, so length times breadth is 10 × 13 = 130. Multiply 130 by the height to find 65 and the answer is 5.

30. **26 km.** You need to count the squares. The six squares from Moverly to Bundock equal 12 km. There are seven squares from Bundock to Avoca, which means that this distance is 14 km.

31. $\mathbf{\frac{1}{2}}$**.** There are 6 out of 12 parts that are half coloured.

32. **D.** The net is a trapezoidal prism. You have to imagine how it will look when it is folded along the lines.

33. **5 m.** If a 10 metre pole is $\frac{2}{3}$ the height of its shadow then a shadow of 7.5 m is from a pole of 5 metres in height.

34. **18.** There are 72 tiles and for every four tiles there are 1 white and 3 black. Four tiles goes into 72 tiles 18 times. This means that you need 18 white and 54 black tiles.

35. **26.** The numbers are added together to give the next number in the series, so 2 + 4 = 6 and 4 + 6 = 10 and 6 + 10 = 16 and finally 10 + 16 = 26.

36. **9 in 19.** You start with 20 numbers and 10 of them are even. You pick the first number and this is even, so this leaves 19 numbers and nine of them are even numbers. It means that you have 9 chances out of 19 of picking an even number.

37. **11.** The average age is 13 so that means the total of all the ages is 13 × 3 = 39. You are told that the two girls are aged 13 + 15 = 28, so that means 39 − 28 = 11.

38. **$84.** It is $50 for the first 100 calls and then each call costs 17 cents. So for 200 more calls it will be 200 × 17 cents = $34.
$50 + $34 = $84.

39. **500.** If $\frac{3}{4}$ is 375 then one-quarter is 125 (divide 375 by 3). To find the original number, multiply 125 by four.

40. Here is the complete answer:

Chances	Sentences
3	When I toss a coin once it will land on heads.
2	I will eat some take away food next week.
4	I will be involved in an accident next week.
5	I am zero centimetres tall.
1	I was born.

41. **A.** A has by far the largest area. The area of the target that is C is only about one-fifth of the area that is A. The target area B is also smaller than A; it is just over a half of A.

42. **30.** The answer is 30 because 15 times 30 equals 450.

NUMERACY TEST 4 (pp. 56–62)

1. **6087**

2. You should have coloured or shaded **any nine** out of the 12 rectangles. See the shaded diagram below as an example:

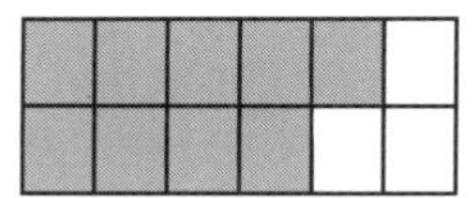

3. **7.** Any numbers from 47500 to 48499 could be rounded to 48000.

4. **6.** Nine students scored six and this was the highest for any of the scores.

5. **88.** The numbers decrease by three:
100 97 94 91 88.

6. **$32**

7. **602309**

8. **If I toss a coin once, it will land heads or tails.** There are only two ways it can land—heads or tails. (I suppose it may be theoretically possible for it to land on its edge.)

9. $4\frac{1}{2}$

10. **89637 < 94362.** Do you know what the symbols mean? < is less than; > is greater than; = means equals; ≠ means not equal.

11. **75%.** There are 100 squares in the figure and 75 are coloured; this makes it 75%.

12. ☆☆☆☆☆☆☆. The sequence is 1, 3, 5 then 7. The symbols change continuously.

13. **A.** The others are slightly different. Here is the original and the copy.

Original

A

14. **$12.85** (The sum is $25.80 minus $12.95)

15. **5.** This is not an easy question. The rope is 9.95 m and the lengths are 1.99 m. One way is to divide 9.95 by 1.99 which gives 5. Another way is to look at the answers and multiply each one by 1.99 to see which one gives 9.95. You know that one of the answers has to be correct. A really straightforward way is to estimate—you know that 1.99 m is almost 2 m and 9.95 m is almost 10 m so there are about five 2 m lengths needed.

16. **143 and 99.** They add up to 242 which can be rounded down to 240.

17. **10.** It is important to do the multiplication first, then the subtraction: $28 - 6 \times 3$ equals $28 - 18 = 10$.

18. **300 litres.** The trick here is to first convert the 1.5 kilolitres to 1500 litres. This is just a question in which you change units from kilolitres to litres.

19. **3 out of 6 chances.** There are three possible even numbers (2, 4 and 6) out of six numbers on a dice so it is 3 out of 6 chances.

20. **Flip.** This is a horizontal flip. It may be hard for you to see so get a parent or teacher to help you.

21. **B.** This is shown below. The pattern is shown in the top row. The coloured and white shapes change position and there is also a double line in the second figure.

Underneath there is another figure with the same pattern of coloured and white shapes (a coloured square and a white triangle in a rectangle). In the missing space you should expect to see a rectangle where the coloured and white shapes change position and where there will also be a double line in the second figure.

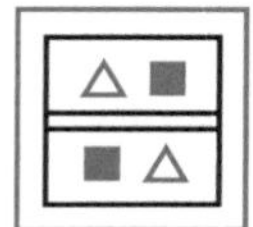

22. A. 

23. 64 cm². This is the area of a triangle which is half the base (8 cm is half the base) multiplied by the height (also 8 cm). If you forget this formula then it is also half the area of the rectangle.

24. **.** The closeness of the symbols is shown below.

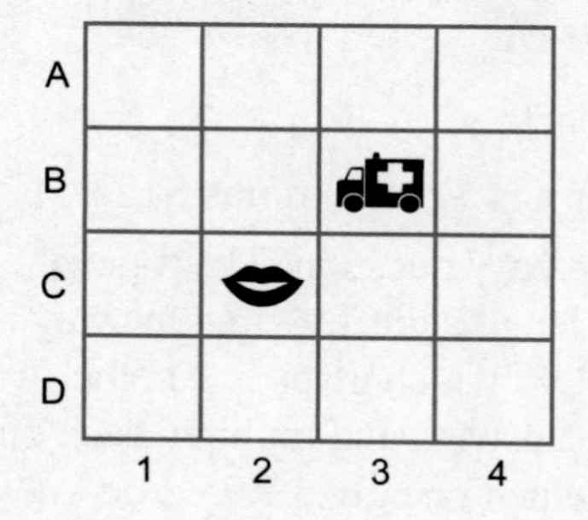

25. C. A tessellation is a pattern made up of shapes that fit together. They don't have gaps between them or overlaps.

26. 120°. This is a regular hexagon with all sides of the same length and all internal angles are 120 degrees.

27. Germany. Here is the chart of values:

USA	216682937
Japan	73285000
Germany	47975377
Italy	36994581
France	34597000
UK	31202111

28. 10 km

29. 1000 cm³. The volume of a prism is the length times the breadth times the height. Remember that volume is always given in cubic units.

30. 12 noon.

31. $\frac{1}{2}$. This is because 8 out of the 16 squares are half shaded.

32. B. 

33. 11. The numerals less than 6875 are: 5678, 5687, 5768, 5786, 5867, 5876, 6578, 6587, 6758, 6785, 6857.

34. 100 metres. The three fields are 13 500 m² so each field is 4500 m². If the width is 45 metres then the length of a field must be 100 metres because 100 × 45 = 4500.
The first step is to find the area of one soccer field—then it is easier because you have been told its width.

35. 6250. The numbers reduce by 1250.

36. 1 in 8. Let H stand for heads and T stand for tails. When you toss three coins, you can get HHH (three heads) or TTT (three tails) or other combinations. There are eight combinations: HHH, HHT, HTH, HTT, THH, THT, TTH, TTT. So three tails (TTT) is one out of eight.

37. 51 000 tonnes. There are two steps in solving this problem. The first is to find 15% of 60 000, which is 9000. Subtract 9000 from 60 000 and you are left with 51 000.

38. $184. The total bill is $334. You add the other items and these come to $150 so the balance is $184.

39. 1280. You know that 960 is three-quarters. So one-quarter must be 960 divided by three which is 320. Add 320 to 960 to give 1280.

40. Here is the most likely list from the choices given:

Chances	Sentences
0	The earth is flat.
1	Everyone you know was born on a day of the week ending in '-day'.
0.5	A randomly chosen person is male.
0.75	There will be bushfires in the summer in Australia.
0.25	The next person you meet will have been born in Autumn.

41. 70 km. Here is the shape with the amounts for all sides shown. It is merely a matter of adding the lengths of each side.

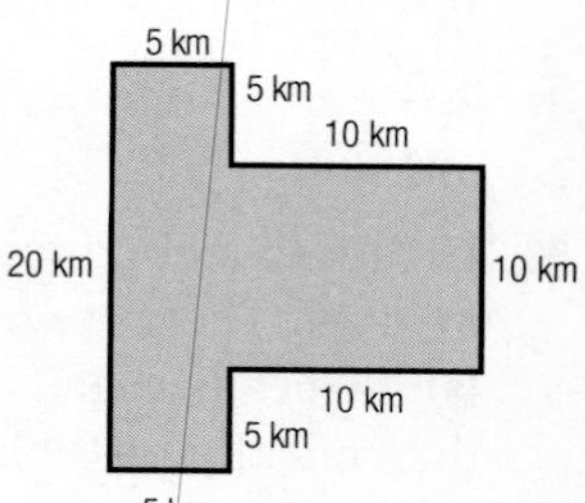

42. $\frac{3}{4}$. A half is equal to two quarters, so two quarters plus half a quarter is three-quarters.

ANSWERS TO READING TESTS

READING TEST 1 (pp. 65–71)

1. **You might find it on a Christmas card.**
2. **It is like a manual calculator.**
3. **the Middle-eastern people**
4. **for working out problems**
5. **the Greeks**
6. **5 units, tens, hundreds, etc.**
7. **the beads in the middle**
8. **663**
9. **This person has a poor memory.** This is from a humorous poem written by Lewis Carroll, who also wrote *Alice in Wonderland*. He was also a mathematician and liked to write amusing stories to entertain his nephews and nieces. Some parts of this may be a little difficult to read because the language is old fashioned, so do not be afraid to ask for help.
10. **42**
11. **It did not matter because he had seven extra coats and three pairs of boots.**
12. **The worst problem was that he could not remember his name.**
13. **fourth paragraph.** This is the paragraph where he is called *Hi, Fry me!*, *Fritter my wig!*, *What-you-may-call-um!*, *What-was-his-name!* or *Thing-um-a-jig!*
14. **a word that has a powerful effect.**
15. ***intimate friends* and *enemies***
16. **courage**
17. **Many people know that it is important to wash your hands.**
18. **Many people wash but don't dry their hands.**
19. **several thousand**
20. **germ**
21. **Bacteria are micro-organisms because there can be many thousands on a hand.** Bacteria are micro-organisms or microbes because they are so tiny. They are so small that many thousands can fit into a hand.
22. **The best way is to wipe with a paper towel and then hot air-dry for 20 seconds.** The article states that the best procedure is to get as much of the dampness off with a paper towel and then to hold your hands under a hot air-drier.
23. **The next best alternative is to wipe carefully with separate paper towels.**
24. **Around half did not even wash their hands.**
25. **It is recommended that they wash and dry their hands and use a paper towel.**
26. **cleanliness.** Hygiene has to do with cleanliness.
27. **2 4 1 3.** The correct order is: (1) Rub your hands together with soap until they are soapy; (2) Rinse your hands; (3) Dry them with a clean towel; (4) Turn off the water.
28. **4**
29. **Gerry's father**
30. **It is part of a larger story called *Spooked*.**
31. **Gerry refused to stay with his aunt.**
32. **She insisted quietly.**
33. **because he cannot be alone**
34. **Gerry was angry when he ran from the room.**
35. **to step inside the wardrobe**
36. **Gerry was aiming to make his parents sorry if the spook attacked him.**
37. **feel sorry for Gerry.**
38. **a ghost**
39. **soothe his anger.** His mother left him in the wardrobe to calm down.

READING TEST 2 (pp. 73–82)

1. **to tell children how to behave**
2. **A Goop is a naughty character.**
3. **The message is not to let anything turn you from your purpose.**
4. **The Kid thought he was an adult because he had horns.**
5. **the killing of animals**
6. **A.** This shows two girls trying to reach the fruit on the high wall. They cannot reach but try to find an answer. One girl brings a rock on which to stand. This is a different type of question.
7. **C.** This shows a girl darning a sock. If she does this now when the hole is small then it will save it getting larger and needing more work to repair in the future.

8. **nothing.** Jim sold it for eight quid but lost the money gambling.
9. **Bill was delayed because he went back to look for the packhorse.**
10. **Jim was stalling for time.** He was trying to delay telling Bill that he had lost the money from the sale of the horse.
11. **A Sketch of Mateship.** This is the actual title of the story. It is a story about being friends even when someone lets you down.
12. **There is no point in seeking revenge; friendship is more important.**
13. **ACBD**
14. **This text is near the start of a story.** Actually it is from Chapter 1 of the book Animal Farm, which you may read in your high school lessons in Year 7 or 8.
15. **because old Major wanted to tell the animals about his dream**
16. **Old Major was Willingdon Beauty.**
17. **the dogs**
18. **Muriel is the goat.**
19. **because everyone wanted to hear what Old Major had to say**
20. **The pigs settled down in the straw immediately in front of the sheep and cows.**
21. **settled down comfortably**
22. **Boxer**
23. **because Benjamin was not happy with things**
24. **This passage is from a fable about animals.**
25. **all of the above.** Jacques-Yves Cousteau was a scientist, an underwater explorer, an author, a documentary filmmaker and a French Naval Officer.
26. **1910**
27. The word **spellbound** has a similar meaning to the word *fascinated*.
28. **A**. He may have bought the other things when he was older, but he bought the camera as a child.
29. **a film about real life**
30. **navy** rhymes with wavy; **mask** rhymes with task; **feature** rhymes with creature; **series** rhymes with queries; **machine** rhymes with clean
31. The following statements are true:

    He was a famous scientist and explorer.
    He joined the French Naval Academy.
    He bought the *Calypso* in 1950.

    Make sure that you read the answers carefully. Jacques Cousteau did not invent the aqualung, he *perfected* it.
32. **perfecting the aqualung**. Although he accomplished everything listed here, pay attention to the words *greatest diving achievement.*
33. ***Calypso* is an oceanographic research ship.**
34. **because she was awarded two Nobel prizes**
35. **physics and chemistry**
36. **the discovery of pure radium and polonium and isolated metallic radium**
37. **a blood disease**
38. **radiation**
39. **for helping humanity through science.**

READING TEST 3 (pp. 84–91)

1. **ACBD**
2. **information about beaches.** This is from a tourist guide in a section called 'Splash out at the beaches'.
3. **breaks**
4. **the baker's cart**
5. **The advantage in being a baker is eating the cakes.**
6. **because he is riding a horse and cart**
7. **an umbrella.** A *parasol* is a small or light umbrella/sunshade.
8. **a route**
9. **Both these poems give reasons for liking and not liking a job.**
10. **governess**
11. **Ada Cambridge was happiest with learning by herself.**
12. **The Rev. George Frederick Cross was first sent to Wangaratta.**
13. **Ada Cambridge is best remembered for *Thirty Years in Australia*.**
14. **a serious difficulty**

15. **because her health broke down**
16. **a story**
17. **Huang An looked younger than his age.**
18. **because it is afraid of the light from the sun or the moon**
19. **because he was compared to the age of the tortoise**
20. **King Darius**
21. **a cave or a hole**
22. **so that Daniel could not escape**
23. **a ring with a small seal.** These rings were stamped on hot wax as a form of signature in ancient times.
24. **to ensure that the rock was not moved**
25. **for one night**
26. **because the King was worried**
27. **He served God all the time.**
28. **An angel who closed the lions' mouths saved Daniel from the lions.**
29. **King Darius was very happy.**
30. **There is not enough information in the text to decide whether the events did occur.** Note that you cannot make a judgement only from this text.
31. **strapper**
32. **to press with the nose**
33. **Southern Cross**
34. **Most people thought that Phar Lap was not a racehorse.**
35. **one**
36. **when Phar Lap was aged three.** Note that it may have been a dream when he was a two-year-old also but you are not informed of this in the passage. Be careful not to make assumptions.
37. **People started to take notice of Phar Lap in the spring of 1929.**
38. **Phar Lap's racing style is described as smooth and powerful.**
39. **It means that people began to feel that Phar Lap was like their own horse.**

READING TEST 4 (pp. 93–100)

1. **Healthy food makes you stronger.** The first nine questions have been taken from our Year 3 NAPLAN book. This will allow you to monitor changes and improvements in performance. These questions were specially selected as they covered the different levels of achievement.
2. **fresh fruit**
3. **bread, rice and pasta**
4. **once every now and then**
5. **when you eat it too quickly**
6. **The Taj Mahal**
7. **Shah Jahan**
8. **21 years**
9. **an exclamation**
10. **7.** There are seven ingredients: pineapple, strawberries, mint, watermelon, pawpaw, mango and a secret ingredient.
11. **chemical.** This may have been a little difficult for you. If you are not certain, then eliminate those answers that you are sure are wrong, then take a guess from those that are left over.
12. **there is a free gift.**
13. **a toy**
14. **The offer will not last long.**
15. **deal.** This may have been hard for you. Remember to ask for help if you are not sure of the answers.
16. **a movie poster.** *Commandos Strike at Dawn* is the title of the film being advertised. It may have been a difficult question for you. Remember to ask for help if you are not sure of the answers.
17. D
18. **sale**
19. **for advertising**
20. **11**
21. **to score more goals than the opposing side**
22. **Players need to get the ball past the opposition and shoot it in the goal post**. If you are not certain which answer to choose, eliminate those answers that you are sure are wrong. Then make a guess from those that are left over.

23. **artificial**
24. **The ball is never hit with the flat side of the stick**. Did you pay attention to the word *never*?
25. **changed**
26. **It is meant to be a person's weak point.**
27. **It is the only part of his body that was not dipped into the water.**
28. **Achilles fought in the battle against Troy.**
29. **Hector's brother**
30. **nonsense poem.** 'Jabberwocky' was written by Lewis Carroll. It is from the novel *Through the Looking-Glass, and What Alice Found There* (1871) and is thought to be one of the greatest nonsense poems ever written in English.
31. **slithy; mimsy; fumious; frabjous.** *Slithy* could come from lithe and slimy; *mimsy* could be from flimsy and miser; *fumious* could be made from fuming and furious; and *frabjous* could be a combination of fabulous and joy. The other words are 'real' words.

    For questions 32 to 35, here are the words and their possible meanings. You may have found this quite difficult but don't worry as it's not straightforward at all.
32. *brillig*—**C (four o'clock in the afternoon)**
33. *gyre*—**D (to go round and round)**
34. *wabe*—**A (a grass plot)**
35. *raths*—**E (green pigs)**
36. **'It seems to fill my head with ideas.'**
37. **a myth of heroism**
38. **An adult is narrating the poem.** You know this because the words *my son* and *my beamish boy* are used.
39. **joy**

See the Glossary on pages 164–167 for an explanation of grammar and punctuation terms.

CONVENTIONS OF LANGUAGE TEST 1 (pp. 102–108)

1. **but**
2. **rise**
3. **to know**
4. **look**
5. **have**
6. **narrowest** (Please note: There are no tricks intended in any of these questions. In the NAPLAN Tests, the questions are specially selected and designed to test your knowledge.)
7. **apple**
8. **He said, "What do you mean I lost?"**
9. **Later that day, John finally called to tell me where he was.**
10. **Gerry's books were due back at the library on Wednesday.** Be careful with possession: plural nouns do not take an apostrophe, e.g. *books*.
11. **The boys' bikes were locked up outside the library, but when they went to leave, the bikes were gone.** The reason the apostrophe is after the 's' is because more than one boy is being talked about. You know this by the hint in the question *they went to leave*. If it were just singular, it would read *The boy's bikes were locked up*.
12. **Marc, who hit the tennis ball into the neighbour's window, would now have to go and apologise.**
13. **who**
14. The sentence should look like this: **"Josephine, get inside right now", said Granny. "You need to start your homework immediately."**
15. **Mum's job was to read books to the twins while Dad helped Samantha and Elli finish their essays.**
16. **The children.** *They* is a pronoun; it is in place of the noun *children*.
17. **verb.** In this sentence *walked* is a doing word, i.e. a verb.
18. **Close the door.** In the first answer option *close* is a noun; in the second a verb meaning 'shut'; in the third an adjective; and in the last one *close* is an adverb.
19. Our camp was deep in the **A**mazon **R**ainforest.
20. We were eating dinner when disaster **struck**.
21. **My mother and I think** that the newly painted wall looks good.
22. Tommy likes his **new** school because the children are **kinder** to him than at his last.
23. Ethan and Chris always **like** to play handball during lunch.
24. **their**
25. **rang**
26. **great**
27. **rain**
28. **straight**
29. **journey**
30. **friend**
31. **heart**
32. **city**
33. **sweat**
34. **dimming**
35. **rolling**
36. **excellent**
37. **airport**
38. **thankful**
39. **bedroom**
40. **birthday**
41. **particularly**
42. **mischievous**
43. **concentrate**
44. **entrance**
45. **library**
46. **through**
47. **disappeared** (Please note: There are no tricks intended in any of these questions. These words are commonly misspelt.)
48. **past**
49. **probably**
50. **heading**

CONVENTIONS OF LANGUAGE TEST 2 (pp. 111–116)

1. **so**
2. **since**
3. **doing it**
4. **I wonder if Connor will arrive on time.** This is an indirect question (that is, it does not require an answer) and therefore doesn't need a question mark after it. Be careful not to put a question mark at the end of an indirect question. If it was written as a question within a statement, we do end with a question mark, e.g. *I wonder, "Will Connor arrive on time?"*
5. **better**
6. **in**
7. **from.** If you aren't sure about an answer, then you should just guess. If you have time, you can come back to those questions at the end.
8. **at**
9. **in**
10. **by**
11. **despite.** Don't spend too much time on any one question. Allow around one minute for each question.
12. **gone**
13. **into**
14. **while**
15. **drank.** Be careful of the past tense of some verbs. Present tense of the verb *to drink* is *I drink*, past tense is *I drank*, and the past participle, which is used after a form of the word *have*, is *I have drunk*.
16. **to proceed**
17. **We are**
18. **Sam and Mary**. *They* is a plural pronoun. It stands for more than one person, i.e. Sam and Mary.
19. **Noun**. *Courage* is a noun because it is the name of something.
20. **He is better suited to drawing than writing**. This may have been difficult. Usually an adverb says something more about a verb. It tells how or how much. In the first answer option, *better* is a noun; in the second a verb; in the third an adjective; and in the last one *better* is an adverb.
21. **taller**
22. **The customer, rather angry and impatient, left the store.** A pair of commas is used in the middle of a sentence to identify clauses, phrases and words that are not necessarily adding to the meaning of the sentence. One comma is used before to indicate the beginning of the pause, and one at the end to indicate the end of the pause. A good hint is that if you leave out the clause, phrase or word, does the sentence still make sense? For example: *The customer (rather angry and impatient) left the store.*
23. **The students were preparing for the exams when the fire alarm went off in the principal's office.** Be careful with possession: plural nouns do not take an apostrophe, e.g. *students* and *exams*. Watch out for apostrophes—even adults make mistakes with them.
24. **Michele asked, "Has the mail arrived yet?"** Full stops, question marks and commas always go inside the quotation marks.
25. **was**
26. **squid**
27. **hoe**
28. **through**
29. **chief**
30. **glove**
31. **dwelling**
32. **boring**
33. **hopping**
34. **disguising**
35. **confusing**
36. **permitting**
37. **rabbit**
38. **telescope**

39. **cushion**
40. **xylophone**
41. **toddler**
42. **injured**
43. **two.** Although the word is spelt correctly here, *too* means *also* or *as well*. The English language includes many words that sound the same but are spelt differently, depending upon the context in which they are used. Be careful of these words and get to know the context in which they should be used.
44. **Rescue**
45. **ambulance**
46. **seriously**
47. **occurred**
48. **neighbourhood**
49. **embarrassed**
50. **vicious**

CONVENTIONS OF LANGUAGE TEST 3 (pp. 119–124)

1. **while**
2. **by** (Please note: There are no tricks intended in any of these questions. In the NAPLAN Tests, the questions are specially selected and designed to test your knowledge.)
3. **has.** The word *television* is singular, so the answer is *has*.
4. **went out**
5. **He and I ride our skateboards to school every day.** Does that sentence sound OK to you? Maybe it does, but the others have a pronoun error. If you are having trouble, say the sentence as separate clauses: Him rides our skateboards; *Me rides our skateboards*. This is clearly not right, so *He and I ride our skateboards to school every day* is correct.
6. **We can get to Brisbane more quickly, can't we, if we take the freeway?** This is a question and so requires a question mark. It also requires commas. You can test this by removing the phrase surrounded by the commas and seeing if it still makes sense, which it does, e.g. *We can get to Brisbane more quickly (can't we) if we take the freeway?*
7. **"It's nearly the school holidays. I hope you will able to visit us soon. When will you next be in Perth?"** The third circle should be coloured in. Remember that all punctuation marks, like full stops, question marks and commas, always go inside the quotation marks.
8. **found**
9. **Nick doesn't like brussels sprouts. Neither do I.** *Neither* can be paired with *nor*, but is never paired with *or*. *Either* is used to show two possibilities. It can be paired with *or* but never with *nor*.
10. **Chrissy said to meet with Amy this afternoon, so we went.** This is an example of indirect speech and therefore doesn't need speech marks. Be careful not to put speech marks around an indirect question. If it is written as a question within a statement, you do need speech marks, e.g. *Chrissy said, "Let's meet with Amy this afternoon, so we went."*
11. **Many companies make sugar-free soft drinks, which contain less sugar, but do not quite taste the same.** You can test where the commas should go by removing the phrase surrounded by the commas and seeing if it all still makes sense, which it does—e.g. *Many companies make sugar-free soft drinks (which contain less sugar) but do not quite taste the same.*
12. **clumsiest**
13. **Yvette said, "Time for our piano lesson."** Remember: the first word of the spoken phrase takes capital letters. Also note that the speech marks go around the spoken words.
14. **The women's handbags were stolen and their credit cards were never found.** Remember: plural nouns like *handbags* and *credit cards* don't take an apostrophe.
15. **"Hey, Theo, what do you think?" said Christian. "Do we have time for another game?"**
16. **"You can come back on Wednesday," said Peter.** Remember: the spoken words begin with a capital letter and a comma will end the spoken words.
17. **in order to**
18. **into**

19. **when**
20. **back**
21. **to have**
22. **prettier**
23. **Before**. Don't spend too much time on any one question. Allow around one minute for each question.
24. **them.** (Please note: There are no tricks intended in any of these questions. In the NAPLAN Tests, the questions are specially selected and designed to test your knowledge.
25. **Aaron's history book, which weighs about 3kg, fell out of his locker and onto my foot.**
26. **height**
27. **wheat**
28. **soul**
29. **asked**
30. **month**
31. **hoping**
32. **making**
33. **village**
34. **mistaking**
35. **buttoning**
36. **translating**
37. **bargain**
38. **coffee**
39. **tomorrow**
40. **recommend**
41. **restaurant**
42. **experienced**
43. **applicant**
44. **kitchen**
45. **interest**
46. **excellent**
47. **attention**
48. **deliver**
49. **manager**
50. **January**

CONVENTIONS OF LANGUAGE TEST 4 (pp. 127–133)

1. **from**
2. **although**
3. **are**
4. **and buying**
5. **them**
6. **sheep.** Plural means 'more than one'. *Sheep* is used both as a singular and plural noun.
7. **First floor is women's footwear and formal dresses, and men's shoes are on the fourth floor.**
8. **Brett said, "Neil, please show Andrea to her new office."**
9. **The teacher asked what they were doing.**
10. **We will still be able to play football, won't we, even if it is raining?**
11. **I was not aware that the science project was due today. Neither was Ross.** *Neither* can be paired with *nor*, but never with *or*. *Either* is used to show two possibilities. It can be paired with *or* but never *nor*. Careful: *Nor did Ross* has an incorrect verb. It would be correct if it said *Nor was Ross*. Remember to read the questions very carefully. There is no need to rush through things as you have about a minute per question.
12. **Max, who has applied for entry to several local high schools, really wants to go to Varity College.**
13. **"No Luke," Mum called out, "the call was not for you."**
14. **so**
15. **go ahead**
16. **service?**
17. **require**
18. **We**
19. **back**
20. **to**
21. **are eating** (George and Ahmed are eating kebabs for lunch.)
22. **Michael's** (Anthony is Michael's father.)

23. **,** (Place a comma after *footballer*, that is: *Gerry, who is a first-grade footballer, used to live in my street.*)
24. **better** (John said that his new bike is better than his old one.)
25. **youngest** (Nick is the youngest in the family.)
26. **weak**
27. **shoe**
28. **blue**
29. **cries**
30. **choice**
31. **dance**
32. **soar**
33. **aunt**
34. **batting**
35. **padding**
36. **stripping**
37. **seaweed**
38. **explain**
39. **chemist**
40. **asthma**
41. **stairs**
42. **business**
43. **where**
44. **forty**
45. **becoming**
46. **weird**
47. **religion**
48. **guarantee**
49. **vacuum**
50. **criticise**

Notes

SPELLING WORDS FOR CONVENTIONS OF LANGUAGE TESTS

To the teacher or parent

First read and say the word slowly and clearly. Then read the sentence with the word in it. Then repeat the word again.

If the student is not sure, then ask them to guess. It is okay to skip a word if it is not known.

Spelling words for Conventions of Language Test 1

Word	Example
26. great	It was great to see my cousins.
27. rain	The farmer is waiting for rain.
28. straight	The road ahead is straight.
29. journey	We set out on a journey to the outback.
30. friend	My friend lives nearby.
31. heart	She had a heart operation.
32. city	It is hard to find a place to play in the city.
33. sweat	He will sweat if he plays tennis in this heat.
34. dimming	The sunglasses are dimming the glare.
35. rolling	The ball is rolling toward the goal.
36. excellent	This is an excellent opportunity.
37. airport	He is coming to the airport to meet me.
38. thankful	I am thankful that I have some savings.
39. bedroom	The bedroom is to the front of the house.
40. birthday	His birthday is in October.

Spelling words for Conventions of Language Test 2

Word	Example
26. squid	A squid is a marine animal.
27. hoe	A hoe is used to dig the soil.
28. through	He came through the front of the store.
29. chief	The chief of the tribe was old.
30. glove	Put the oven glove on first.
31. dwelling	A dwelling is where people live.
32. boring	Some subjects in school are boring.
33. hopping	The rabbits are hopping in the paddock.
34. disguising	The criminals were disguising their identity.
35. confusing	The details on the form are confusing to her.
36. permitting	Weather permitting there will be a picnic on Tuesday.
37. rabbit	The dog chased the rabbit.
38. telescope	He looked at the stars through a telescope.
39. cushion	She placed the new cushion on the sofa.
40. xylophone	The symphony orchestra has a xylophone.

To the teacher or parent

First read and say the word slowly and clearly. Then read the sentence with the word in it. Then repeat the word again.

If the student is not sure, then ask them to guess. It is okay to skip a word if it is not known.

Spelling words for Conventions of Language Test 3

Word	Example
26. height	The height of the fence is 120 centimetres.
27. wheat	Wheat is used to make flour.
28. soul	They say that the soul of a person lives forever.
29. asked	They asked for directions.
30. month	December is the last month of the year.
31. hoping	I am hoping to travel interstate next year.
32. making	The carpenter is making a roof for the house.
33. village	There is a small village on the island.
34 mistaking	They are mistaking me for my brother.
35. buttoning	I am buttoning up my coat to protect me from the cold wind.
36. translating	The computer is translating from one language to another.
37. bargain	The shopper was looking for a bargain.
38. coffee	They stopped to have a cup of coffee.
39. tomorrow	Tomorrow is the school sports carnival.
40. recommend	I recommend that you apply for the job.

Spelling words for Conventions of Language Test 4

Word	Example
26. weak	The customer asked for a weak tea.
27. shoe	This shoe was made from leather.
28. blue	The sky is blue.
29. cries	The baby cries when hungry.
30. choice	There is plenty of choice in the supermarket.
31. dance	They performed a traditional dance.
32. soar	At take-off the fighter will soar into the sky.
33. aunt	My aunt is a kind person.
34. batting	The quality of the batting in cricket is assessed by the number of runs.
35. padding	The footballer wore padding to protect his body.
36. stripping	The worker is stripping the wallpaper with steam.
37. seaweed	Seaweed lined the beach after the storm.
38. explain	I tried to explain my situation to the police officer.
39. chemist	The chemist sells medicines.
40. asthma	Asthma involves a difficulty in breathing.

Notes

Notes